Morality, Authority, and Law

Morality, Authority, and Law

Essays in Second-Personal Ethics I

Stephen Darwall

OXFORD
UNIVERSITY PRESS

OXFORD
UNIVERSITY PRESS

Great Clarendon Street, Oxford, OX2 6DP,
United Kingdom

Oxford University Press is a department of the University of Oxford.
It furthers the University's objective of excellence in research, scholarship,
and education by publishing worldwide. Oxford is a registered trade mark of
Oxford University Press in the UK and in certain other countries

Published in the United States of America by Oxford University Press
198 Madison Avenue, New York, NY 10016, United States of America

British Library Cataloguing in Publication Data
Data available

Library of Congress Cataloging in Publication Data
Data available

ISBN 978–0–19–966258–6

For Laura

Contents

The forthcoming companion volume to
Morality, Authority, and Law is:
Honor, History, and Relationship:
Essays in Second-Personal Ethics II

Acknowledgments

Many colleagues, students, friends, and family members have helped me to formulate the ideas in the essays in this volume. The central elements of the second-person framework were first conceived in the stimulating environment provided by the University of Michigan Philosophy Department; I owe so very much to many people there. Since coming to Yale in 2008, I have been fortunate to find wonderful colleagues and students who have helped me to develop my ideas further. I am especially indebted to the participants in a seminar Jules Coleman and I gave at the Yale Law School on law and the reactive attitudes in Fall 2008, a seminar I gave on moral obligation in Spring 2009, and a seminar Matt Smith and I offered on recognition in Fall 2011. I have also had the opportunity to present versions of these essays at many different institutions, conferences, and workshops and have benefited enormously from the feedback I received there. I cannot even try to mention all of these, but I would be remiss not to give special thanks for the invitations that initiated many of these essays.

"Morality's Distinctiveness" was written for a conference on the point of morality at the Humboldt University in Berlin in June 2010. "Bipolar Obligation" was initially presented as the keynote lecture at the 7th Annual Wisconsin Metaethics Workshop at Madison in September 2010. "Moral Obligation: Form and Substance" was delivered to the Aristotelian Society in London in November 2009. "But It Would Be Wrong" was originally given as the keynote lecture at the Social Philosophy & Policy Center conference on moral obligation at Bowling Green State University in November 2008. "Morality and Principle" was written for a volume honoring Jonathan Dancy to be published by Oxford University Press in 2013.

"Because I Want It" was first presented at the Social Philosophy & Policy Center conference on moral knowledge in September 2000. And "The Value of Autonomy and Autonomy of the Will" was written for a conference on autonomy and well-being at the University of Toronto in April 2004.

"Authority and Second-Personal Reasons for Acting" was originally given at a conference on reasons for action in April 2006 at Bowling Green State University. "Authority and Reasons: Exclusionary and Second Personal" was presented at a conference honoring Joseph Raz at the University of Manchester in May 2008. "Law and the Second-Person Standpoint" was written for an issue of *Loyola of Los Angeles Law Review* devoted to *The Second-Person Standpoint*, edited by Robin Kar. "Civil Recourse as Mutual Accountability" was written with Julian Darwall for a conference on civil recourse theory at The Florida State University College of Law in February 2011.

My sons, William and Julian Darwall, continue to indulge a philosophical father with their willingness to think through ideas together. In addition to being a co-author,

Julian has helped to clarify and develop my thoughts about law more generally. And Will has made vivid to me the challenges a second-personal framework faces in theorizing a variety of areas, from political economy to meaningful personal relations. Finally, I thank my wife, Laura Radwell, for her love, support, and belief, and for letting a somewhat hidebound philosopher into her life.

Many of these essays were originally published elsewhere, and I gratefully acknowledge the publishers listed below for permission to republish them (with light revisions) here.

"Bipolar Obligation," in Oxford Studies in Metaethics, vol. VII, ed. Russ Shafer-Landau (Oxford: Oxford University Press, 2012), pp. 333–67. Reprinted with the permission of Oxford University Press.

"Moral Obligation: Form and Substance," Proceedings of the Aristotelian Society 110 (2010): 31–46. Reprinted by courtesy of the Editor of the Aristotelian Society. © 2010.

"But It Would Be Wrong," Social Philosophy & Policy 27 (2010): 135–57. Reprinted with the permission of the editors of Social Philosophy & Policy.

"Morality and Principle," in Thinking About Reasons: Essays in Honour of Jonathan Dancy, ed. David Bakhurst, Brad Hooker, and Margaret Little (Oxford: Oxford University Press, 2012). Reprinted with the permission of Oxford University Press.

"Because I Want It," Social Philosophy & Policy 18 (2001): 129–53. Reprinted with the permission of the editors of Social Philosophy & Policy.

"The Value of Autonomy and Autonomy of the Will," Ethics 116 (2006): 263–284. © 2006 by Ethics.

"Authority and Second-Personal Reasons for Acting," in Reasons for Action, ed. David Sobel and Steven Wall (Cambridge: Cambridge University Press, 2009), pp. 134–54. Reprinted with the permission of Cambridge University Press.

"Authority and Reasons: Exclusionary and Second Personal," Ethics 120 (2010): 257–278. © 2010 by Ethics.

"Law and the Second-Person Standpoint," Loyola of Los Angeles Law Review 40 (2006–2007): 891–910. Reprinted with the permission of Loyola of Los Angeles Law Review.

"Civil Recourse as Mutual Accountability," with Julian Darwall. Florida State University Law Review 39 (2012): 17–41. Reprinted with the permission of Florida State University Law Review.

Introduction

In *The Second-Person Standpoint* (*SPS*), I argue that many central moral concepts, including those of moral obligation, right and wrong, and moral rights, have an irreducibly second-personal structure. By this I mean that these concepts implicitly refer, in a way other ethical and normative concepts do not, to claims and demands that must be capable of being addressed second personally. For example, I argue that it is part of the very idea of a moral (claim) right that the right holder has the authority to make the claim of the person against whom the right is held and hold him accountable for compliance. As P. F. Strawson argued influentially in "Freedom and Resentment" a half century ago, accountability is second personal (as he put it, "inter-personal") in its nature (Strawson 1968: 77). When we hold people accountable, whether others or ourselves, we take a different perspective on them and implicitly relate *to* them in a way that is different than when we view them in an "objective" or third-personal way.

I argue that the second-personal character of central moral concepts has fundamental implications for the kinds of reasons it takes to justify beliefs and attitudes that involve these concepts. Although nothing can rule out consequentialist moral theories on conceptual grounds alone, I maintain that it does follow from my analysis, as it did indeed from Strawson's, that there is a fundamental conceptual difference between the good and the right, and that considerations showing that an action would be desirable, even from an impartial point of view, are not "reasons of the right kind" to establish by themselves the action's deontic status—its being either morally obligatory, prohibited, or permissible.

In the essays that follow and in this volume's successor (*Honor, History, and Relationship: Essays in Second-Personal Ethics II*), I investigate issues, argumentative threads, and implications that I was only able to touch on briefly in *SPS*. The essays in the current volume are divided into three sections. Those in the first section concern different aspects of *morality*—what is distinctive about morality as an ethical concept, whether the fact that an action is morally wrong is *itself* a reason against doing it that is additional to the considerations that make the act wrong, whether substantive moral norms follow from morality's second-personal form, whether morality could be particularistic and not require general principles, and, finally, the metaethical character of "relational" or "bipolar" obligations that one person has *to* another.

The two essays in the second section concern different aspects of *autonomy*. The first distinguishes different concepts of autonomy, most importantly, between autonomy as a good, whether personal or impersonal, and autonomy as something we can claim or demand, such as a right to shape our own lives. It discusses what Kant called "autonomy of the will" and argues that there is a way of interpreting Kant's notion in which it is a presupposition of any justifiable claim to autonomy. The second essay approaches autonomy from what may seem an unexpected direction: how an agent's desires and will can give her reasons for acting. It argues that these do create reasons, but not owing to an "internal reasons" thesis of the sort associated with Bernard Williams (Williams 1981b). Rather, an agent's own desires and will gives her reasons in the same way another's do, as a form of respect for her autonomy and second-personal authority.

The essays in the final section are all concerned with different aspects of authority and law. The first two discuss Joseph Raz's influential "normal justification thesis," according to which claims to the (practical) authority to direct someone can be justified by a showing that his following this direction would enable him to comply better with reasons for acting he independently has. Raz's thesis poses a potential challenge to a second-personal account, since if it were true, second-personal reasons to comply with a practical authority might derive from non-second-personal reasons. I argue in the first essay that putative justifications of this kind are insufficient because they do not account for authority's conceptual tie to accountability. Nothing can establish that someone has authority over us in a way that gives rise to a duty to obey without establishing that we are accountable for obedience. Razian "normal" justifications have no tendency to show this. In the second essay, I discuss Raz's claim that satisfying the conditions of the normal justification thesis can show that a putative authority's direction creates a "preemptive" reason for acting as she directs and "exclusionary" reasons against acting on competing reasons. Against this, I argue that reasons for acting of these kinds can be created only by genuine authorities we are accountable for obeying. I conclude that practical authority is irreducibly second personal, despite Raz's arguments.

The final two essays sketch a second-personal approach to law and, more specifically, to the law of torts. The first indicates how fundamental issues of jurisprudence concerning the nature of law and the differences between criminal and private or civil law might be illuminated by a second-personal framework. The second takes up a leading theory in tort law, civil recourse theory, and argues that it is best elaborated in second-personal terms as a form of mutual accountability.

The essays in this volume need not be read consecutively. I assume that most readers will have more interest in one topic or another and will proceed accordingly. There are significant connections between these essays, however, as I hope will become evident. A core set of ideas about second-personal concepts and reasons, and the second-person perspective, runs throughout. Since the essays are not meant to be read in any particular order, I have not seen how to avoid some repetition in laying out the core ideas. I apologize for this, but hope that readers will find the repetition more helpful than annoying.

To provide a more specific idea of what to expect, the essays might be briefly summarized as follows.

Morality

"Morality's Distinctiveness" begins with Anscombe's and Sidgwick's characterization of the difference between ancient ethics and "modern moral philosophy" and argues that what is distinctive about morality as it is conceived in modern ethical thought is the conceptual centrality of irreducibly second-personal notions, such as obligation and accountability (Anscombe 1998; Sidgwick 1964, 1967). The argument proceeds by considering David Hume's famous claim that the distinction between "moral virtues" and estimable non-moral "natural abilities," is purely verbal (Hume 1978, 1985). Hume makes this claim, I argue, because he fails to appreciate the conceptual difference between third-personal evaluative attitudes, like disesteem and contempt, and second-personal Strawsonian "reactive attitudes" like moral blame (Strawson 1968). Hume's failure to see more than a verbal difference between the moral and the non-moral is thus evidence that what is distinctive about morality is its second-personal aspect.

"Bipolar Obligation" investigates the concept of a so-called "relational duty" that is owed *to* someone. Unlike the idea of a moral obligation *period*, bipolar obligations have not only *obligors*, agents who are subject to the obligation, but also *obligees*, those to whom the obligation is owed. They thus entail a correlative claim right that the obligee has to claim *of the obligor* the conduct that the obligor is obligated to the obligee to perform. Although bipolar obligations have figured prominently in recent moral and political theory, little attention has been paid to their metaethics. In what does a bipolar obligation consist? I provide an account of the concept of bipolar obligation that is connected to the account of moral obligation period I present in *SPS*. Both concepts are shown to be second personal, but in different ways. Someone is morally obligated to do something period just in case her doing it is something that anyone (including she) justifiably demands of her as a *representative person*. And someone is obligated *to another* to do something just in case the obligee has the individual discretionary authority to make demands of the obligor *as the obligee* and to hold the obligor *personally* accountable. Moral obligations period conceptually implicate *representative authority*, whereas bipolar obligations involve the obligee's *individual authority*. Both forms of authority are second personal, however, since they implicitly involve address, whether this authority is exercised by first, second, or by third *parties*.

"Moral Obligation: Form and Substance" begins with the second-personal analysis of moral obligation's form that I defend in *SPS* and argues that this analysis has implications for substantive moral requirements. Given what it is to take responsibility for oneself and hold oneself answerable, I argue, it follows that if there are any moral obligations at all, there must also exist a basic *pro tanto* obligation not to undermine one another's moral autonomy.

"But It Would Be Wrong" considers whether the fact that an action would be wrong is *itself* a reason not to perform it. *SPS* defended the conceptual thesis that an action is wrong if, and only if, it would be blameworthy to perform the action without adequate excuse. This is a "warranted attitude" thesis about moral obligation, right, and wrong. It says that something is morally obligatory if, and only if, failing to perform the action would make the agent a justified object of blame were he to omit the action without excuse. Warranted attitude accounts of *value* suggest what Scanlon has called "buck-passing" about value, that being valuable is not itself a reason, but "passes the buck" to reasons for valuing something in which its value consists (Scanlon 1998). Would a warranted attitude account of moral obligation and wrongness, such as that offered in *SPS*, not entail, therefore, that being morally obligatory or wrong gives no reason for action itself? I argue it does not. Although warranted attitude theories of normative concepts entail buck-passing with respect to reasons for the specific attitudes that are inherently involved in the concept, the concepts of moral obligation and wrong are normative, in the first instance, not for action, but for Strawsonian "reactive attitudes" through which we hold people answerable for their actions. On this analysis, moral obligations are demands we legitimately make as representative persons, and the fact that an act would violate such a demand, and so disrespect the authority these demands presuppose, is indeed a reason not to perform a wrongful act that is additional to whatever features make the act wrong.[1]

"Morality and Principle" argues against what Jonathan Dancy calls "moral particularism." Dancy's arguments for this position proceed entirely on the basis of general features of normative reasons for acting rather than anything having to do with morality in particular. Dancy argues that the existence of normative reason for acting need not depend on there being valid general norms or principles from which these reasons derive. But Dancy does not consider whether there might be something about morality in particular that requires the existence of general *moral* principles. I argue that there is. What is distinctive about morality is not that there are impartial or impersonal reasons that favor or support some action, but that action is required or demanded of us—that we are morally obligated to act in the sense of being warrantedly held accountable for doing so and blamed if we do not and lack valid excuse. Though it is no part of the idea of the existence of a normative reason for acting in general that the agent must be able to know about and guide himself by this reason, this is central to the notion of any standard with which we can warrantedly be accountable for complying. A conceptual requirement of public accessibility is thus central to the existence of moral obligations in a way that is similar to one that requires that anything that can count as *law* (and legally obligate) be promulgated. The same considerations that push toward the necessity of general principles in law, for example, legal doctrines expressed in a judge's *ratio decidendi*, make them no less necessary in morality.

---

[1] Mostly, when I speak about our representative authority to *demand* obligatory conduct, I do not mean that just any person has standing to make the demand in speech or to reproach others for violations. Like Strawson, I hold that we implicitly make the demand through our "proneness" to demanding reactive attitudes (Strawson 1968: 92–3).

Autonomy

How can an agent's desires or will give him reasons for acting? This is the question with which "Because I Want It" is concerned. Not long ago this question might have seemed silly, since it was widely believed that all reasons for acting must be based in agents' desires.[2] The interesting question, it appeared, was not how what an agent wants could give him reasons, but how anything else could. In recent years, however, this earlier orthodoxy has been turned on its head, as a growing number of philosophers have come to stress the action-guiding role of reasons in deliberation from the agent's point of view. What a deliberating agent has in view is rarely his own will or desires as such, even if taking something as a reason is intimately tied to desire. Desires are "backgrounded"; what is in the deliberative foreground are the objects of desire and their features (Pettit and Smith 1990). Although a central argument of my *Impartial Reason* (1983) proceeded along these lines, I argue here that there is a generally unappreciated way in which an agent's will, desires, preferences, and concerns *do* give him reasons that outstrip any he has to have these attitudes, namely, analogously to the way another person's can give him reasons. To fail to take another person's will, desires, concerns, and so on, into account, say, because one thinks, however correctly, that she lacks good reason to have these attitudes, constitutes a kind of disrespect. I argue that self-respect speaks in favor of taking one's own actual will and concerns into account beyond the reasons one has to have these attitudes. This means, perhaps ironically, that what makes an agent's will normative for her is her capacity to take a second-personal attitude toward herself.

"The Value of Autonomy and Autonomy of the Will" begins by distinguishing the bewildering variety of things "autonomy" has been use to refer to in moral and political philosophy. Kant's famous doctrine of autonomy of the will, that the will is "a law to itself independently of any property of the objects of volition," can seem completely disconnected to any of these. I argue, however, that Kant's idea can be interpreted in a way that is indeed connected to autonomy in a familiar sense, but not autonomy as a good, rather as something to which we can claim a right, namely, a right of independence or self-determination. This is owing to the second-personal character of the concept of claim rights and inescapable presuppositions of the second-person standpoint. When we claim a right to something, we have to assume that the person against whom we claim it can recognize and be moved by the legitimacy of our claim against him and not just by the desirability of states of affairs. The *right* and the *desirable* are fundamentally distinct concepts, and though the latter does not presuppose autonomy of the will, the former does.

---

[2] For discussion of the "desired-based reasons thesis" see Darwall 1983: 25–82.

Authority and Law

SPS argues that the concepts of authority, legitimate demand, accountability, and of distinctive, second-personal reasons for complying with these demands form a circle of irreducibly second-personal concepts, that each concept entails the others, and that no proposition that involves only concepts outside the circle can entail any proposition involving concepts within it. "Authority and Second-Personal Reasons for Acting" considers a potential challenge to this claim from Raz's "normal justification thesis," which holds that the normal way of justifying someone's claim to authority over another person is that the second would comply better with the reasons that apply to him anyway were he to treat the first's directives as authoritative. I argue against Raz's thesis that it provides "reasons of the wrong kind" for authority. The argument is analogous to Strawson's argument in "Freedom and Resentment" that the fact that it would be desirable to blame someone cannot show that what he did is *culpable*, that blame is a fitting response to what he has done (Strawson 1968). Similarly, the fact that it would be desirable, because one would better comply with independent reasons, to treat someone's directives as authoritative, cannot show that obedience is called for in the way it is to genuine authority. Hence it cannot follow that someone actually *has* the relevant authority.

"Authority and Reasons: Exclusionary and Second Personal" takes on a second aspect of the "normal justification thesis," namely, Raz's claim that when the thesis's conditions are met, the putative authority's directives provide pre-emptive and exclusionary reasons for acting. I argue that this is not true owing to considerations similar to those that show that the normal justification thesis is mistaken about the grounds for practical authority. Raz is right that genuinely authoritative directives create pre-emptive and exclusionary reasons, but that is because genuine authority entails accountability for compliance. Practical authority is thus revealed to be internal to the circle of second-personal concepts; the pre-emptive and exclusionary character of reasons created by legitimate demands cannot be accounted for independently of their second-personal character.

"Law and the Second-Person Standpoint" discusses how a second-personal framework can shed light on jurisprudential issues concerning the nature of law. If the concept of practical authority is irreducibly second personal, it would not be surprising that fundamental legal ideas should turn out to be second personal also. I argue that this is indeed the case. Even if law and legal authority are *de facto* matters, they nonetheless purport to have authority *de jure* and, therefore, that those subject to law are genuinely obligated and answerable for compliance. In this way, the law purports to give citizens second-personal reasons, and this explains their putatively pre-emptive and exclusionary character. A second-personal framework can also explain fundamental differences between distinct branches of law. Criminal law is structurally analogous to the "moral law"; it creates obligations that are analogous to moral obligations *period*. Just as the moral community or representative persons have the authority to demand compliance with moral obligations, so also are cases in criminal law appropriately brought by "the people" and their representatives (prosecutors). Matters of private law, by contrast, concern legal obligations that, like bipolar moral obligations, are owed to obligees. They therefore entail claim rights held specifically by obligees. It follows from the argument of "Bipolar Obligation" that they entail obligees' individual discretionary authority to hold obligors personally accountable. It is a reflection of this that cases in tort and contract law are not brought by the state or by the people, but by putative victims, and that successful cases involve damages payable to them.

"Civil Recourse as Mutual Accountability," written with Julian Darwall, concerns a prominent theory in the law of torts: civil recourse theory. The main theoretical divide in tort law is between consequentialist (including economic) approaches, on the one hand, and justice-based approaches, on the other. The major justice-based approaches are, respectively, corrective justice theories and civil recourse theories. Corrective justice theories hold that obligors who injure and violate the tort rights of obligees have a derivative duty of repair and that the function of tort law is to enforce that duty. Civil recourse theorists argue that corrective justice theories fail to capture the distinctive standing of victimized obligees. The function of tort law is not to correct injustice or enforce a duty of repair, but rather to provide a forum in which victims can get recourse and take action against their tortfeasing obligors. Civil recourse theorists sometimes characterize this as involving a kind of retaliation or revenge. We argue that civil recourse theory is right about the special standing (*individual authority*) victims have to hold the tortfeasor accountable, but that it risks failing to appreciate what tortfeasors' accountability to victims consists in, since it fails properly to distinguish between accountability and retaliation or vengeance. Accountability's second-personal structure entails that it involves not returning disrespect for disrespect, but a respectful demand for respect. Accountability is always fundamentally reciprocal.

I
Morality

1

Morality's Distinctiveness

"Morality," as philosophers currently use the term, refers to something different than it does when someone speaks of the morality of ancient Athens or that of Pashtun tribes of contemporary Afghanistan. Neither is it the same as any individual's morality. What we have in mind in these latter uses are social *mores* or customs, or norms and values to which some individual subscribes. *Moralities* are identified socially or psychologically, via their acceptance by some individual or group. They are thus items that can be studied by the empirical social sciences, understood broadly, perhaps, to include empathic or hermeneutic *Verstehen* no less than detached observation. *Morality*, as we philosophers now understand it, however, is an essentially normative rather than an empirical concept, however broadly "empirical" might be understood.[1] Moreover, "morality" in this sense admits of only a singular use. There are many actual and possible *moralities* (embodied psychologically and socially), but there is only one *morality*. And it has an apparent necessity that renders any distinction between the possible and the actual moot. Morality presents itself, in the words of the seventeenth-century Cambridge Platonist Ralph Cudworth, as "eternal and immutable" (Cudworth 1996).

An anthropologist, historian, or historical sociologist might inform us about some society's or group's morality, but expertise of these kinds would not constitute competence on the normative question of what *morality* requires, even on what morality requires of people who belong to that society or group. Facts about the *mores* actually in place would of course be relevant to the latter question, but they would not settle it.

To be sure, social groups and individuals usually understand their moralities in inherently normative terms as well and may make no distinction between *their* morality and the normative standards and convictions to which they are committed. I take it, however, that the concept of morality in the sense we philosophers are interested in is a concept that comes onto the scene only when reflective distance of this kind has been achieved to refer to standards that have normative force independently of their acceptance, independently, that is, of the morality's being *theirs* or, for that matter, of its being *anyone's*.

If morality is inherently normative, it is not constituted by just any normative standards. Most obviously, there can be normative questions, like what we should

---

[1] I take it that this conceptual claim does not beg any metaphysical or epistemological questions.

believe, that we do not generally include within the ethical. But morality in the sense we currently are interested in is not constituted by just any *ethical* standards either. We can use "moral" and "morality" in any way we like, of course. But though the terms are sometimes used broadly as synonyms for "ethical" and "ethics," the sense I have in mind here is what Gibbard calls "morality's" "narrow sense" (Gibbard 1990: 40–3).

It is evidence that philosophers generally use "morality" more narrowly than "ethics" that the word does not appear in English translations of Aristotle's *Ethics* or Plato's *Republic*, though it sometimes does in commentaries on these texts.[2] The questions that Plato and Aristotle are interested in concern the good life, virtue, and noble or fine (*kalon*) action. And though these can find their way into philosophical discussions of morality, when they do, they typically have a distinctive inflection (concerning, for example, *moral* virtue and goodness) or they are treated as relevant, but not what is primarily at issue (for example the relation of the good—what Frankena called "non-moral value"—to moral goodness and moral right and wrong; Frankena 1973: 62). No one doubts that Plato and Aristotle count among the greatest ethical philosophers, but neither has much to say about morality in our current sense. Arguably, neither had the concept.[3]

Ancient Ethics and Modern Morality

Elizabeth Anscombe noted this feature of ancient ethics in her famous "Modern Moral Philosophy" (published in 1958), as did Henry Sidgwick, almost a century before. Anscombe argued that the "modern" concepts of "*moral* obligation and *moral* duty," hence "of what is *morally* right and wrong, and of the *moral* sense of 'ought' " are not to be found among the ancients (1998: 26).[4] As she put it picturesquely: "If someone professes to be expounding Aristotle and talks in a modern fashion about 'moral' such-and-such, he must be very imperceptive if he does not constantly feel like someone whose jaw has somehow got out of alignment: the teeth don't come together in a proper bite" (27).

The modern concept of morality, according to Anscombe, is modeled on the idea of law, essentially including "juridical" notions of obligation, culpability, and guilt (30–1). The point is not that the modern view makes no distinction between the moral and the legal. Rather it identifies a peculiar kind of law that differs conceptually from local, national, or even from international law, as it does also from any *society's morality* or

---

[2] This can be confirmed by a search of electronically available translations, such as W. D. Ross's and Terence Irwin's translations of Aristotle's *Nicomachean Ethics*, or Benjamin Jowett's or Paul Shorey's translations of Plato's *Republic*. See Kraut 2006 for an excellent account of why it is wrongheaded to take Aristotle's "*dein*" to refer to moral duty, obligation, or rightness.

[3] Similarly, Nietzsche's critique in the *Genealogy of Morals* is targeted specifically on morality rather than on ethics in general; indeed, it is itself partly an ethical critique: of "the value of [morality's] values" (Nietzsche 1998: 8). For an excellent discussion see Clark 1994.

[4] Of course, Anscombe was a critic of modern moral philosophy as she characterized it.

mores. So understood, human beings are subject to morality, what Kant calls the "moral law," not by inhabiting any earthly jurisdiction or by being part of any given social order, but just because we are moral agents in the company of others.

Sidgwick draws a similar contrast but with a different emphasis. "[I]n Platonism and Stoicism, and in Greek moral philosophy generally," Sidgwick writes, "but one regulative and governing faculty is recognised under the name of Reason—however the regulation of Reason may be understood; in the modern ethical view, when it has worked itself clear, there are found to be two—Universal Reason and Egoistic Reason, or Conscience and Self-love" (Sidgwick 1964: 198).[5] Sidgwick's own philosophical views raise interesting issues about how to interpret the relation between "Universal Reason" and "Conscience." According to Sidgwick's famous dualism of practical reason, there are two fundamentally independent rational dictates: Rational Prudence, "one ought to aim at one's own good," and Rational Benevolence, "as a rational being I am bound to aim at good generally" so "the good of any other individual as much as [my] own" (Sidgwick 1967: 381–2).

Sidgwick holds that only the latter is a distinctively *moral* obligation. Only then does he say that one is "morally bound" (382). But why? What does Sidgwick take to be special about morality and its "ought" that distinguishes it from the normative force of prudence?

Sidgwick's dualism might seem to provide the answer. Prudence is what is desirable, good, or rational from the agent's point of view or out of concern for her, so perhaps morality concerns what is desirable, good, or rational from a more inclusive or abstract perspective, in Sidgwick's memorable phrase, the "point of view of the universe" (Sidgwick 1967: 382). Perhaps the dictates of conscience or morality are simply the voice of reason from this universal point of view.

However, Sidgwick also stresses, like Anscombe, that "conscience" in modern ethical thought is essentially conceived with "quasi-jural notions" of obligation, "duty," and right (Sidgwick 1967: 106). This is important to add for two reasons. First, the ideas of moral obligation, right, and wrong cannot be captured in terms of what is desirable or rationally advisable from an impersonal or impartial, moral point of view (Darwall 2006). To see this, just consider whether or not it is a conceptually open question whether, given that an action would be most advisable, or desirable from a moral point of view, the action is morally *required* or whether it would be morally wrong to omit it. It seems obvious that this is a substantive normative question that is left open by the concepts involved.[6] In other words, it is a conceptually open question whether there can be such a thing as supererogation, actions that are morally advisable but not obligatory. Someone who asserts that possibility is clearly not saying something self-contradictory or otherwise conceptually confused. It clearly seems possible, moreover, for two people coherently to disagree in their normative convictions about

---

[5] For an excellent discussion of this passage, see Frankena 1992.
[6] Neither does it seem that the openness of the question might be due to lack of conceptual clarity.

whether morality always requires us to do what it would be morally best for us to do. But if these are conceptual possibilities, then the concepts of moral obligation, right, and wrong, must be different concepts from those of what it is desirable or advisable, or undesirable or inadvisable, from the moral point of view.

In *The Second-Person Standpoint*, I argue that the reason this is so is because the concept of moral obligation is conceptually tied to that of moral responsibility or accountability. It is a conceptual truth that what we are morally required or obligated to do, what it would be wrong for us not to do, is what we are warrantedly held accountable for doing and blamed for not doing if we omit the action without a valid excuse. Moral philosophers from Grotius on made a fundamental distinction between legitimate demands, on the one hand, and rational "counsel," on the other, and placed moral obligations squarely on the demand side of the ledger (Darwall 2012b).

Second, although it is certainly true that philosophers in the modern period began to take seriously the non-eudaimonist possibility that considerations of impersonal or impartial good provide normative reasons independently of whether the agent himself benefits (Francis Hutcheson is an excellent example), this thought is importantly different from the kind of supreme rational authority that modern moral philosophers, like Butler and Kant, came to claim for morality (Hutcheson 2004). Even Hutcheson (and Sidgwick himself) did not think that what is advisable or desirable from an impartial, impersonal, or universal point of view rationally trumps considerations of self-interest. They thought that the claims are either equally weighty or incommensurable. When philosophers in the modern period have claimed rational supremacy for morality, their claim has been that the moral "ought" is overriding *when it is interpreted in terms of moral requirement and obligation*. They have claimed that the fact that an action is, all things considered, morally *obligatory* (and so wrong not to do) invariably is or entails sufficient reason to do it independently of the agent's good or interest.

Sidgwick's contrast is therefore that whereas ancient Greek philosophy and pre-modern thought deriving from it (including classical natural law theories deriving from Aquinas) were eudaimonist, taking the agent's good to be the only ultimate source of normative reasons for action, many thinkers of the modern period came to believe in a juridical, distinctively obligating normative order, morality, that purports to provide a source of reasons that is distinct from, and can potentially conflict with, prudence or rational self-interest, however broadly these are conceived.[7]

For Anscombe, Sidgwick, and their followers, the concept of morality is a distinctively modern concept.[8] Though it has roots in the Stoic idea of natural law, divine law of the Abrahamic religions, and the classical natural law tradition deriving from Aquinas, the concept of morality that Anscombe and Sidgwick have in mind originates with the early modern natural law tradition of Grotius, Pufendorf, and the philosophers who followed

---

[7] So understood, morality or the "moral law" differs from law more properly so called in having *de jure* authority or normativity whether or not it has authority *de facto*.

[8] Including Schneewind 1998; Rawls 2000; and Darwall 1995, 1999, and 2012b.

them (Darwall 2012b).[9] Natural law, as these philosophers theorized it, is a set of juridical, obligating norms of right and wrong that any human moral agent is subject to independently of the contingencies of any given social or political order. It is what philosophers now call "morality."

In what follows, I want to explore what is special about morality. If, that is, Anscombe, Sidgwick, and their followers are correct about its provenance, then what is distinctive about the modern concept of morality?[10] It is a commonplace that morality, as the moderns conceive it, distinctively concerns agency and the will—how agents conduct themselves with respect to what is up to them. As Mill says in *The Subjection of Women*, "The principle of the modern movement in morals and politics, is that conduct, and conduct alone, entitles to respect" (Mill 1869: Ch. IV, ¶5, p. 325). I shall suggest that the reason this is so is because moral obligation as the moderns conceive it is tied conceptually to accountability and that this brings into play a set of attitudes, evaluations, and ways of regarding one another as mutually accountable moral agents or wills. What is distinctive about morality in the sense we moderns have in mind is that it consists of norms that any responsible agent can warrantedly be *held to* (by himself and others) as one mutually accountable agent among others. I have argued in the past that since accountability is inevitably a second-personal affair, so likewise is moral obligation (Darwall 2006). If its "quasi-jural" character is, therefore, a distinguishing element of our concept of morality, it will follow from my arguments that so also is its second-personal character.

Here, however, I would like to approach these points somewhat indirectly by considering Hume's famous claim that the distinction between moral and non-moral virtues is at best verbal. Hume is led to this conclusion, I shall argue, because he does not sufficiently appreciate the second-personal character of the attitudes that are distinctive of morality. My hope is that seeing how a failure to appreciate the second-personal character of central forms of moral assessment leads fairly naturally to Hume's conclusion can help us to see that the difference between the moral and the non-moral is tied, at least in part, to morality's second-personal character.

Hume's Claim: "Moral Virtues" vs. "Natural Abilities"

"No distinction is more usual in all systems of ethics," Hume writes in the *Treatise*, "than that betwixt *natural abilities* and *moral virtues*" (3.3.4.1). Under "natural abilities," Hume includes involuntary "mental qualities" like wit, intelligence, and "good humour" that are "on the same footing with bodily endowments" in being "almost invariable by any art or industry" (3.3.4.1, 3.3.4.4). Moral virtues contrast with these,

---

[9] Grotius and Pufendorf's French translator, Jean Barbeyrac, frequently uses "*moralité*" ("morality") in discussing their natural law theories. See, for example, his *Historical and Critical Account of the Science of Morality*, appended to his translation of Pufendorf's *Law of Nature and Nations*.

[10] For a critique, see Irwin 2008. I criticize Irwin in Darwall 2011a and 2012b.

according to the writers that Hume is criticizing, in distinctively concerning the *will*; only character traits that are expressed in voluntary choice are genuine moral virtues. One such writer, especially salient to Hume, was Hutcheson. Hutcheson held that moral good and virtue are realized only in agents' motives and, therefore, that "no external circumstances of fortune" or "involuntary disadvantag[e] can exclude any mortal from the most heroick virtue" (Hutcheson 2004: 234).[11]

Hume and Hutcheson are both sentimentalists, but Hume has a further, intramural disagreement with Hutcheson that is intimately related to their difference over whether there is a real difference between moral virtues and estimable natural abilities. Hutcheson holds that judgments of virtue and vice, moral good and evil, involve distinctive irreducible sentiments ("simple ideas" that Hutcheson calls "approbation" and "condemnation," respectively) that differ from esteem for natural abilities. But though Hume titles the section of the *Treatise* in which he develops his own sentimentalist account "Moral Distinctions Deriv'd From a Moral Sense," using Hutcheson's term for the human sensitivity to simple ideas of moral approbation and condemnation, Hume quite explicitly rejects Hutcheson's theory that judgments of vice and virtue involve any such "original instinct" (Hume 3.2.1.6–7). Hume holds that moral judgments are made through the same psychological mechanism, sympathy, that is involved in esteem and disesteem quite generally, whether moral or non-moral.[12]

Hume recognizes that there is something "modern" about the idea he is opposing, since he contrasts it with a tendency among "the antients" to include "under the title of moral virtues" "qualities" that are no less "involuntary and necessary" than wit, "judgment and imagination"—characteristics like "constancy, fortitude, and magnanimity" (3.3.4.3). Only the fortunate are in a position to show Aristotelian magnanimity, for example. For the more recent writers that Hume has in mind, however, this disqualifies magnanimity from being a genuine moral virtue.[13]

Hume was profoundly suspicious of this modern idea. As he saw it, the mere performance of an act of whatever kind "has no merit" in itself. "When we praise any actions, we ... consider the actions as signs or indications of certain principles in the mind and temper" (3.2.1.2). And whether those principles should be regarded as moral virtues or as estimable natural abilities is at best "merely a dispute of words" (3.3.4.1). Philosophers who enter into it "encroach upon the province of grammarians" (*Enquiry*, Ap4.1). Worse, Hume harbored a proto-Nietzschean suspicion that what really lay behind the modern tendency was an attempt by religionists to reduce the ethical to self-abnegating

---

[11] When Hutcheson sketches a way of estimating moral good, he consequently argues that what matters is the ratio of the good someone produces to his abilities and opportunities (Hutcheson 2004: 126–34). Unless we discount for fortune in this way, we don't home in on a person's moral goodness, according to Hutcheson, since these can only concern his will.

[12] I discuss this difference between Hume and Hutcheson and its relevance to their respective relations to utilitarianism in Darwall 1994.

[13] We should note for the record, however, that Hume thinks that "all moralists" would agree with "the antients" in classifying Aristotelian magnanimity as a "moral virtue" (3.3.4.3).

obedience to divine sanction and command. "Upon the whole," Hume wrote to Hutcheson, "I desire to take my *Catalogue of Virtues* from Cicero's *Offices*, not from the *Whole Duty of Man*," referring to a text of his Calvinist upbringing (Burton 1846: 144).

So far as Hume can see, there is only one putative rationale for restricting moral virtue to the voluntary, and it is at once beside the point and mischievous. Intentional conduct "may be chang'd by the motives of reward and punishment," he writes, so "legislators," "divines, and moralists, have principally applied themselves to . . . regulating . . . voluntary actions, and have endeavour'd to produce additional motives for being virtuous in that particular" (3.3.4.4). But even if the desire to avoid sanctions can lead someone to perform an *act* that is the normal expression of a virtue, say, a beneficent act that might otherwise have been motivated by benevolence, a desire to avoid sanctions is a motive of the wrong kind for virtue. The resulting conduct will be, say, beneficent without being benevolent, so not really virtuous. Thus the fact that voluntary conduct responds to sanctions is at best beside the point; truly virtuous conduct does not. Worse, the attempt to read the involuntary out of the catalogue of virtues on these grounds smacks to Hume of an ecclesiastical agenda to stifle and suppress benign aspects of human nature that should be resisted. Better, like the ancients, to think of ethical virtue not in terms of obedience to any kind of law, but as intrinsically estimable qualities and traits, whether these are voluntary or not (hence moral or non-moral).

Put this way, Hume's complaints about "modern moral philosophy" resonate with more recent critiques like Nietzsche's in the nineteenth century and those of Anscombe, Williams, and others, in the twentieth. Hume may not have had as sophisticated an appreciation or genealogy of *ressentiment* as Nietzsche, but he is certainly in the same neighborhood when he rejects the "monkish virtues" of "self-denial" and "humility" on the grounds that

A gloomy, hair-brained enthusiast, after his death, may have a place in the calendar; but will scarcely ever be admitted, when alive, into intimacy and society, except by those who are as delirious and dismal as himself. (*Enquiry* 9.1.3)

Anscombe's famous manifesto against "modern moral philosophy" sounds themes not altogether dissimilar to Hume's when she argues that modern moralists have helped themselves to a law conception of morals without the theological metaphysics necessary to give it authority and that ethical philosophers would do better to return to the kind of ancient virtue ethics found in Aristotle (Anscombe 1998). And Bernard Williams carries elements of Hume's and Nietzsche's critique forward when he argues that the modern concept of morality tends toward an all-consuming obsession that subjugates the self and alienates us both from ourselves and from each other (Williams and Smart 1973: 111–18, 1981a, 1985). Better to return, as Williams does in *Ethics and the Limits of Philosophy*, to the broad Socratic question of how one should live (1985: 1).[14]

---

[14] See Baier 1993 for a related critique of Kant's ethics and defense of Hume.

Third-Personal Sentimentalism

Now Hume takes judgments of virtue to concern a certain kind of warranted sentiment or response. As we shall see, he allows that there are subtle differences between
the response that admired natural abilities often stimulate and that more typically
inspired by the motives and traits that moderns like Hutcheson place within a catalogue
of genuine moral virtues. The former most frequently give rise to "esteem," while the
latter tend to be the object of "love." But Hume's point is that, whatever their
differences, these responses are fundamentally similar—both are disinterested pleasures
we feel in contemplating a person's qualities, hence pleasures any spectator can be
expected to feel toward the quality when she contemplates it on a "general survey"
from an observer's point of view (3.2.2.24; 3.3.5.1).

I believe that Hume is right about some of this. But when we properly diagnose why
he is, we see something important that his account misses. I shall argue that what is
common to love and esteem, as Hume understands them, is that they are essentially
third-personal observer's responses. In this way, they are like aesthetic responses. It is
no accident, therefore, that Hume often refers to virtue as moral beauty (e.g., 3.1.1.22;
3.2.1.8). The crucial point is that neither Humean esteem nor love involves any form
of *relating to* its object, actual or imaginary. Consequently, one can have either response
without having to presuppose any capacities in its object to relate back in some way
that might reciprocate the response.

Humean love and esteem differ in this way from the distinctive responses that
P. F. Strawson called "reactive attitudes," which Strawson influentially argued mediate
moral accountability (Strawson 1968). In *SPS*, I argue that central moral concepts,
most obviously that of moral obligation, are connected to accountability conceptually
and, therefore, to reactive attitudes through which we hold ourselves accountable
(Darwall 2006). When you and I feel reactive attitudes—whether "personal" reactions
like resentment or guilt or "impersonal" ones like indignation or moral blame—we
implicitly address demands *to* the objects of these attitudes; we take up what Strawson
called an "inter-personal" (what I call a "second-personal") standpoint toward someone and imaginatively *hold* her responsible (Darwall 2006). We view her from the
perspective, as Strawson says, of "involvement or participation in a human relationship" with her, as opposed to from an "objective" point of view. As I sometimes put it,
reactive attitudes come with an RSVP, an implicit bid for the other's recognition of the
authority we assume to justify our implicit demand. The responses that mediate moral
accountability—holding someone responsible—are thus second personal rather than
third personal. Blame, in other words, is not a form of disesteem. Blame is second
personal; disesteem, even moral disesteem, is third personal.

In being tied to accountability, moral obligations are connected conceptually to the
second-personal reactive attitudes that mediate it. It is a conceptual truth, I argue, that
what is morally obligatory is what it would be blameworthy (that is, would warrant
the reactive attitude of moral blame) were the agent to perform the action without

adequate excuse (Darwall 2006). Blame and guilt implicitly address moral demands to their objects and bid for their object's recognition of the demand's legitimacy. In this way, they purport to place bearer and object into a relationship of reciprocal second-personal recognition.

When you view someone "objectively," by contrast, Strawson says, "though you may fight him, you cannot quarrel with him, and though you may talk to him . . . you cannot reason with him" (Strawson 1968: 79) Strawson's contrast between talking to or fighting with someone and "quarreling" with him may not be immediately clear, but Strawson is evidently leaning on "quarreling's" juridical roots in the idea of making an *objection* or asserting a *claim*.[15] It is this second-personal character of reactive attitudes that enables them to mediate mutual accountability. And it is also this aspect that explains a reactive attitude's distinctive focus on, and its implicit assumptions about, its object's *will*. I shall argue that the responses that Hume points to lack this interpersonal or second-personal aspect that is in play whenever you and I hold one another and ourselves to account morally.

Being bound by a moral obligation is thus different from being subject to just any norm or standard, say a standard of excellence or virtue, or even a standard of base-level performance that determines being "up to standard." It is part of the very idea of moral obligation that one is accountable for compliance, whether to God, as theological voluntarists thought, or to one another (and ourselves) as equal members of the moral community, as Strawson and I would urge. And it is part of the very idea of having the standing to hold someone responsible, oneself or someone else, that one has the authority to expect or demand some conduct. Nothing like this is any part whatsoever of the general idea of applying a standard to someone, even one of minimally competent performance. If I try to play the trombone, then, like anyone else, I am subject to standards for trombone playing, which determine whether my playing is minimally competent, excellent, or whatever. But I am not answerable or accountable for complying with these standards in the way that we are with moral obligations. For that to be true, reactive attitudes, like blame or guilt, would have to be warranted.

It is the idea of authoritative demand and what we presuppose when we address putatively legitimate demands and hold someone accountable for compliance with them that creates a focus on the capacity for moral agency and its exercise. From Hume's perspective, characteristics of a person's will are simply one of a variety of things that we may evaluate about her and esteem or love her for, including, perhaps, her powers of trombone playing, and there is no more reason to think that they are objects of a fundamentally different kind of evaluative response than there is to think that we have a different kind of response to fine trombone playing. We can admire

---

[15] The *Oxford English Dictionary* gives the following definition: "To make a complaint, protest, or objection; to find fault, take exception," and the following etymology: "after Middle French *quereler* to assert one's claim to (a right, property)" <www.oed.com/viewdictionaryentry/Entry/155979>.

people for their skill and accomplishments on the trombone no less than for their steady commitment to just and honest dealing. From this point of view, the modern focus on the will can seem a kind of fetish.

My Strawsonian counter-claim is that reactive attitudes, like moral blame, that are involved in assessing moral responsibility are *essentially* interpersonal (second-personal) responses to someone's will (Darwall 2006). They implicitly address a putatively authoritative demand on another's will, thereby express the will of the person who has the attitude, and call for reciprocation in the will and practical reasoning of their objects. They are not just one kind of disesteem among others.

Hume's Argument

We can turn now to the specifics of Hume's critique of the modern distinction between estimable natural abilities and moral virtues. Hume allows, again, that there are frequently differences between the responses that are normally inspired by natural abilities and those to which modern moral philosophers' virtues more typically give rise. Natural abilities often inspire "esteem" rather than the "love," which, Hume and Hutcheson agree, is the appropriate response to a moral virtue like benevolence.[16] But although natural abilities like "good sense" and "genius" beget esteem, Hume thinks that others, like "wit" and "humour" give rise to love (3.3.4.2). And things are complicated further, since, although many virtues, more usually so called, beget love, there are others that we naturally respond to with esteem.

The characters of *Caesar* and *Cato*, as drawn by *Sallust*, are both of them virtuous, in the strictest sense of the word; but in a different way: Nor are the sentiments entirely the same which arise from them. The one produces love; the other esteem: The one is amiable; the other awful: We could wish to meet with the one character in a friend; the other character we wou'd be ambitious of in ourselves. (3.3.4.2)

Admirable natural abilities are more typically objects of esteem than of love, qualities we are likelier to be ambitious of in ourselves than desirous of in a friend. But Hume thinks this is not always true, since we appropriately respond to wit and humor with love also and want them in friends no less than in ourselves. But neither are all moral virtues objects of love rather than esteem. Courage and other virtuous traits that Hume collects under "greatness of mind" inspire awe rather than love, so Hume contrasts them with "benevolence" and "goodness."

Despite these differences, Hume holds that love and esteem are "at the bottom the same passions, and arise from like causes" (3.3.4.2n; see also 2.2.2.10). According to Hume's psychology, both love and esteem are pleasurable sentiments that arise by sympathy (in his technical sense of an idea of a feeling's being transformed into the feeling itself) when we contemplate things that are related to someone in some way

---

[16] In the next several paragraphs, I am indebted to discussion with Julian Darwall.

that brings pleasure to him or others.[17] When I contemplate someone's benevolence, for example, my mind is carried by an association of ideas to its normal consequence, pleasure in others, which sympathy transforms into pleasure in me, the observer. This pleasurable sentiment then takes the other as object by Hume's "double relations" of sentiments and objects, and love for the benevolent person results. When I contemplate someone's riches, natural beauty, or genius, my mind is similarly carried by association to the pleasure of the person who has these qualities, which sympathy then transforms into pleasure in me. Here, again, this pleasurable sentiment in me can take the other person as its object, via the requisite double relations, and I love the other person.

The superficial difference between love and esteem arises, according to Hume, because we naturally "compare" our position to others, and this comparison can compete with sympathetic pleasures. So if I am ambitious of riches, natural beauty, or genius, and I contemplate someone who has more of these, this can, by the same double relations, tend to make me feel humility also. Esteem is produced when love and humility are mixed together, resulting in a sentiment that, although "more severe" or "serious" than love, is nevertheless still a pleasure (3.3.4.2n).

In spite of this superficial difference, Hume's view is that love and esteem are fundamentally the same response; both are pleasurable sentiments felt on contemplating someone's qualities. Of course, not even Hume is willing to count someone's riches and fine house as part of his virtue or merit. He restricts the latter to a person's "mental qualities," although it seems doubtful that he can do so on other than verbal grounds since his view of the relevant psychology seems in all respects the same (3.3.4.1). We need not bother with that, however, since we are interested in what is common to love and esteem of mental qualities in general and why Hume thinks that the usual distinction modern moralists make *within* these is only verbal. The central point is Hume's contention that what makes something a merit or demerit, praise-worthy as a virtue or "blameable" as a vice, whether it is a "moral virtue" concerned with voluntary choice or not, is that it is appropriately the object of a pleasurable or painful sentiment when contemplated "on a general survey," that is, from a *third-person point of view* (3.3.5.1).

In the second *Enquiry*, Hume attempts to finesse the issue by speaking in more general terms of "merit" and "demerit." He admits that "some blameable or censurable qualities are called *defects*, rather than vices" (Ap4.1). But he claims, again, that this is merely a verbal preference that does not mark any underlying evaluative difference. Whatever mental qualities "are the object of love or esteem . . . form a part of personal merit." And those that "are the object of censure or reproach . . . detract from the character of the person possessed of them," whether they have to do with voluntary choice or not (Ap4.1). Moreover, Hume claims that even the usual verbal preference is

---

[17] For a discussion of Humean sympathy and how it functions in his account of the moral sentiment, see Darwall 1994.

not consistently marked. "Who did ever say, except by way of irony, that such a one was a man of great virtue, but an egregious blockhead?" (Ap4.2).[18] "A blemish, a fault, a vice, a crime," Hume adds; "these expressions seem to denote different degrees of censure and disapprobation; which are, however, all of them, at the bottom, pretty nearly of the same kind or species" (Ap4.22).

Now again, I follow Strawson in holding that Strawsonian reactive attitudes have an ineliminable "inter-personal" or second-personal aspect that suits them to holding people responsible. But there is nothing in praising and blaming responses, *as Hume understands these*, that involves any such imaginative address or, consequently, any presupposition that the object of the address is capable of recognizing its validity and regulating his own will by the legitimacy of the demand that is implicitly addressed. The perspective from which we feel Humean esteem, love, disesteem, and hatred, and so judge merit or demerit, is a third-person standpoint. It is possible to be put off this point by the fact that Hume frequently uses "blame" to refer to disesteem of demerit in all its forms. When one looks at these uses in context, however, it becomes clear that by "blame" Hume does not mean anything that is implicitly addressed to its object, as when we hold someone to blame as *culpable* with Strawsonian reactive attitudes. Rather, Hume uses "blame" to refer to any attribution of defect whether it is "a blemish, a fault, a vice, or a crime" (Ap4.22).[19]

When someone feels disesteem or disdain for an "egregious blockhead," there is clearly no implicit demand that the object of his disdain stop being so stupid or answer for his stupidity. Neither is the disdain intelligible only on the assumption that its object is capable of understanding what a blockhead he is. To the contrary, it is even more intelligible on the assumption that he is not. And those who feel the disdain (as opposed, say, to blame for "acting like an egregious blockhead") are far likelier to express their disdain, whether actually *or* imaginatively, to other *cognoscenti* than to the blockhead himself. The contrast with second-personal reactive attitudes like moral blame could not be starker. When we blame someone for something, we implicitly hold her answerable in a way that implicitly addresses a putatively legitimate demand to her to desist; we bid for her recognition of the demand's legitimacy and for her to take responsibility for her conduct, including through the reciprocating reactive attitude of guilt. In so doing, we cannot help but presuppose that the object of our attitude is a moral agent who is capable of the relevant recognition and reciprocating understanding and attitudes. The implicitly second-personal aspect of reactive attitudes makes this presupposition unavoidable. You cannot coherently attempt to enter into a second-personal relation with someone except on such an assumption.

For Hume, on the other hand, moral assessments are fundamentally aesthetic. "The approbation of moral qualities . . . proceeds entirely from a moral taste, from certain

---

[18] "One whose head is blockish or 'wooden'; an utterly stupid fellow." *Oxford English Dictionary*.

[19] According to *Past Masters*, "blame" appears 36 times in Books II and III of the *Treatise*. I conjecture that in no instance is it used to express a Strawsonian reactive attitude.

sentiments of pleasure or disgust, which arise upon the contemplation and view of particular qualities or characters" (3.3.1.15). Disgust is thus, for Hume, a kind of "blame," but obviously it is not one that implicitly involves interpersonal relating or address. Indignation or anger at the weather is a kind of anthropomorphizing, seeing the weather as something that is appropriately held responsible and to which demands to change are appropriately addressed. Not so with disgust at a foul taste or smell or even, indeed, with disgust at moral corruption or wrongdoing. Finally, as I remarked, above, Hume frequently speaks of virtue and merit as "moral beauty," and of vice and demerit as "moral deformity." The perspective throughout is one of aesthetic distance rather than any standing to relate to others and address demands, much less that of common membership in a moral community.

Morality, Accountability, and Hume's Critique

Recall Hume's suspicion that modern moralists suppose a real distinction between moral virtue and natural abilities because they want, mistakenly, to model morality on divine law. As Hume sees it, their desire to restrict the moral to the voluntary derives from their misidentifying moral virtue with the desire to avoid sanctions. Hume is of course right that there is nothing virtuous about such a desire. But Hume misunderstands the way that sanctions enter into the modern concepts of moral accountability, culpability, and guilt, and, consequently, the resources that modern moral theory has, and has made use of, to avoid the misidentification of which Hume accuses it.

A useful example is an early modern natural lawyer who actually holds that morality is a law God imposes on his creatures that is made valid by God's superior authority: Samuel Pufendorf. Pufendorf has a philosophically subtle and penetrating theory of what such a view of morality must be committed to if it is to avoid the kind of criticism Hume lodges. Pufendorf explicitly distinguishes between deference to superior power from the desire to avoid sanctions, on the one hand, and the kind of motivation that must be available to an agent under genuinely obligating law, on the other. To put the point in terms made famous by H. L. A. Hart, there must be a distinction between being *obliged and obligated* (Hart 1961: 6–8). For Pufendorf, God can impose genuine law on his creatures only through *their recognition* of his authority so to direct them. His theory brings into play a whole battery of concepts—accountability, imputation, and authority—along with the capacities to operate with these concepts in practical thought.

Pufendorf makes a fundamental distinction between merely imposing oneself on another('s will) and that being done legitimately, with authority. And he connects this to an equally basic, and reciprocal, distinction within the obligated agent's motivation and practical reasoning between being moved by fear of a threatened sanction ("sense of an impending evil"), on the one hand, and being moved by respect for the legitimacy of the sanction (seeing that the evil "falls upon him justly"), on the other (1934: 91). In the latter case, Pufendorf says, the obligated will must be able "to judge itself worthy of some censure, unless it conforms to a prescribed rule" (1934: 91). Only then, he says, does the "obligation affect the will morally" (1934: 91). The "main difference between obligation and compulsion" is that "in the latter the mind is forced to something by merely external violence contrary to its intrinsic inclination, while whatever we do from obligation is understood to come from an intrinsic impulse of the mind, and with the full approbation of its own judgment" (1934: 386).

We can put these points in Strawsonian terms. When we hold ourselves answerable for complying with legitimate demands, we take up an "inter-personal" or second-personal perspective on ourselves and make ourselves vulnerable to reactive attitudes like guilt that are the first-party reciprocals of second-party resentment or third-party indignation or moral blame. As Pufendorf sees it, only God has the standing or authority to resent violations of his legitimate demands. But if God's demands are genuinely legitimate, therefore genuinely obligating rather than merely obliging, then they must warrant not just God's resentment, but also the violator's feeling guilt, and *anyone's* moral indignation or blame. Mill calls guilt a kind of "internal sanction," but it is important to appreciate that guilt is not merely painful, or the (painful) fear of further (external) sanctions (Mill 1998: Ch. III). It is the painful sense of having done wrong, having violated a legitimate demand that comes, not just from someone else, say God, but also that one implicitly makes of oneself, through blaming oneself in feeling guilt.

Modern moral theorists who follow Pufendorf and Strawson are thus committed to agreeing with Hume that the moral motive is not the desire to avoid sanctions. But they disagree with him that modeling morality on law is committed to this. To the contrary, in their view, an adequate juridical theory of morality is committed to *denying* it. Moral obligations are what we are accountable for doing just as one moral agent among others, and that requires that moral agents be able to hold themselves accountable in their own practical thought, finding there distinctively moral motivation for acting as they are obligated that cannot be reduced to the desire to avoid sanctions.

A further indication of Hume's failure to appreciate the role of accountability, and accountability-seeking attitudes, in moral thought can be found in his theory of justice. Justice, for Hume, is an "artificial virtue." For issues of justice to arise at all, a mutually advantageous "convention" must exist (literally, a *convening* of individual wills into something like a joint resolution, however implicit) to comply with specific "rules," the rules of justice, that structure mutually advantageous social practices, specifically, those of property, contract, and promise (3.2.2.9–10). Hume distinguishes two "obligations" to justice. The "natural obligation" is the self-interested motive everyone has to see that mutually advantageous practices are maintained (3.2.2.23). And what Hume calls the "moral obligation" is the sympathy-created third-personal esteem and love that arise when one considers the benefits that justice has for all (3.2.2.23–4).

Hume's conventional account of justice is of course brilliant in its way, but it faces well-known problems in accounting for the motivation to be just. As Hume himself realizes, neither self-interest nor any sympathy-created concern responding to the interests of others can reliably motivate just acts, since justice may sometimes require acting contrary both to individual *and* to collective interest, as in Hume's example of repaying a loan to a "seditious bigot" rather than putting the loaned money to some higher social purpose (3.2.2.22). Interpreters find different attempted Humean solutions to this problem, including, for example, Hume's doctrine of "general rules." My interest here, however, is not so much to pursue this issue as to note Hume's insensitivity to the connection between justice and accountability and to the role of accountability-seeking attitudes, like resentment. Since the perspective of moral assessment is steadfastly third personal for Hume, this should come as no surprise.

We should note that the kind of justice with which Hume is here concerned is tied conceptually to rights, indeed, to rights of the kind that Grotius dubbed "perfect" rather than "imperfect." What is in question is not some notion of equity or desert that generates no legitimate demand or enforceable claim. Property, promise, and contract all involve individual right holders who have, by virtue of their right, a standing or authority to claim or demand certain treatment. We should also note that a central feature of the modern concept of morality is that it develops in tandem with the idea of universal (perfect) rights, which include "moral powers," as Pufendorf calls them, to acquire property and undertake (perfect) obligations to, and rights against others through promise and contract, to consent to others' acts that would otherwise wrong them, and so on.

Moreover, as Grotius himself makes clear, perfect rights bring into play a distinctive kind of accountability, namely, *to the individual right holder*, that is additional to the accountability that is always involved whenever moral obligation is in question. A perfect right, Grotius says, is a "*Faculty*" of the person that includes the standing or authority to "*deman[d] what is due*" to him (2005: I, 139). An imperfect right, by contrast, is not a "*Faculty*" but an "*Aptitude.*" Under this heading, Grotius includes considerations of "*Worth*" and "*Merit*" that can recommend actions as more or less worthy or meritorious, but that no one has standing to *demand* (2005: I, 141). Grotius notes that "Ancients" like Aristotle, and "Moderns" who follow him, may take considerations of the latter kind to be included within what they *call* "justice" and "right." (It is what Aristotle and his followers include under "distributive justice."[20]) Nonetheless "Right, properly speaking, has a quite different Nature": "doing for [others] what in Strictness they may demand" (2005: I, 88–9).

Perfect claim rights entail obligations *to the right holder* and this brings in a form of accountability that is distinctively *to her*. The right holder has an *individual* authority, which she can exercise at her discretion and not as a representative of the moral community, to demand that moral obligations to her be complied with in general, to hold others accountable for how they treat *her* in particular, to authorize or consent to actions that would otherwise violate her rights, to claim compensation or not at her discretion, to forgive or not, and so on.[21]

---

[20] On the curious difference between this traditional Aristotleian and our contemporary notions of distributive justice, see Fleischacker 2004: 17–28.

[21] I discuss this further in relation to correlative relational or bipolar obligations in Darwall 2012.

The accountability-seeking attitude that is distinctively in play in injustices that violate claim rights is therefore *resentment*. Only the victim can warrantedly resent a violation of her rights. And the question of whether to forgo, suspend, or attempt to work through resentment and perhaps forgive is a question only for her. Others have no standing to exercise her individual authority on these matters unless they have somehow been authorized to do so, if she is competent, by her.

Consider, then, the way resentment enters into Hume's theory and compare that to Adam Smith's. Smith holds that we judge whether harm to some victim was unjust by projecting ourselves impartially into the perspective of the victim (as someone in her position) and assessing whether there is reason to resent the injury, in Smith's words, whether resentment is a "proper" response (Smith 1982: 79). Moreover, although not always consistently, Smith understands resentment as attempting "not so much to make [the person who harms us] feel pain in his turn, as . . . to make him sensible that the person whom he injured did not deserve to be treated in that manner" (Smith 1982: 95–6). The implicit aim of reactive attitudes is thus that others answer for their treatment of us by acknowledging our authority to demand different treatment.

Compare the following remarkable passage from Hume's second *Enquiry*.

Were there a species of creatures, intermingled with men, which, though rational, were possessed of such inferior strength, both of body and mind, that they were incapable of all resistance, and could never, upon the highest provocation, make us feel the effects of their resentment; the necessary consequence, I think, is, that we should be bound, by the laws of humanity, to give gentle usage to these creatures, but should not, properly speaking, lie under any restraint of justice with regard to them, nor could they possess any right or property . . . (*Enquiry* 3.1.18).

Resentment, for Hume, is not an attitude that is tied to justice conceptually or that mediates its distinctive form of accountability. Rather, resentment functions to create costs for the resented that have to be figured into their calculation to determine whether accepting rules that give victims specific *convention-based* authorities and rights would be mutually advantageous or not. If others' power is sufficiently inferior to ours, then restraining our treatment of them by such rules will not be advantageous to us, and we will consequently owe them no obligations of justice.

Hume's approach to justice thus alternates between self-interested calculations of advantage (the "natural obligation") and third-personal assessments of overall benefit (the "moral obligation") in a way that makes him blind to justice's distinctively interpersonal (second-personal) character. Here again, Hume fails to appreciate the distinctive character of accountability-seeking attitudes that moral assessments, in this case of justice and injustice, involve.[22] From the third-person perspective of esteem and

---

[22] There are passages, however, where Hume is far from tone deaf to reactive attitudes. Here is a remarkable one from the chapter on "Liberty and Necessity" in the first *Enquiry* in which, much like Strawson in "Freedom and Resentment," Hume says that resentment is relatively imperious to theoretical views of causal determinacy: "A man who is robbed of a considerable sum; does he find his vexation for the

disesteem, the features of will that moral evaluation brings distinctively into view seem simply one valuable or disvaluable feature among others.

As against Hume, I have been arguing that our (modern) concept of morality is a juridical one that includes a conceptual connection between moral obligation and moral accountability. It is no accident that Hume's third-personal theory of moral evaluation blinds him to these features. I take it, therefore, that Hume's conclusion that the distinction between the moral and the non-moral is merely verbal is actually evidence that morality's connection to fundamental forms of accountability is where the real difference between the moral and the non-moral lies. What makes morality distinctive among normative notions is its network of juridical ideas, including forms of accountability that assume, in the idea of morality, a fundamental *de jure* normativity, one that is lacking in any *de facto* system of law, that is, in law, more properly so called.[23]

loss any wise diminished by these sublime reflections? Why then should his moral resentment against the crime be supposed incompatible with them?" (Hume 1985: 102). I am indebted to Hsueh Qu for pointing me to this passage.

[23] I am indebted to participants at a conference on the point of morality held at the Humboldt University in Berlin in July 2010 and to audiences at various universities for very helpful comments.

2

Bipolar Obligation

Philosophers generally use "moral obligation" as a synonym for "moral requirement" or "moral duty," to signify acts it would be morally wrong not to do. But there is another, older use of "obligation" that refers more specifically to bonds or ties that exist between moral agents and some (usually other) individual, group, or, perhaps, entity, *to* whom they are obligated or have a duty. Obligations of this latter sort are sometimes called "relational" or "directed" obligations or duties (e.g., Gilbert 2004). Following Weinrib and Thompson's discussions of their "bipolar" normativity, however, I will call them *bipolar obligations* (Weinrib 1996; Thompson, 2004). Bipolar obligations always involve a relation between two "poles": an agent who is obligated (the *obligor*) and an individual, group, etc., *to* whom she is obligated, tied, or bound (the *obligee*).

For example, someone making a promise is generally thought to become obligated to her promisee in a way she is not to third parties and that is not fully captured by saying that keeping the promise is her moral obligation *period*, as we might say, and that breaking it would be wrong; promise breaking also *wrongs the promisee*. Moreover, a promisee has a distinctive normative standing or authority in relation to the promiser that third parties do not have. The promisee can release the promiser from his obligation to keep the promise, insist on the promise's being kept, claim some kind of apology if it is not, forgive the promiser, and so on. In these ways, the promiser has a duty *to* the promisee that goes beyond the keeping of her promise simply being her moral duty. The promiser/promisee relation gives rise, we might say, to an obligor/obligee relation (Darwall 2011b; Watson 2009).

To be sure, we speak of a "bond" or "tie" with "unipolar" obligations or moral obligations *period*, also. An agent under a moral obligation (period) is also said to be morally bound. But any bond that is part of the concept of moral obligation period is not to anyone or anything; it is simply *to do* something, whether the action is owed to anyone or not. So far as the concept of moral obligation (period) is concerned, there might be obligations that are not owed to anyone, or at least, that go beyond any that are. Perhaps there is an obligation not wantonly to destroy beauty or not to foul the environment that is like that. But it does not matter whether there is or not. Even if there were no instance of moral obligation that did not also involve a bipolar obligation, we could still distinguish between the concepts of bipolar obligation and moral obligation period.

The existence of an obligee is part of the concept of a bipolar obligation, though it is not of moral obligation period. The latter exists just in case it would be wrong not to do something (either *pro tanto* or all things considered—it will not matter for our purposes). That is insufficient, however, for a bipolar moral obligation. For a bipolar obligation to exist some action must *wrong an obligee*; it must constitute a *wronging* and not just a wrong period.

My topic in this essay is the metaethics of bipolar obligation, more specifically, bipolar obligations whose violations *wrong* their obligees, that is, bipolar moral obligations. I do not mean to suggest that bipolar moral obligations can be weighed against moral obligations period. We can assume, consistently with anything I want to say in this essay about the distinctiveness of bipolar moral obligations, that the central practical question facing a moral agent is nonetheless what, all things considered, she is morally obligated period to do.[1]

In *The Second-Person Standpoint* and elsewhere I have argued that moral obligation period is a second-personal concept and that the reasons provided by moral obligations are second-personal reasons (Darwall 2006, 2007b; see also Darwall 2010a). What makes a concept or reason *second personal* in my sense is that it is tied to *address* conceptually. Address is always second personal by definition, since it must have an *addressee*, if only implicitly. What makes the concept of moral obligation second personal, I argue, is its conceptual connection to moral responsibility or *accountability*, which entails a standing to address (and be addressed by) legitimate claims and demands.

I follow a number of philosophers, including Mill, Richard Brandt, and Allan Gibbard, in arguing that moral obligation, duty, right, and wrong are conceptually tied to moral responsibility and therefore to moral *blame* (Mill 1998: Ch. V; Brandt 1979: 163–76; Gibbard 1990: 41). What is morally obligatory is not just what there are good moral reasons to do, however weighty these reasons might be. It is what it would be morally *wrong* not to do. And moral wrong is not just any kind of moral failing. An act is morally wrong if, only if, it would be *blameworthy* if done without excuse. As Mill put it, "There are other things . . . which we wish that people should do, which we like or admire them for doing, perhaps dislike or despise them for not doing, but yet admit that they are not bound to do" (Mill 1998: Ch. V. ¶14). In these cases, Mill adds, "it is not a case of moral obligation; we do not blame them."[2] It is a conceptual truth that an act is morally wrong, if, and only if, it is blameworthy if done without excuse.

---

[1] I will assume that if X is morally obligated to Y to do A, it follows that X is morally obligated period to do A, at least other things being equal.

[2] Also: "We do not call anything wrong, unless we mean to imply that a person ought to be punished in some way or other for doing it; if not by law, by the opinion of his fellow creatures; if not by opinion, by the reproaches of his own conscience" (Mill 1998: Ch. V. ¶14).

Half of my argument, then, has been that moral obligation, right, and wrong are tied to accountability and to moral blame conceptually. In the other half, I have followed Strawson's famous argument in "Freedom and Resentment" that responsibility or accountability is always implicitly, as Strawson put it, "inter-personal" or, as I prefer to put it, "second personal." We hold one another and ourselves morally responsible through distinctive attitudes ("reactive attitudes") such as resentment, indignation, guilt, and, I argue, moral blame, through which we implicitly address putatively legitimate demands.

Strawson didn't give a formal definition of reactive attitudes, but their central features are clear from the role they play in his argument about moral responsibility and freedom of the will. Strawson's core idea is that reactive attitudes involve a characteristic way of regarding the individuals who are their objects that commits the holder of the attitude to certain assumptions about the object individual and her capacities to regulate her will. Unlike "objective attitudes," like disdain, disgust, and annoyance, reactive attitudes are "participant attitudes" that are essentially characterized by "involvement or participation with others in inter-personal human relationships" (Strawson 1968: 79). There is always a second-personal element to reactive attitudes. Through the attitude we *hold* its object to something and thereby implicitly make a demand *of* (and so implicitly address the demand *to*) him or her. As Strawson put it, "the making of the demand is the proneness to such attitudes" (Strawson 1968: 96). The reason that reactive attitudes distinctively implicate freedom of the will, then, is that we can intelligibly address a demand to someone to regulate her will appropriately only if we suppose that she can so regulate it as a result of recognizing our demand's legitimacy. The supposition is, as Gary Watson says, a "constraint on moral address" (Watson 1987: 263, 264). In this way, reactive attitudes like moral blame are unlike other critical attitudes, like disesteem, contempt, and disgust, which lack an intrinsically addressing, second-personal element, whether these latter take a distinctively moral form, as in moral disesteem or disgust, or not.

Strawson makes a distinction, which will be important in what follows, between *personal* and *impersonal reactive attitudes*. A personal attitude, like resentment, is felt as if from the perspective of an involved party, while impersonal reactive attitudes are felt as if from an uninvolved, third party's standpoint. It is, nonetheless, important to Strawson's argument, as it will be to mine, that both personal *and* impersonal reactive attitudes are essentially "inter-personal" in his sense, or *second personal*, in mine, since they both implicitly address demands. Thus "first-party" reactive attitudes, like guilt, second-party attitudes, like resentment, and third-party attitudes, like indignation or moral blame are all *equally* "inter-personal" in Strawson's sense and so second personal, in mine.[3] "Second person" does not mean "second party."

---

[3] The first two are personal reactive attitudes; the third is an impersonal reactive attitude.

Some Preliminaries

What, then, is the relation between moral obligation period and bipolar obligations? R. Jay Wallace has pressed a line of objection to my account of the former that leads him to speculate that the ideas *second-personal reason* and what I call *second-personal authority* that are implicit in my account of moral obligation period, should themselves be understood in terms of bipolar obligations. On the approach Wallace suggests, "what makes a reason second personal is...that it is implicated in a structure of relational or 'bipolar' normativity" (Wallace 2007: 26). Wallace's worry, which I will address below, is that there is no way to make good on the notion of a presupposed (second-personal) *authority* to make demands that I hold to be implicit in "impersonal" reactive attitudes like moral blame, hence in moral obligation period. There may be a clear enough notion of what it is for someone to have the authority to *create* a distinctively second-personal reason by making a legitimate demand of someone, as when, for example, a sergeant orders her troops to fall in. But moral blame is not like that. Moral demands do not come into existence through being made in blaming someone. But neither do I, nor does Strawson as I read him, want to say that blame is purely epistemic. Blame seems to have a *practically* directive quality that can't be understood solely in terms of directing someone's attention to the existence of a reason—at least, to a reason that doesn't itself consist in a legitimate demand. It may seem unclear, however, how to understand this idea.

Wallace's suggestion, as I understand it, is that the framework of second-personal reasons, legitimate claims and demands, etc. that I am attempting to theorize is only at home with bipolar obligations. In other words, the distinctive kind of normativity involved in bipolar obligations is more basic than that of second-personal reasons, legitimate claims and demands, and so on. Rather than the former being understood in terms of the latter, "what makes a reason second personal," Wallace suggests, is "that it is implicated in a structure of relational or 'bipolar' normativity" (Wallace 2007: 26). But this raises an obvious question. What exactly *is* "bipolar normativity"? How are we to understand the metaethics of bipolar obligation?

That will be our question here. I shall argue that Wallace's suggestion is precisely backwards. My claim is that there is no adequate way of understanding *both* moral obligations period *and* bipolar obligation except in second-personal terms, so that "second personal" cannot just be a synonym for "bipolar." Bipolar obligations do implicate a distinctive species of second-personal authority and reason, and so entail a distinctive kind of accountability, which distinguishes them from moral obligations period. But moral obligations period are also tied to accountability conceptually, albeit a different species, and are therefore no less second personal than are bipolar obligations. To put the point in a rough and preliminary way, obligees have an *individual authority* to hold their obligors accountable as the particular individual in bipolar relation to *them*, whereas anyone, including third parties, the obligee, and the obligor him- or herself, share a *representative authority* (as representative persons or members of the moral community) to hold obligors accountable for complying with moral obligations period.[4] The ideas of second-personal authority and reason are thus more general than is that of bipolar normativity. So the former cannot be understood in terms of the latter. To the contrary, the latter is a species of the former.

Moreover, I shall argue also that there is a conceptual tie between these two species of the genus of second-personal authority and reasons. Although moral obligations period do not analytically entail bipolar obligations, bipolar moral obligations *do* entail moral obligations period. If X is under a moral obligation to Y to do A, then X is, other things equal at least, under a moral obligation period to do A. Actions that wrong someone (violate a bipolar obligation) are also wrong period, all else being equal, at least. If this is right, it follows that the individual authority that is involved in bipolar obligations cannot exist without the representative authority that is involved in moral obligations period. Since both individual and representative authority are second-personal notions, it will follow further that bipolar normativity cannot be explicated without the general ideas of second-personal authority and reasons.

Before we begin, I need to make two important preliminary clarificatory remarks. First, we will be interested in understanding the nature of genuinely *normative* bipolar obligations. Since part of what we want to know is whether, as Wallace suggests, there might be a basic kind of "bipolar normativity" that can explain the normativity of second-personal reasons, we can ignore bipolar obligations that are not inherently normative in the sense of entailing normative reasons for some action or attitude. For example, there are social or conventional obligations like those of custom, etiquette, or law, at least as legal positivists understand it, that may not entail normative reasons. There may well be normative reasons to follow custom, etiquette, or the law, or to have reactive attitudes toward failures to do so, but nothing in the concept of custom, etiquette, or law, on a positivist view, at least, seems to *entail* that there are (Foot 1972). Even if they purport to provide us with reasons, none of custom, etiquette, or law would cease to exist as such if these normative reasons were not to exist.

Second, I shall take our topic to be the nature of bipolar obligations and normativity that do not simply reduce to moral obligations period, including a moral obligation to treat others as though one had bipolar obligations to them or even to accept that one does. If it turns out that anything plausibly regarded as a bipolar moral obligation can be reduced to moral obligation period in this way, then no special or distinctive bipolar normativity or obligation exists in the sense in which we are interested.

These clarificatory points turn out to have important implications for how we should understand some normative moral theories' attitude toward bipolar obligations in our current sense. Consider, for example, an indirect consequentialist view like rule consequentialism. Rule consequentialists would likely agree that optimific social rules

---

[4] How they may respectively hold violators accountable also differs. For example, individual obligees arguably have standing to express resentment to their obligors in complaints in a way that representative persons do not necessarily have standing to express their blame.

will include bipolar conventional *rule-defined* obligations. The most socially useful practice of promising, for instance, is likely structured by rules that tie promisers to promisees in various ways, giving title to promisees to hold promisers personally accountable for fulfilling promises, to release promisers from their obligations to promisees, and so on. If that is so, rule consequentialists will hold that it would be morally wrong to violate such socially useful bipolar rules, even if doing so would be optimific in the case at hand. All this is familiar ground.

However, rule consequentialists do not accept that these conventional *rule-defined* bipolar obligations are inherently normative or have any inherent moral force in themselves, hence that they have any basic "bipolar normativity." According to rule consequentialism, conventional bipolar obligations get whatever normativity they have thanks to be their being socially useful and hence something we have a moral obligation period to follow. Rule consequentialism thus denies that genuine moral obligations can themselves be bipolar. There are just moral obligations period to comply with bipolar-obligation-defining conventional rules.

Earlier I mentioned that the original use of "obligation" was to refer to something essentially relational or bipolar. Originally, "obligation" was used to refer to the upshot of an act of *obliging*, where the latter was thought to include such actions as bestowing a favor, entering into an agreement or contract, swearing an oath, and the like.[5] According to this usage, by doing a good service, for example, a benefactor obligates her beneficiary to her as a debt of gratitude. By entering into an agreement or making a contract, the parties obligate themselves to one another to perform as agreed. By swearing an oath to or before someone, the swearer obligates and makes himself accountable to the person to or before whom he swears for that to which he swears. And so on. Obligations in the original sense of the word were always owed by an obligor to an obligee.

Now it might seem obvious that the relations to which the original use of "obligation" referred are bipolar obligations in the sense in which we are interested. But actually, this is far from obvious, as can be appreciated by reflecting on the very different attitudes that Nietzsche takes in Chapter 2 of *On the Genealogy of Morals* toward what he calls "personal obligations" and debts, on the one hand, and the idea of moral obligation, on the other (Nietzsche 1998: Ch. 2). Nietzsche has no complaint against what he regards as an earlier notion of debts owed to others except when this idea is conceived in (he thinks later) distinctively moral terms as warranting a guilty conscience and moral blame. Only then are obligation and debt conceived in the objectionable sense of what Bernard Williams called "the morality system" or what Brian Leiter calls "morality in the pejorative sense" (Williams 1985; Leiter 1995).[6]

---

[5] *The Concise Oxford Dictionary of English Etymology*, online. This earlier use helps explain why writers like Hart and Rawls sometimes reserve "obligation" to such voluntary undertakings (though Hart also famously distinguishes between being obliged, in the sense or being compelled, from being obligated) (Rawls 1971: 113; Hart 1958: 100–5; Hart 1961: 6–8).

[6] See also the excellent discussion in Clark 1994.

"Personal obligation had its origin," Nietzsche writes, "in the oldest and most primitive relationship among persons there is, in the relation between buyer and seller, creditor and debtor" (Nietzsche 1998: II.8). Nietzsche objects only to "the moralization of these concepts (their being pushed back into conscience...)" (Nietzsche 1998: II.21). He has no problem with the notion that people who fail to pay their debts should expect personal responses like anger, retaliation, and so a kind of primitive "punishment" from their creditors (see especially Nietzsche 1998: II.4). What he rejects is the idea that actions can warrant moral blame or guilty conscience, that is, a feeling that appears to hold someone accountable *impartially*, as if from anyone's point of view. Such putatively impartial or impersonal feelings are, Nietzsche holds, repressed, distorted, unhealthy, and self-deceptive versions of a personal *ressentiment* that the weak and their priestly spokesmen are incapable of discharging or even acknowledging.

Since Nietzsche refuses to countenance "personal obligations" in moral terms, he counts as rejecting the category of bipolar obligations as we are conceiving of them. Bipolar obligations in our sense *are* moral obligations, since their violation wrongs the obligee. They differ, of course, from moral obligations period. But I shall take it that they entail moral obligations period. Any violation of a bipolar obligation that genuinely *wrongs* the obligee must also be morally wrong period, other things equal, at least. Clearly, this is no part of the concept of "personal obligations" as Nietzsche conceives of them.[7]

So do early uses of "obligation" pick out bipolar obligations in our sense? That depends on whether their referents are conceived in implicitly moral and normative terms. And that is probably an indeterminate matter until those using the term can make the kinds of distinctions we now do between social, legal, and financial obligations, which are conceived as distinct from, and as not analytically entailing, moral obligations (or, indeed as having any intrinsic normativity), on the one hand, and obligations that bind morally, that is with morality's distinctive normativity, on the other. It is, that is, indeterminate until those who use the term have assimilated the very conceptual changes that Nietzsche criticizes.[8]

As I mentioned, I shall claim that the ideas of second-personal reason, authority, accountability, and so on, are more general than that of bipolar obligation. Bipolar obligations involve a distinctive second-personal relation between obligor and obligee that includes the obligee's being warranted in addressing certain demands to the obligor on his own behalf and at his own discretion, and in holding the obligor

---

[7] It follows that the retaliatory responses that Nietzsche is discussing, including *ressentiment* as he understands it, differ from reactive attitudes, as Strawson and I understand them. Nothing within retaliatory responses involves the distinctively "inter-personal" or second-personal structure that Strawson and I are pointing to. For further discussion, see Darwall 2010b and Darwell forthcoming b.

[8] In Darwall 2012b and Darwell forthcoming b, I argue in favor of Anscombe and Sidgwick's view that the idea of morality conceived in terms of distinctively moral obligation is a modern conception and not one found, for example, in ancient Greek ethical writers like Plato and Aristotle.

personally accountable. Here I shall claim that bipolar obligations always involve an assumed *individual authority* or standing that the obligee has with respect to the obligor that others do not have. When victims hold their victimizers responsible through Strawsonian "personal reactive attitudes" like resentment (Strawson 1968: 72), or for that matter, when they decide to forgo holding their victimizers responsible, or forgive them, as is their prerogative, obligees presuppose this *individual authority* with respect to their obligors.

Because of the conceptual relation between (bipolar) wronging and doing wrong period, however, this individual authority cannot exist by itself. This is a significant second point. If moral wrong and obligation period are best analyzed in terms of what, if unexcused, warrants moral blame, and if, as Strawson and I argue, third-party or "impersonal" reactive attitudes like blame also implicitly address demands, then these attitudes, like personal ones, must presuppose an authority as well, only one that, unlike individual authority, is *non-discretionary* and that anyone has as a *representative* person or member of the moral community. Thus whereas bipolar obligations and associated personal reactive attitudes presuppose *individual authority*, moral obligation period and associated impersonal reactive attitudes like indignation and moral blame presuppose *representative authority*.

It is worth stressing again the importance for Strawson's argument in "Freedom and Resentment," as for my argument here, that both personal and impersonal reactive attitudes are essentially interpersonal or second personal. Both must consequently presuppose some form of second-personal authority. My claim is that they presuppose different species: individual authority and representative authority. I shall conclude that the ideas of second-personal authority and second-personal reasons are more general than that of "bipolar normativity." The metaethics of bipolar obligation involves a distinctive species of second-personal authority, which cannot exist without the existence of representative authority also.

Bipolar Obligations and Individual Authority

Having clarified the outlines of our topic—bipolar obligations that place obligor and obligee in a distinctive *moral* relation—we can now focus on it more sharply, beginning with a number of insightful observations from Michael Thompson's important article on bipolar normativity (Thompson 2004). Thompson distinguishes between the "monadic" normativity involved in rule- or law-based "deontological concepts," including moral obligation period, and a bipolar normativity that is implicated in concepts that concern "relations of right" between individuals. Thompson calls the latter "dikaiological" rather than "deontological" concepts because of their conceptual connection to rights and justice (*dike*).[9] Monadic deontological categories define a deontological order:

---

[9] Apparently, this term was first introduced in Glassen 1959. I am indebted to Arthur Ripstein for this reference.

(1) Doing A is wrong (impermissible).
(2) Not doing A is morally obligatory.
(3) Doing B is morally permissible (not wrong).
(4) Not doing B is not morally obligatory.

Dikaiological concepts, by contrast, define a *dikaiological order*:

(5) X wronged Y by doing A.
(6) X has a duty to Y not to do A.
(7) Y has a right against X that X not do A. (Thompson 2004: 335, 338)

A dikaiological order defining relations of right is bipolar in that the agents referred to in propositions (5)–(7) are "like the opposing poles of an electrical apparatus." Propositions (5)–(7) "represent an arc of normative current as passing between the agent-poles," X and Y (Thompson 2004: 335). And this normative relation or "current" is "internally related to two points of view that might be taken on it" from the perspective of "each of its poles," X and Y, respectively (Thompson 2004: 371).

Hohfeld famously put this point by saying that (6) and (7) express the same "legal relation" (Hohfeld 1923: 65–75). Following Thompson, however, we might do better to substitute "dikaiological" for Hohfeld's "legal," since the relation is not simply deontological; it is dikaiological. X doesn't simply have a duty not to do A; X has this duty *to* Y. And this bipolar duty entails a claim right that Y has against X that X not do A. Claim rights and bipolar obligations are, in the jargon, conceptually "correlative."[10]

Thompson notes that a dikaiological structure and relations of right need not be moral, as we observed earlier. Dikaiological, bipolar relations can be represented also in a set of conventions, customs, law, or even in games. Dikaiological concepts can be "shifted," Thompson says, "into various gears, or sung in various keys": moral, conventional, customary, legal, or "ludic" (Thompson 345–6). For the reasons I mentioned earlier, however, we are interested only in the dikaiological structure that is part of morality: bipolar moral obligations and correlative moral claim rights.

These include reciprocal moral obligations and claim rights that moral persons have: "what we owe to each other," in Scanlon's phrase (Scanlon 1998). But nothing in the concept of bipolar moral obligations restricts them to these. We might suppose, for example, that we also have bipolar obligations *to*, and not just moral obligations period with respect to very young children, for example, or other animals, neither of whom

---

[10] This might be questioned, since it might be argued that some bipolar obligations do not entail claim rights. It sounds strained, for example, to say that anyone to whom one owes a debt of gratitude thereby has a claim right to one's gratitude. There is not space adequately to discuss this point here, but I would suggest that though the full force of a claim right is arguably lacking in such cases, there nonetheless must exist some similar second-personal standing, for example, to take ingratitude personally and hold the ungrateful person responsible in some way, in order of us to be able to say properly that there exists a bipolar obligation of gratitude. In any case, for present purposes I shall simply assume with Thompson and Hohfeld that bipolar obligations entail correlative claim rights. I am indebted for discussion here to Rowan Cruft.

are reciprocally obligated to us. For our purposes, however, we may restrict ourselves to genuinely interpersonal bipolar moral obligations.

Thompson maintains that the concept of *person* in the relevant sense is itself dikaiological, defined within a dikaiological structure. We are persons, in this sense, "in relation to" others: X in relation to Y and Y in relation to X (Thompson 2004: 353). To be thus a person just is to have the relevant obligations to and rights against other persons. The concept of person differs in this way from the concept of agency or that of a free will.

Agents act, think, and regard one another as persons in this sense when they see each other within a dikaiological framework of relations of right to one another. In so doing, they perforce relate *to* one another, if only implicitly and in thought.[11] Individuals are thus persons in relation to other persons, not in the way a brother has a biological relation to his siblings, but as when he relates to them *as* his siblings. To act and think as a person in this sense is to do so within an essentially interpersonal, or second-personal, reciprocally recognitional space. As Thompson puts it in Heideggerian terms, thinking and acting as persons involves our "being-toward-others" (Thompson 2004: 358). Recognizing your sibling or that someone is your sibling is thus different from acknowledging or recognizing someone *as* your sibling with whatever bipolar obligations that might involve. Similarly, to recognize someone as a person is to relate to him as having basic rights against and obligations to one that are the reciprocals of the obligations and rights one has to and against him. It is, in this sense, to respect him as a person, or as *another* person (as someone "just like me") (Darwall 1977, 2006).

This means that a second-personal element is essential to the concepts of moral obligations to and rights against, as well as to the concept of moral person that is definable in relation to these. We can bring this out more clearly by considering Joel Feinberg's theory of claim rights, the entailed reciprocals of bipolar obligations (Feinberg 1980). Suppose you hold that it is not just wrong (and contrary to a moral obligation) period to step unbidden on other people's feet, but also that doing so violates their rights. What does this latter thought involve?

We can easily imagine a society (Feinberg's "Nowheresville") in which it is thought morally wrong to step on others' feet, unless, say, they desire or do not mind one's doing so, but where the latter is not seen as a giving of consent that can be understood only within a bipolar dikaiological order. So viewed, others' will and preference would appear simply as features of the moral landscape that bear on moral obligations period. Others would not yet be regarded as having any prerogative or authority to consent, where consent is conceived as something that can be given only through a second-personal address that reciprocally presupposes the authority to release one from what would otherwise be a bipolar obligation *to* the other.

Consent can only be given second personally and is dikaiological by definition (Ripstein 2009: 111–132; Darwall 2011b). It involves the exercise of a "normative

---

[11] For a discussion of recognition respect for persons as second personal in this way, see Darwall 2006: 119–47.

power," in this case, to release someone from a bipolar obligation he would otherwise have, say, not to step on your feet (Raz 1972 and 2002: 98–104). Normative powers, in general, are dikaiological authorities or standings to enter into reciprocally recognizing second-personal engagements with others that alter bipolar obligations and claim rights holding between the parties, but which engagements also presuppose that the parties are already obligated to one another in various ways. Other essentially bipolar dikaiological normative powers include the authority to make promises, to enter into agreements and contracts, and even such prosaic normative capacities as are exercised when we ask someone to do something or accede to a request (Watson 2009; Darwall 2011b; Enoch 2011).

Normative powers can only be exercised second personally, through a reciprocally recognizing transaction with another person. And their exercise both presupposes specific authorities, rights, and bipolar obligations, which are reciprocally recognized by the parties to the transaction as existing independently of the transaction, and creates new ones as a result, for example, a promiser's obligation to a promisee.

The power of consent is but one of an ensemble of normative powers or authorities that enter into the having of a claim right against someone, and therefore into another's having a bipolar obligation to one. These powers or authorities are all, moreover, essentially second personal. Feinberg emphasizes that the right holder's standing or authority to demand or *claim* her rights enters into the very idea that she has a claim right. "It is claiming," Feinberg writes, "that gives rights their special moral significance" (Feinberg 1980: 151). The authority to claim our rights "enables us to 'stand up like men,' to look others in the eye, and to feel in some fundamental way the equal of anyone" (Feinberg 1980: 151). When we regard persons as having a claim right that others not step unbidden on their feet, part of what we think is that each person has a distinctive set of individual authorities over others' conduct with respect to *his* feet that he doesn't have with respect to the treatment of other people's feet. Among other normative powers, each has the power to consent to and thereby authorize and render permissible treatment of his feet that would otherwise wrong him.

Right holders also have a distinctive authority to hold others answerable for violations of *their* rights that third parties do not have. The point is not that third parties have no authority. To the contrary, I shall claim that any special authority right holding obligees have can exist only if there is also an authority, *representative authority*, which they share with third parties, as well as with any obligor who might violate their rights. The point is that there is a special *individual* authority an obligee has to hold the obligor personally answerable that can, like the power of consent, be exercised only by the right-holding obligee herself at her discretion.

One way to see this is to reflect on forgiveness (see, e.g., Griswold 2007). Just as it is uniquely up to the right holder to decide whether or not to consent or waive her right (assuming the right is one that can be waived), so is it distinctively up to a victim whose right has been violated, whether to forgive someone who has violated it. No one else has the same authority or standing.[12] Moreover, just as the power to consent can exist only against the background of bipolar obligations and rights that are in force without consent, so also can the authority to forgive exist only against the background of a distinctive authority that obligees and right holders have to hold others personally responsible. Forgiveness involves the victim's somehow moving past holding his victimizer personally responsible, for example, as Butler believes, through the personal reactive attitude of resentment (Butler 1900: Sermon IX).

Similarly with apology. An apology is, by definition, addressed to someone who receives it and who has the authority to accept it or not. If a victim comes upon an unaddressed admission of guilt and expression of sincere regret in her victimizer's diary, she has not discovered an apology.[13] Apologies are a way of holding oneself personally answerable to an obligee whose authority to hold one thus answerable is thereby reciprocally recognized. It is a second-personal acknowledgment of having violated a bipolar obligation to the obligee and of the obligee's special authority to hold one answerable for it.

Similarly also with the distinction made in law between the legal authority or standing to bring cases in civil and in criminal law, respectively. It is uniquely up to a(n alleged) victim to decide whether or not to bring a case in the civil law of contracts or torts. If a wronged or injured party would prefer not to pursue a tort action and seek compensation, the state and other citizens do not generally have the authority to pursue it on her behalf. It is not, however, up to a(n alleged) victim to decide whether or not to pursue a criminal case, including for the very rights violation of which she has been victim. That is up to "the people" and their representatives. The criminal law is to the moral law as civil law is to the dikaiological order of bipolar moral obligations.

These points about *de facto* legal authority reflect underlying beliefs we hold concerning *de jure* authorities that are central to our going concept of morality. They reflect the belief that obligees (right holders) have an *individual moral authority* with respect to obligors against whom they hold claim rights. Obligees have an individual authority to claim rights *they* specially hold, for example, to insist on a promise or a contract made *to or with them* being kept, and to hold obligors individually or personally answerable to them for violations if it is not, for example, to complain, seek apology or compensation, forgive, and so on. And similarly for the authority that is presupposed by the exercise of any normative power that is implicated in a dikaiological structure of bipolar obligations and claim rights. In each case, persons relating to one another second personally within a dikaiological order reciprocally presuppose that the obligee has an individual authority to make demands of the obligor and hold him personally responsible.

Summing up this section, bipolar moral obligations entail a distinctive discretionary second-personal authority that obligees have to make claims and demands of obligors and

---

[12] Though others who are specially related to the victim may have some standing, it is nonetheless not the same.

[13] Though she might if she came across something with the same content addressed to her.

hold them personally responsible. And this distinctive *individual authority* is related conceptually to a distinctive reason for acting that, because of its conceptual tie to an authority to address claims and demands, we can usefully call "second personal." Among the various reasons that exist for not stepping on others' feet, some, such as that it would cause pain and inconvenience, are logically independent of any authority anyone might have to make claims and demands of others (or themselves). But consider the fact that stepping on another's foot would violate her right. Or equivalently, that it would violate a (bipolar) obligation to her. I have been arguing that this reason *is* tied conceptually to the other's individual authority to make claims and demands of one and hold one personally accountable for compliance. In the terms of *SPS*, then, this reason is a second-personal reason. It is a reason that would not exist but for its connection to an authority to address (second-personal) claims and demands. Bipolar normativity thus involves a distinctive kind of second-personal authority and reason.

The Distinctive Normativities of Moral Obligation Period and Bipolar Obligation

Persons have no *individual* authority to hold others personally responsible for violations of moral obligation period—with respect to the "moral criminal law," as it were—even if, indeed, the content of the moral obligation period is identical to or coextensive with respecting their moral right, that is, with a bipolar moral obligation *to them*. Whether to hold a person responsible for doing wrong, as opposed to wronging someone, is up to no one *in particular*. But if moral obligations period are genuine moral *demands*, who has the authority to make these demands? The answer that I take to be implicit in Strawson's work, and that I defend and develop in *SPS*, is that moral obligations period analytically entail a non-discretionary second-personal authority we all *share* as representative persons or members of the moral community to hold ourselves and one another accountable and demand compliance with moral obligations period. Thus where bipolar obligations presuppose the individual authority of the obligee, moral obligations period presuppose a representative authority that any person has as a representative person or member of the moral community to hold themselves and others accountable for compliance through impersonal reactive attitudes.

To make this idea plausible, let us step back a bit and ask, first, what makes any normative notion normative? And second, what are the distinctive normative aspects of the concept of bipolar obligation and moral obligation period? I assume that what makes a concept normative is that it analytically entails normative reasons for some attitude or other.[14] Credibility concerns there being reasons to believe some proposition or person. Desirability is normative for desire. Choiceworthiness is normative for

---

[14] This may not be quite right, since there might be normative requirements (such as "wide scope" oughts) that cannot be understood in terms of normative reasons (Broome 1999). However, we can ignore this complication for present purposes.

choice. The estimable is normative for esteem. And so on, for every normative notion.[15]

On this assumption, we should then ask, for what attitudes are moral obligation period and bipolar obligations distinctively normative? Now it might seem that the obvious answer is that both are normative for action. What we are morally obligated to do, whether period or to someone, is what we have good reason (perhaps conclusive reason, if the obligation is all things considered), or at least moral reason, to do. But however true that might be, I think it can fairly readily be seen that the concepts of moral obligation period and bipolar obligation differ from the concept of what there is good or conclusive reason, or even, good or conclusive moral reason, to do.

The normative notion that is distinctively concerned with action, intention, and choice is *choiceworthiness*, that is, there being normative reason to choose, intend, or do something. Obviously, the concept of moral obligatoriness differs from this concept, if only because there are reasons to act that have nothing to do with morality at all.

But neither is moral obligation period simply a proper part of the choiceworthy, the morally choiceworthy: what there is moral reason to do, or what there is reason to do from the moral point of view, either *pro tanto* or all things considered. This can be seen by reflecting on the fact that it is at least conceptually open that there might be actions that are recommended, however conclusively, by moral reasons, however weighty, that are nonetheless not morally required. In other words, the possibility of super-erogation, of action above and beyond the call of moral duty, is not closed by the concept of moral obligation. To the contrary, many of us believe that morality can recommend action, maybe even strongly recommend it, without yet requiring it or making it morally obligatory (period). And we clearly are not being incoherent or conceptually confused in having this belief.

Whether there is such a thing as supererogation is a substantive normative question rather than a purely conceptual one. If an act consequentialist maintains that it is always wrong not to perform the action that morality most recommends, and a Rossian deontologist denies this, it would seem that they can be disagreed about this while sharing the same concept of moral obligation (indeed, that they could not be thus disagreed unless they did). Similarly, it would seem that what the Rossian asserts is not contradictory or conceptually confused, as it would have to be if the concept of the moral obligatory were the same as that of the morally choiceworthy, or most morally choiceworthy. So the concept of moral obligation must differ from that of moral choiceworthiness.

The morally obligatory is what morality *demands*, what can legitimately be demanded of us and what we are therefore accountable for as moral agents. This means, I argue, following Mill, Brandt, and Gibbard, that the concept of moral obligation is normative in the first instance for the distinctive attitudes through

---

[15] I defend this more fully in Darwall 2010a.

which we hold one another and ourselves morally responsible, namely, "impersonal" Strawsonian reactive attitudes such as moral blame (Darwall 2006, 2007b). The concept of moral obligation (period) is that of an action's being blameworthy, that is, a fitting object of the attitude of moral blame (equivalently, what there are normative reasons of the right kind to blame), if the action is done without adequate excuse.[16]

This does not mean, I hasten to add, that moral obligation is not *also* normative for action. It means that since its *distinctive* conceptual normativity is for impersonal reactive attitudes like moral blame, obligation's normativity for action must follow in some way from this. I argue that this is indeed the case (Darwall 2006, 2007b), owing to blame's conceptual connection to accountability. To hold someone accountable through moral blame is incompatible with seeing him as having had sufficient reason to act as one is blaming him for doing. Blame can be defeated either by excuses (which admit wrongdoing, but plead extenuation) or by justifications (which defeat also the charge of having violated a moral demand). It is incoherent to blame someone for wrongdoing while accepting that he had sufficient reason to act as he did. Moral obligation's normativity for action thus follows from its normativity for blame.

If the distinctive normativity of moral obligation period is for impersonal reactive attitudes, the natural conclusion is that the normativity of bipolar obligations (and correlative claim rights) is for personal reactive attitudes like resentment.[17] It is a conceptual truth that something violates a bipolar obligation (and so a correlative claim right) if, and only if, the action would warrant resentment if done without excuse. If this is right, then, to capture the special normativity of bipolar obligations, bipolar normativity, we have to account for the distinctive second-personal element involved in holding people personally accountable, for example, through an attitude of resentment that implicitly addresses a demand to the resented agent, presupposes an *individual authority* to do as the individual tied to him in a bipolar "practical nexus," and makes a claim on him to recognize this authority.[18] Part of what it is for an obligor to have a moral obligation *to* an obligee, and for the correlative claim right to obtain, therefore, is that the obligee has a set of individual authorities to claim the right and hold the obligor personally responsible for complying with it in the ways we have discussed.

---

[16] In Darwall 2010a, I discuss how moral obligations create normative reasons for acting. I also discuss how the "right kind of reasons" problem is relevant the fittingness of these attitudes. Note, by the way, that the idea is not that the concept of wrong is identical with that of blameworthiness. An act can be wrong though not blameworthy if the agent has a valid excuse. The conceptual connection is that an action wrong if, and only if, it would be blameworthy if done without excuse.

[17] And, perhaps, resentment's first-party correlate, a form of guilt in which we feel distinctively responsible for someone's injury.

[18] I take the phrase "practical nexus" from Thompson.

We can present the links I have been making in Figure 1:

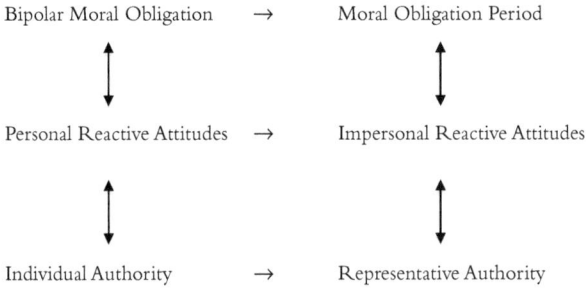

Bipolar Moral Obligation   →   Moral Obligation Period

Personal Reactive Attitudes   →   Impersonal Reactive Attitudes

Individual Authority   →   Representative Authority

Figure 1

The items in each column entail one another, and each of the items in the left column entails the item in the right column that is in its row. Since moral obligations period might exist with no corresponding bipolar obligation, items in the right column do not entail items in their rows in the left column.

To conclude this section, we should note that an obligee or right holder need not actually claim her right or demand compliance with it in order for the right to exist, or that the right consists wholly in any demand that she has the individual authority to make.[19] If that were so, then, for example, you would lack any right that people not step unbidden on your feet until you bid them not to or bid them not to do so unbidden. As we shall see, no moral obligation period, and so no bipolar moral obligation or moral claim right, can exist unless *non-discretionary* demands exist that do not depend on being made by anyone with the individual authority to make them or not. Even so, a connection to the discretionary individual authorities we have discussed is surely part of the concepts of bipolar moral obligation and claim right. Failure to account for this distinctive second-personal aspect will miss an essential element.

Connecting Individual Authority to Representative Authority

It follows from our argument thus far that just as the distinctive normativity of moral obligation period is to be understood in terms of warrant for impersonal reactive attitudes, so also is the distinctive normativity of bipolar obligation explicated in terms of warrant for personal reactive attitudes. In this last section, we shall consider the relations between these points and Wallace's claim that second-personal notions are best understood in terms of bipolar normativity. My counter-claim can perhaps now be more clearly appreciated. Since all Strawsonian reactive attitudes, whether personal or impersonal, are "inter-personal," in Strawson's sense, or "second personal," in mine,

---

[19] I am indebted here to Wallace's comments in Wallace 2007 and to discussion with Kelly Heuer.

both bipolar normativity *and* the normativity of moral obligation period are second personal, albeit in different ways. The distinctive second-personal authority involved in bipolar obligations is *individual authority*, whereas that involved in moral obligation period is *representative authority*. These are different species of second-personal authority (standing to address claims and demands and hold accountable). An obligee has a distinctive discretionary authority as the particular individual to whom an obligor is bound in bipolar obligation to hold the obligor personally responsible. And any person has a (non-discretionary) authority as a representative person or member of the moral community to hold anyone, himself and others, accountable for complying with moral obligations period through impersonal reactive attitudes.

Wallace recognizes what I am calling the second-personal element of bipolar obligations. He agrees that the obligee has a "privileged basis for complaint" "that uninvolved third parties lack" against the obligor if a bipolar obligation is violated and that the obligee can "authorize," and so make permissible, acts that would otherwise violate her rights through consent (Wallace 2007: 29). Wallace's objection, as I understand it, is that these second-personal elements come for free as aspects of bipolar obligation and normativity, that bipolar obligations are the only place where second-personal notions are at home, and therefore that bipolar normativity is the more fundamental idea.

My counter-claim is that impersonal reactive attitudes presuppose authority no less than do personal ones, and that this representative authority is no less second personal than is the individual authority that personal reactive attitudes presuppose. Strawson and I argue that moral blame is always essentially "inter-personal" because it implicitly makes a demand of (and so addresses the demand to) its object. Even "impersonal" reactive attitudes are "participant" rather than "objective" attitudes. In this way, blame differs from other negative critical attitudes, even within the moral sphere, like disesteem, contempt, and disgust. Unlike the latter, the former have an implicit RSVP.

Now this latter point is common ground between Wallace and me. (I actually came to the idea partly through Wallace's insightful writings on responsibility; Wallace 1994.) Here is how he puts the point.

I do not mean to deny that reactive sentiments involve implicit claims; I myself have argued at some length that there is a distinctive stance of holding people to a demand or expectation that is constitutively connected to the Strawsonian reactive attitudes and that is indeed among their defining characteristics. (Wallace 1994) To the extent this is the case, we might say that reactive emotions "address" demands or normative expectations to the agents who are their targets. (Wallace 2007: 30)

But if impersonal reactive attitudes like moral blame implicitly address demands, it also seems obvious that they don't make *naked* demands. Holding someone morally responsible for an action through moral blame isn't an exercise in brute force, except perhaps on a debunking Nietzschean analysis. Blame addresses a demand *as legitimate*, so it necessarily assumes an authority to make the demand. And this is what makes it second personal, in my sense. It addresses a demand as putatively legitimate to an addressee, presupposes the authority to do so, calls the addressee to recognize this authority (has an RSVP), and so on. My claim is that when we blame someone, whether someone else or ourselves, we implicitly address a demand, not at our own individual discretion, but as a representative person, on behalf of the moral community, as it were. Impersonal reactive attitudes like moral blame thus presuppose a *representative authority* that is complementary to the individual authority that is presupposed by bipolar obligations.[20]

Sometimes, Wallace seems to deny that blaming and implicitly holding someone to a demand presupposes any authority to do. Here is what he says:

> When I become indignant about Mugabe's treatment of Zimbabwean dissidents, I assume that he had good reason to comply with the demand that I hold him to for humane treatment of his political opponents. But this reason does not derive from my "authority" to hold him to the demand. If anyone's authority is at issue here, it is surely the authority of Mugabe's political opponents, who are in a privileged position to complain when he arranges for them to be beaten and intimidated. (Wallace 2007: 31)

Wallace and I are agreed that the only discretionary *individual* authorities involved are those of the dissidents, which uninvolved third parties lack. The issue is whether impersonal reactive attitudes presuppose a further complementary authority, *representative authority*. Wallace and I are agreed also that any reason for acting that blame presupposes does not depend on any authority that the blaming individual *distinctively* has, and therefore, *a fortiori*, that the reasons do not depend on a demand being made by any individual.

I am claiming, however, that the reason that blame expresses, namely that the action violates moral obligation period, does depend on there being an authority to make demands of any moral agent that anyone, whether a dissident, an outside party, or Mugabe himself, shares as a representative person or member of the moral community.[21] Individuals don't make moral demands in the way an obligee might demand that an obligor comply with a bipolar obligation or demand an apology for its violation. Rather, when we blame someone, we add our voice to or second, as it were, a demand that we must presuppose is made of everyone by the moral community or representative persons as such.

To hold that impersonal reactive attitudes like blame do not presuppose representative authority is to be committed to the dilemma that either blame is purely epistemic, seeking simply to inform its object of a moral standard or of the legitimate demands

---

[20] It might be objected that not all third parties have representative authority, in particular, those who have violated moral demands themselves do not. It would be hypocritical of them to make any demands of others, since they have not complied themselves. However, even if this is the case, impersonal reactive attitudes would still presuppose a shared representative authority that all persons have unless they have failed to comply with the relevant demands themselves. I am indebted to Julia Markovits for this objection.

[21] See note 20.

that only others have the authority to make or press, or that it has practically directive force, but only brutely or nakedly. Some of the things Wallace says suggests he might take the first horn, although it is hard to see how he could consistently with the broadly Strawsonian interpretation of impersonal reactive attitudes to which he seems otherwise committed (in Wallace 1994). The most that "holding someone to an expectation" could then mean is something like directing the person's attention to it. But it seems impossible to grasp the second horn without lapsing into Nietzschean cynicism about morality.

As a way of consolidating these points, consider again the relation between the special way in which an obligee can hold an obligor responsible for complying with a bipolar obligation and the form accountability takes with moral obligation period. As Wallace says, an obligee has a "privileged basis for complaint." But what exactly does this mean? Suppose, for example, that Mugabe's victims complain to him about their mistreatment. What attitude could Mugabe take that would adequately recognize the legitimacy of their complaints and their authority to hold him accountable for complying with their demands? What is it like to acknowledge someone's legitimate complaint against oneself in the relevant sense?

I take it as obvious that obligees' distinctive privilege of complaint does not just mean that an obligor has to "listen" to the complaint in a way that someone might be required to give another person the space to vent or spout off, or even be required to absorb the cost of bearing the "slings and arrows" of being their complaint's object, that is, to accept that cost without complaint. One can do those things without accepting or recognizing the legitimacy of the complaint itself. Any response of Mugabe's that would adequately acknowledge the legitimacy of the dissidents' complaint and their special authority to make it would have to involve an internal *acceptance* of the complaint's legitimacy, which was also communicated second personally. And any such internal acceptance, I take it, would have to involve Mugabe's taking his victims' resentment to be warranted, not just as an understandable expression of their own sense of injury nor as a form of retaliation that it would be unjust of him to seek to avoid, but in the sense that his own actions of unjustly abusing them were *culpable*. The attitude that would reciprocate his victims' resentment in the sense of being its proper reciprocal would thus be a form of guilt. Mugabe could internally accept his culpability only by *blaming himself*, and so making a demand of himself not as just from his victim's standpoint, but as from anyone's including his own as a representative person or member of the moral community. As Adam Smith insightfully remarks, what resentment is "chiefly intent upon, is not so much to make our enemy feel pain in his turn, as ... to make him sensible that the person whom he injured did not deserve to be treated in that manner" (Smith 1982: 95–6).

If this is right, then there is a conceptual connection between bipolar obligation (along with claim rights) and moral obligation period. If X has an obligation to Y to do A, and Y therefore a claim right against X that X do A, then X's failure to do A would not only wrong Y, it would be wrong period, other things equal, at least.[22] Mugabe cannot adequately recognize his personal responsibility for injuring and thereby wronging his victims without also accepting that his actions were wrong period. And he cannot do that, unless he can believe this wrongdoing excusable, without blaming himself, that is, by implicitly making a demand of himself that he sees to be warranted from an impartial third-party perspective and accepting his own culpability. And this presupposes representative authority. It follows that the individual authority that Zimbabwean dissidents have to object to Mugabe's abuses, cannot exist unless there is also a representative authority that everyone shares along with the dissidents, including third parties and Mugabe himself, to hold Mugabe accountable through directive impersonal reactive attitudes like moral blame.

To conclude: the metaethics of bipolar obligation parallels that of moral obligation period. Both are second personal, but in different ways. Bipolar normativity involves a distinctive individual authority that obligees have to make demands of and hold obligors responsible. And moral obligation period entails a representative authority that anyone shares as a representative person or member of the moral community. It follows that the concept of bipolar obligation is not more fundamental than those of second-personal authority and second-personal reasons. The second-personal authority and entailed second-personal reasons that are distinctive of bipolar obligations are not, and cannot be, the only kind. The idea of second-personal authority is a more general notion, and it is required to understand the metaethics of both bipolar obligations and moral obligations period.[23]

---

[22] There are familiar legal cases in torts where someone can claim compensation for *non-culpable* transgressions of rights (and so, by Hohfeldian entailment, a bipolar legal obligation). Jules Coleman calls these "infringements" rather than "violations" of rights in Coleman 1992. Whether we say that the victim is *wronged* in such a case is probably a semantic choice. Whichever choice we make, it seems that although the victim has a warranted claim to compensation, she would not have warrant for *resenting* the violation. To bring such cases within the spirit of the analysis in the text, we might say that a claim right is either infringed or violated if it would warrant resentment if done without excuse *or justification*, where a justification defeats a charge of wrongdoing (violating a moral obligation period) as well as of culpability.

[23] I am indebted to participants in the 2010 Wisconsin Metaethics Workshop and to audiences at the University of British Columbia, the CUNY Graduate Center, and the University of Wyoming, and the 2011 APA Pacific Division Meetings, as well as participants in a conference on claim rights at Princeton University for helpful comments. I am especially indebted to my commentators on two of those occasions, Henry Richardson and Julia Markovits.

3

Moral Obligation: Form and Substance

I believe it is possible to make an argument from the *form* that moral obligations necessarily take to some basic *substantive* propositions about what moral obligations we have. In what follows I sketch how I think this can be done. By "moral obligation" I mean something narrower than what moral reasons recommend, even conclusively, namely, what morality *requires* or *demands*—in other words, what it would be morally *wrong* not to do. My contention is that a proper understanding of what it is for morality to require or demand something can enable us to derive at least some basic moral obligations.

I draw from an analysis of moral obligation that I defend in *SPS* (Darwall 2006). There I argue that moral obligation is conceptually tied to moral responsibility, specifically, to a fundamental answerability we have to one another (and ourselves) as representative persons or members of the moral community. Who are this "we" and "us"? Anyone, I argue, with the psychic capacities necessary to enter into relations of mutual accountability. I call these capacities *second-personal competence*, for reasons that will emerge presently. Moral obligations are what we *as* second-personally competent persons are answerable for *to* one another (and ourselves) *as* representative second-personally competent persons. This, I shall say, is moral obligation's *form*.

Because accountability to someone entails the latter's *authority* to demand and *hold one* to conduct ("second-personally"), I claim that accountability necessarily involves a *second-personal* relation and authority. In the case of moral demands, the requisite standing is not any *individual authority* anyone has to exercise at his or her discretion. It is rather a *representative authority* we all, all second-personally competent persons, have to hold one another and ourselves to moral demands. We exercise this authority, I claim, when we have Strawsonian "reactive" attitudes like indignation or moral disapproval toward people and blame them when they violate moral obligations without excuse (Strawson 1968).[1]

So far this says nothing about *what* we are morally obligated to do, about the *substance* of our obligations. Moral obligation's form seems only to dictate that whatever its

---

[1] More precisely, as I shall explain presently, what Strawson calls "impersonal" reactive attitudes.

substance is is something we warrantedly expect of one another and ourselves. I shall argue, however, that its form does indeed constrain moral obligations' substance. But before I start, I should set aside two arguments to this conclusion that I reject.

Some philosophers have held, first, that other-regarding content of some kind is simply built into the concept of morality or moral obligation. Whether the idea is that morality essentially has the point or "object" of benefiting human or other sentient life or of solving collective action problems that arise from the unrestrained pursuit of self-interest, views of this kind make "teleological" content intrinsic to the concept of morality (Foot 1958; Warnock 1971; Baier 1958; see also Falk 1965). My argument will depend on no such putative teleological conceptual truths, which I am inclined to reject, in any case. I shall assume that the concepts of morality and moral obligations are best identified *formally*, by their role in our attitudes and practical reasoning, not by any beneficial point or purpose.

Second, it might be thought that by analyzing moral obligation in terms of account-ability, I have already conceptualized it in terms of *what we owe to one another* and so implicitly assumed that moral obligations are in their nature "directed" or "bipolar," thereby constraining any content or substance they might plausibly be supposed to have to familiar obligations we have to each other (Scanlon 1998; Gilbert 2006; Thompson 2004). It is important to see, however, why this is not the case. Seeing this, moreover, will also help us focus more precisely on the central issue with which we shall be concerned.

As Hohfeld pointed out, any (bipolar) obligation that A owes *to* B entails a correlative claim right that B has *against A* (Hohfeld 1923: 65–75). I follow Feinberg (1980) in holding that claim rights are to be understood in terms of a distinctive standing or authority that the right holder (or obligee) has to make claims against the person obligated to her (the obligor) and, I add, to hold the obligor accountable to her for complying with them. This means that bipolar obligations *to someone* are understood in terms of an *individual authority* that the obligee or right holder uniquely has to, among other things, claim her right or forgo it by consent, hold her obligor answerable and resent the injury if her right is violated, seek remedy or not at her discretion, and, perhaps, to forgive (Darwall 2012). Only she or her representatives can do these things.[2]

Thus while, as I said at the outset, the form of moral obligation *period*, as we might call it, involves a fundamental answerability we have to everyone, ourselves included, *as representative persons*, hence their and our *representative authority*, bipolar obligations *to* others, even, any we might have to every other person, implicate a *different* standing or authority that others have *as individuals* to hold us answerable, hence imply their *individual authority*. Assuming that the form of moral obligations period involves a fundamental answerability to one another and ourselves *as representative persons*, therefore, does not

---

[2] It is a reflection of this that it is up to the injured party whether or not to bring a tort action at law, whereas criminal actions are appropriately brought by the people and their representatives.

commit us to the assumption that these obligations are, or even that they entail any that are, *owed to one another*. Bipolar obligations to others implicate individual authority; moral obligations (period) imply representative authority. And it is conceivable that the latter could hold without the former. There might be moral obligations period, say, not wantonly to destroy natural beauty, where there are no corresponding bipolar obligations.

Still, the reverse cannot be true; individual authority must surely entail representative authority. If A is genuinely obligated *to* B to do X, then A must be also be morally obligated to do X period, at least other things being equal. In other words, an action cannot violate a right or bipolar obligation and hence *wrong the obligee*, unless, other things being equal, it would be *wrong period*.[3] So if an action wrongs someone, it violates both the victim's individual authority as well as, other things being equal, a representative authority she shares with the wrongdoer.

We are concerned, however, with the relation in the other direction. We have seen that nothing in the idea of moral obligations as involving answerability to one another *as representative persons* entails anyone's *individual authority* of a kind that is conceptually implicated in bipolar obligations *to* and correlative claim rights against. For example, although a moral obligation not to foul the environment involves, on the analysis I am proposing, our being answerable to one another as representative persons for avoiding environmental degradation, that does not necessarily mean that this is something we *owe to each other*, since no one may have the *individual authority* to demand this conduct or not at his discretion, no one may have a relevant claim right. Moreover, as far as the concepts go, it might be that *all* moral obligations are obligations (period), there being no valid obligations *to* or rights against. Although individual authority apparently entails representative authority, the converse does not seem to hold.

Moral Obligation and Accountability

I believe that an argument can nonetheless be made from moral obligation's form as fundamental answerability to one another as representative persons to a basic substantive moral obligation period, *and* to reciprocal, bipolar obligations, to respect and not undermine one another's moral autonomy. I shall not be attempting to derive a substantive normative proposition from a putative analytic definition or conceptual truth. My argument will be hypothetical. *If*, I shall argue, there are any moral obligations, i.e., substantive normative truths about what we are obligated to do, *then* these must include the basic substantive obligations to which I shall point. Before I begin to make this argument, however, I need to say more about the general outlines of the account of moral obligation from which I shall be drawing.

---

[3] I say "other things being equal," because not all wrongings, hence violations of bipolar obligations and correlative claim rights involve wrongdoing, all things considered. On this point, see Coleman (1992: Ch. 11).

Formal accounts of moral obligation have tended to be advanced in terms of its categorical character and/or its putatively supreme authority. While both features seem necessary, we can fairly easily see that both are, even jointly, insufficient.

Note first that a conceptual gap exists between the ideas of, on the one hand, what morality recommends, however strongly, and, on the other, what it demands or requires. To see this, ask yourself whether you think that the possibility of supererogation is conceptually open. In other words, would someone who thinks that an action might be conclusively morally recommended but not morally required or not wrong not to do, be involved in some kind of self-contradiction or conceptual incoherence? It seems clear that she would not.

Whether supererogation is possible is a substantive normative issue that is not settled by the concept of moral obligation alone. But if that is so, then moral obligation must be a distinct concept from that of what morality recommends, even conclusively. But notice next that moral reasons are no less categorical when they recommend conduct than when they demand it—their validity and recommending power is no less independent of their relation to the agent's ends or interests (Foot 1972). And finally, notice that, so far as the concepts go, moral reasons might recommend an act and *also* outweigh reasons for acting otherwise without its necessarily being the case that the action is morally required or that not doing it is morally wrong. It seems conceptually possible that there might be cases where an agent does nothing wrong though she acts against the balance of moral reasons, even when these outweigh reasons of other kinds. Such an agent would of course be subject to rational criticism, but not necessarily, it seems, to moral *blame*.

If all this is correct, then the concept of moral obligation must differ from that of what moral reasons recommend, however categorical or overriding these reasons might be. What fills the gap, as I see it, is the concept of accountability and moral blame. Moral obligations are moral *demands*, and moral demands are whatever we are legitimately *held* to or answerable for, that is, where violations are *blameworthy* if the agent lacks a valid excuse. As Mill put it, "we do not call an action wrong, unless we mean to imply that a person ought to be punished in some way or other for doing it" (Mill 1998: Ch. 5). "Punishment" may sound overly strong, but Mill includes blame and "the reproaches of [the agent's] own conscience." What it is, consequently, for an action to be morally obligatory and its omission to be morally wrong, is for it to be something whose omission would warrant blame and feelings of guilt, were the agent to omit the action without excuse.[4]

Even though moral reasons do not necessarily constitute moral obligations even when they override, overridingness is nonetheless closely related to moral obligation. It is, however, the conceptual connection to accountability and blameworthiness that explains moral obligation's overridingness and not the other way around. If an action is

---

[4] Note that moral wrongness and blameworthiness are still distinct concepts, since an action may be wrong though not blameworthy because of the existence of an excuse.

morally obligatory, then it is blameworthy not to do it without excuse. But an action cannot be blameworthy when there was adequate justification for doing it, so actions can be blameworthy (and hence violate moral obligations) only if the reasons to comply with moral obligations outweigh reasons not to.

Accountability, Authority, and Second-Personal Demands

I will assume that an analysis of moral obligation that ties it conceptually to accountability and warrant for reactive attitudes like blame and guilt is broadly correct. Our question will then be whether anything about what we are obligated to do follows from this account of its form. I shall argue that it does, more specifically, that an argument can be made from the equal *representative authority* implicit in this account of moral obligation's form to a fundamental obligation to respect and not undermine moral autonomy as well as to a basic reciprocal bipolar obligation that entails every person's *individual authority* to demand treatment of this kind.[5]

I begin with some points about moral responsibility that derive from P. F. Strawson's "Freedom and Resentment" (Strawson 1968). Strawson coined the term "reactive attitude" to refer to a set of mental states that play a distinctive role in holding people morally responsible, whether another person, as in indignation, resentment, or moral blame, or oneself, as in the emotion of guilt. Strawson didn't give a formal definition of these attitudes, but their central features are clear from their role in his argument about moral responsibility and freedom of the will. Strawson's central idea is that reactive attitudes involve a way of regarding the individuals who are their objects that commits the holder of the attitude to certain assumptions about the object individual and her capacities to regulate her will. Unlike "objective attitudes," like disdain, disgust, and annoyance, reactive attitudes are essentially characterized by "involvement or participation with others in inter-personal human relationships" (Strawson 1968: 79). There is always an essentially "inter-personal," or as I shall say, *second-personal* element to reactive attitudes. Through the attitude we *hold* its object *to* something and thereby implicitly make a demand *of* him or her. As Strawson puts it, "the making of the demand is the proneness to such attitudes" (Strawson 1968: 92–3). The reason that reactive attitudes distinctively implicate freedom of the will, then, is that we can intelligibly address a demand to someone to regulate her will appropriately only if we suppose that she can so regulate it as a result of recognizing our demand's legitimacy. The supposition is a "constraint on moral address" (Watson 1987: 263, 264).

---

[5]   Again, on the substantive normative assumption that we are morally obligated to do something or other; i.e., that *some* moral obligations exist.

Consider the difference between the kind of disdain expressed by the put-down, "He is 'an egregious blockhead'" (in Hume's memorable phrase; Hume 1985: 314), and an attitude of indignation or moral blame (as might intelligibly be expressed even by, "Stop acting like an egregious blockhead"). Unlike the latter, the former is unfettered by any constraints on address that inevitably arise when we take a second-person perspective toward someone. Disdain is not standardly addressed to its object; if it has any addressee, indeed, that is likelier to be others we think capable of appreciating why its object is a worthy target. When we blame someone for something, however, we implicitly make a demand *of him* to act differently and, if he has not, to take responsibility for not having done so, where taking responsibility is essentially an *interpersonal* matter (holding himself answerable to us (and, indeed, to himself) as representative persons).[6] In so regarding him, we perforce see him as intelligibly so regarded, as someone who is *competent* to take such an attitude toward himself and guide himself by it. We see him as capable of entering into reciprocal human relationships of mutual accountability.

Disdain involves no such assumptions. One can hardly imagine Hume, believing that his disdain's object is too thick to appreciate his own blockheadedness or to be capable of changing it, withdrawing his put-down as not expressing a fully intelligible attitude. Moral blame, on the other hand, holds its object to a demanded standard and to its object's holding himself to that standard by making himself answerable for compliance. So it is not fully intelligible, or, at least, it is unwarranted in its own terms and not just unfair, when its object is someone we know lacks the psychic capacities necessary to do this. It just does not make sense to blame someone for dull-wittedness, unless one is under some illusion about the human ability to take responsibility for mental endowments. No matter how regrettable or unfair it might be, however, disdain for dull-wittedness is surely an intelligible attitude.

Strawson makes an important distinction *within* reactive attitudes between "personal" and "impersonal" ones. This can be confusing, since one may lose track of the fact that *all* reactive attitudes, even impersonal ones, must be "inter-personal" (or second personal). *Personal* reactive attitudes are those, like resentment and guilt, that are felt as if from the perspective of a participant in the events giving rise to it ("first" or "second parties"), whereas *impersonal* reactive attitudes, like indignation or moral blame, are felt as if from a third party's point of view. One cannot resent or forgive injuries to people with whom one lacks some personal connection, but this is no impediment to moral blame or disapproval. Nonetheless, however "impersonal," blame is not an "objective" attitude in Strawson's sense. It is just as "inter-personal" or second personal as personal reactive attitudes like resentment or guilt.[7] Thus

---

[6] Guilt, as will become clear presently, is interpersonal (or second personal) in this sense. See note 8.

[7] "The same abnormal light which shows the agent to us as one in respect of whom the personal attitudes, the personal demand, are to be suspended, shows him to us also as one in respect of whom the impersonal attitudes, the generalized demand, are to be suspended" (Strawson 1968).

although impersonal reactive attitudes are as if from the perspective of a third party, they are not third-personal attitudes in the usual sense; they involve the same second-personal element of implicit address as do personal ones, only as if from the perspective of a representative person rather than any individual's standpoint.[8]

The difference between *warranted* personal and impersonal reactive attitudes tracks the distinction between individual and representative authority and, consequently, between bipolar obligations *to* and moral obligations *period* (Darwall 2012). On the account we have been assuming, it is a conceptual truth that unexcused violations of moral obligations *period* warrant impersonal reactive attitudes like indignation and blame. Likewise, it is a conceptual truth that unexcused violations of bipolar obligations *to* someone, and hence of the latter's claim rights, warrant personal reactive attitudes like resentment from the obligee or right holder of the obligor, at least other things being equal.

The same points can be put by saying that personal and impersonal reactive attitudes implicate different *authorities* to make the demands they implicitly address. When we feel moral disapproval or blame toward people for violating a moral obligation (period), we implicitly address demands not as individuals, but as representative persons; indeed we implicitly demand that those we blame make the same demand of themselves from the very same perspective. When, however, someone has violated a claim right you had against him, hence an obligation he had *to you*, he has not just done wrong—he has *wronged you*. So you have a distinctive *individual* authority as the victim to hold him answerable, for example, to resent the wrong, which you can exercise or not at your discretion. You can seek compensation or not, forgive or not, and so on. No one else has the standing to do these things, except perhaps to represent you if you cannot speak for yourself. To sum up: *Warranted impersonal reactive attitudes, and thus moral obligation period, implicitly involve representative authority; and warranted personal reactive attitudes, and thus obligations to and correlative claim rights against, implicitly involve individual authority.*

Second-Personal Competence as Sufficient for Moral Obligation

We are now in a position to begin our positive argument. We can begin with Strawson's point that when we take someone to be morally obligated and hold him responsible with an impersonal reactive attitude, we have to attribute to him whatever

---

[8] Similarly, *second personal* does not imply *second party*. Guilt, like any reactive attitude is second personal, since it involves implicit address, but it clearly is not a second-party attitude. In feeling guilt, one implicitly addresses a demand to oneself. Finally, any second-personal attitude is also first personal. Address, whether implicit or explicit, is always from someone (an individual (I) or a collective (we)).

psychic competences are necessary to enter into mutually accountable, interpersonal relationship.[9]

What, then, does second-personal competence involve? In addition to whatever capacities we might include under rational agency, I take it to follow from Strawson's argument that, for human beings, at least, it includes the capacity for reactive attitudes, in addition to imaginative and empathetic abilities necessary to put oneself in others' shoes, including those of a representative person. But further, second-personal competence also includes the capacities to make and regulate oneself by normative judgments about what attitudes are *warranted* from these points of view. This need not mean that moral obligation is tied conceptually to *human* psychology. So long as a being has the capacity to take a second-person standpoint toward others and himself, make judgments about what demands would be warranted from this perspective, and regulate his conduct through making the relevant demands of himself, the being counts as second-personally competent.

The Strawsonian insight, as I interpret it, is that second-personal competence is both necessary and sufficient for moral obligation. Strawson clearly holds that second-personal competence is necessary. But the thought that it is also sufficient finds no less support in the reflections he relies on in linking moral obligation and answerability.

It is uncontroversial that fundamental moral obligations apply equally to all *moral agents*. When utilitarians say that we are morally obligated to do what will maximize utility or to comply with rules whose acceptance maximizes utility, they do not mean that we are so obligated *as human beings*, as members of a certain biological species. Like other moral theorists, they take it that there exists a set of capacities, which we collect under the term "moral agency," that are both necessary and sufficient to make one subject to moral obligations. Not every human being has these capacities, indeed, though it is uncontroversial that normal adult human beings do. Nothing ties moral agency to species membership.

It follows from the letter of Strawson's argument that moral agency includes second-personal competence. Otherwise second-personal competence would not be necessary for moral obligation, since moral agency, however we understand it, is supposed to be sufficient. The only way that second-personal competence might then not be sufficient for moral obligation is if moral agency included additional features, features that, when added to second-personal competence, make up an ensemble of capacities sufficient to make whomever has them subject to moral obligations.

What might such additional features be? No specific knowledge seems to be explicitly required. We do think, of course, that people can be held morally responsible, and so be

---

[9] This is often not an all or nothing affair, of course. But we can abstract from these complexities and assume that what we might call "full" moral obligation and moral responsibility presuppose "full" second-personal competence. So understood, second-personal competence is what Rawls called a "range property" or concept, much as Rawls treated the capacity for "moral personality" in *A Theory of Justice* (Rawls 1971: 509). All that matters is that one is above a certain threshold.

properly held subject to moral obligation, only on the assumption that they can know, appreciate, and regulate themselves by the obligations with which we take them to be answerable for complying. But we do not take it as a defense or excuse that someone simply lacked the relevant knowledge, at least when it concerns the moral obligations of the most basic sort. We presume that moral agency includes the capacities necessary to acquire and appreciate this knowledge, at least in principle.

Neither do we suppose that any specific contentful motivational state, like benevolent concern, is necessary to be subject to moral obligation. Our sense that we can legitimately demand that people not harm others, for example, is in no way conditional on agents being able to care about their potential victims and their welfare for their own sakes. We do not treat lack of benevolent concern as an excuse or mitigating factor. Even beings who, like Kant's "unfortunate man" who are "by temperament cold and indifferent to the sufferings of others" would seem to have some basis to appreciate the legitimacy of the moral demand not to harm, for example, if they would make such a demand of others and can see that no such demand can be warranted except impartially (Kant 1996b 438).[10]

If moral agency involves no additional features, however, and if second-personal competence is necessary for moral responsibility and obligation, it follows that the capacity for moral agency is nothing other than second-personal competence. The latter is both necessary and sufficient for moral obligation.

Somewhat unexpected support for this thought comes from Hobbes. After listing the laws of nature in *Leviathan*, Hobbes writes:

To leave all men inexcusable, they [the laws of nature] have been contracted into one easy sum, intelligible, even to the meanest capacity; and that is, Do not that to another, which thou wouldest not have done to thyself. (Hobbes 1994: 15.¶35)

Hobbes must therefore think, along the Strawsonian lines we have been pursuing, that duties imposed by laws of nature are essentially tied to responsibility. If they could not be "sum[med]" into something "intelligible, even to the meanest capacity," violations would be "[e]xcusable" quite generally. But notice also the form that Hobbes's summation takes. Hobbes cannot plausibly mean by "wouldest not have done to thyself" what one would *prefer* not to have done to oneself. I may prefer a world in which others peel me grapes, and, if so, there is a sense in which I would not "have" others forbear to do this. But this would give me no reason to think that I have any duty to peel grapes for others.

Suppose, however, that I would hold others to this, expect it of them, feel indignant and resent it when they do not, and so on. This must be the sense that Hobbes has in mind. The sum of the laws of nature is that one should not act toward others as one would expect or demand of others that they not act toward one and would blame them

---

[10] I do not mean, however, that forms of psychopathology that make one dead to moral considerations or to impartially regulated reactive attitudes cannot excuse.

for doing, were they so to act without excuse. Knowledge of our fundamental moral obligations must apparently take some such form if second-personal competence is to be sufficient for it.

Second-Personal Competence as Ground for Moral Obligation

An obvious problem with formulations of the golden rule as a fundamental moral principle that has long been noticed is that so long as people are prepared to accept others making the same demands of them, nothing rules out their making even the most outrageous demands of others. As Hobbes formulates it, the golden rule is less a fundamental axiom from which basic moral obligations can be derived than a principle of moral consistency or integrity. Still, it highlights moral obligation's second-personal character. Action toward others can be consistent with our moral obligations *as we understand them* only if it is consistent with demands of others we take to be warranted.

We have been assuming that what matters for moral obligation is what demands would be warranted from the impartial perspective we and others share, namely, that of representative person. Moreover, if others are bound by the very same fundamental moral obligations we are, then others must be able to see these demands as warranted from the very same perspective also. It follows that something can be a fundamental moral obligation, then, if, and only if, it involves a demand of *anyone* (i.e., any second-personally competent person) that *anyone* can see to be warranted from the perspective of a representative second-personally competent person.

For moral obligations to exist at all, consequently, there must be fundamental demands that anyone can see to be warranted *from* anyone, as a representative second-personally competent, *to any second-personal competent*, himself or others. But for this to be true, there must be something that anyone subject to such demands could see to warrant them. What could provide such warrant?

Now the process of considering what demands are warranted from the perspective of a representative person is itself an exercise of second-personal competence. So when we hold one another and ourselves responsible from this perspective through exercising second-personal competence, there is a straightforward sense in which we are committed to valuing one another's exercise of this very same competence. A central lesson of Strawson's discussion is that answerability is always a reciprocal, second-personal affair. It is impossible warrantedly to hold others answerable without allowing them the interpersonal space to take responsibility for themselves by making their own autonomous choices. One cannot coherently hold someone responsible for (freely choosing) to do something while simultaneously undermining his ability to make the choice himself or otherwise usurping his agency.[11]

A fundamental (Rawls might say "highest-order") interest in living with others on terms of mutual accountability, exercising and allowing them the liberty to exercise the ability autonomously to make their own moral choices and so take responsibility for themselves as their author is thus built into the second-person perspective of a representative person (Rawls 1980: 525). Since this is so, there is necessarily warrant from this perspective, at least other things being equal, for a demand not to usurp others' moral agency or otherwise undermine the conditions of free moral choice. And this means that if there are any moral obligations at all, there must exist a *pro tanto* moral obligation not to restrict others' moral autonomy in these ways. Here already we have derived some substance from moral obligation's form.

And we can go further. It simply cannot be the case that there is only this one moral obligation, since there can be significant moral choices only if there are other obligations also. But here again, any other moral obligations would have likewise to be things any second-personally competent agent can find warrant for from the perspective of a representative person, through exercising second-personal competence. It seems inconceivable, from this perspective, that the interest in autonomous choice can be contained within some specified moral realm. Part of what it is to respect someone's standing to make her own moral choices, even as one makes moral demands of her, is to leave it up to her how and whether to comply. Otherwise, she will not be complying of her own free choice and so taking responsibility for herself. This means that the interest in exercising second-personal competence involves an interest in being accorded the interpersonal space necessary to lead one's own life more generally. And if that is so, it follows that *pro tanto* demands not to violate autonomy and restrict liberty are also warranted more generally. And there is no reason to think that warranted demands grounded in this interest would not also extend significantly wider, to include, for example, obligations of mutual aid and non-maleficence, as well as others.

Moreover, this interest can also ground the *individual authority* to lead one's own life that constitutes a claim right to do so, that is, not just the wrongness of usurping moral autonomy or otherwise violating the conditions of free moral choice, but also its wronging *the individual moral agents involved*. There is absolutely nowhere to stand to object reasonably to any second-personally competent agent's claim to make his or her own moral choices. We can hardly warrantedly hold him responsible as representative persons for taking individual responsibility *for himself* without thereby committing ourselves to according him a distinctive *individual authority* to hold us responsible for letting him do that. Thus although we can distinguish analytically between a representative person's perspective from which we and he have the very same authority for

---

[11] For an interesting analysis of paternalism as involving illegitimate usurpation of agency, see Shiffrin 2000.

holding people responsible for letting people make their own moral choices and his individual standing to object to our failing to let *him* do so, it would seem that any interest in the exercise of autonomous moral choice that can provide warrant for the former impersonal reactive attitudes and demand must also be able, impartially, to warrant the latter personal reactive attitudes and demand as well.

Obviously, this is only a beginning sketch of how one might seek to derive moral obligations and claim rights from materials that are available within a second-person standpoint. I hope it is clear, however, that if moral obligation's form consists in a fundamental answerability we have to one another, then its substance must include basic obligations to allow one another to take responsibility for ourselves.[12]

---

[12] I am indebted to members of the audience at the Aristotelian Society in December 2009, where this was initially presented, for very helpful discussion.

4

"But It Would Be Wrong"

At a critical juncture in the Senate Watergate Hearings in 1973, H. R. Haldeman testified about a taped conversation he had heard between President Richard Nixon and the White House lawyer, John Dean. Nixon and Dean were discussing the possibility of raising hush money to meet the demands of one of the Watergate burglars, E. Howard Hunt, so that Hunt wouldn't spill the beans about the break-in at the Democratic National Committee. The President asked how much money would be required, and Dean answered, "Probably a million dollars—but the problem is that it is hard to raise." Nixon replied, "There is no problem in raising a million dollars, we can do that." Then, according to Haldeman, Nixon added the following, soon to be famous, phrase: "But it would be wrong."[1] We now know that Nixon did not actually say this, but it seems clear what Haldeman's intention was in saying he did.[2] Haldeman wished to portray Nixon as implying that if paying off Hunt would be wrong, then there was good reason, decisive reason in fact, not to pursue that course of action and that it should therefore not be considered further.

Here arises a recently discussed philosophical problem (Scanlon 1998: 11, 2007; Dancy 2000; Stratton-Lake 2003; Zimmerman 2007). Does the fact that an act would be wrong provide any reason *itself*, let alone a decisive reason, not to perform it? The question is not whether there is adequate reason to avoid wrong-doing. Recent discussion has tended to take it for granted that there is. The question rather is whether the fact that an action would be wrong is itself a reason of any kind, whether especially strong or conclusive or of any strength whatsoever. Various considerations have led some philosophers to think that it is not (including Dancy 2000; Stratton-Lake 2003; Zimmerman 2007). Briefly, these include the following.

---

[1] "Counterattack and Counterpoint," *Time* (August 13, 1973).

[2] Here is what the transcript of the March 21, 1973 tape says: "PRESIDENT: How much money do you need? DEAN: I would say these people are going to cost, uh, a million dollars over the next, uh,—two years. (Pause) PRESIDENT: We could get that. DEAN: Uh, huh. PRESIDENT: You, on the money, if you need the money, I mean, uh' you could get the money. Let's say—DEAN: Well, I think that we're going—PRESIDENT: What I mean is, you could, you could get a million dollars. And you could get it in cash. I, I know where it could be gotten. DEAN: Uh, huh." (Watergate Trial Conversations, Nixon Presidential Library and Museum, <http://nixon.archives.gov/forresearchers/find/tapes/watergate/trial/transcripts. php>.)

An action is wrong only if there are reasons that make it wrong, *wrong-making features* of performing the action or *"grounds"* of its wrongness.[3] So it seems that it should be these features of the action, the features that make it wrong, that are the reasons not to perform the wrongful act, not the fact that the action would be wrong itself. Such a further reason would seem superfluous, if not indeed to involve a kind of double counting.

It is sometimes pointed out also that a morally good person is moved directly by wrong-making features of the wrongful act rather than by the fact that the act would be wrong; the former and not the latter are *the good person's reasons* for acting as she does.[4] Someone who is moved primarily by overall moral verdicts, such as an action's being wrong, rather than by the grounds of the verdict, has been said to have a kind of "moral fetish," rather than being truly morally good. Thus even Haldeman's fantasy endowed Nixon with something less than moral goodness. It was as if the fact, say, that paying Hunt off would subvert justice left Nixon entirely unmoved until he realized that that made the act morally wrong.

Of course, from the fact that a morally good person's reasons are typically morally relevant features, rather than the moral status these features bestow upon an action, it hardly follows that moral wrongness is not itself a reason for acting. Even if it is not a reason for a morally good person, it might still be for those who are no better than morally mediocre. Or it might be a reason even for the morally good, though not a reason they typically act on.

Yet a further line of thought in favor of holding that moral wrongness is not itself a reason comes by analogy with T. M. Scanlon's "buck-passing" theory of value (Scanlon 1998: 95–100). According to Scanlon, being good or having value is not itself a reason to have any attitude or take any action with respect to the valuable thing. Rather value "passes the buck" to the good- or value-making features of the valuable thing, and it is these features that provide reasons for the relevant (valuing) attitudes and actions toward it. That the thing is valuable or good does not provide a further reason for the relevant attitudes or actions. If a buck-passing account is plausible for evaluative (good-making) properties, however, then why would it not be for deontic (right- or wrong-making) properties also? Why not think that, as with goodness or value, moral

---

[3] The latter term derives from Dancy 2000. When I speak of "good-making" or "right-" or "wrong-making" properties in what follows, I will have this sense in mind, namely, *grounds* or *normative reasons* for something's value, rightness, or wrongness. We might call this a *normative* sense, as opposed to a *metaphysical* sense of good-making or right- or wrong-making features—i.e., the features in which something's being good, right, or wrong consists metaphysically. I shall be arguing that an act's wrong-making features in the normative sense—i.e., the grounds of or normative reasons for something's being wrong—do not exhaust the reasons not to perform the wrongful act; that the fact that the act is wrong is itself a reason. I should not be understood as claiming that if there is some complex fact or facts in which this latter fact consists metaphysically, the fact that an act is wrong is a reason that is additional to *these* facts, since on the hypothesis in question, that is what the fact of an act's being wrong would itself consist in. I have been helped here by discussion with, among others, Janice Dowell and Peter Schulte.

[4] Cf. Michael Smith on the *de dicto* desire to avoid wrongdoing as opposed to *de re* desires to avoid actions of wrong-making kinds (Smith 1994: 75–6). However, see Carbonell forthcoming.

wrongness passes the buck to wrong-making features, and it is (only) they that provide reasons for the relevant attitudes and actions, including not performing the wrongful act?[5]

This has not, however, been Scanlon's view. He has taken the position that an action's being wrong is indeed a reason not to do it (e.g., Scanlon 1998: 11 and 2007). In what follows, I shall argue that Scanlon is right; taking a buck-passing approach to normative concepts in general, and to the concepts of moral obligation, right, and wrong, in particular, does not entail that an act's wrongness is not a reason not to perform it. To the contrary, I shall argue, the most plausible buck-passing theory of the concepts of moral obligation and wrong entails that an act's being wrong is a reason not to perform the act that is additional to the act's wrong-making features (in the normative sense of features that *ground* or are normative reasons for its wrongness).[6] I will argue this in three stages. First, in first section, I argue that a buck-passing theory of a normative concept (or similarly, a "warranted" or "fitting attitude" theory of the concept), although entailing that the fact that something instantiates the concept (say, is good, right, or wrong) is not a further reason for the specific attitudes that are conceptually tied to the normative concept, it may not entail that that fact is not a reason for some relevant choice, intention, or *action*, since the conceptually implicated attitude may not entail any relevant action attitude (like intention or choice). Then in the second section, I present a buck-passing theory of the concepts of moral obligation, right, and wrong, according to which these are normative, at least in the first instance, not for intention or action, but for attitudes through which we hold people responsible for their actions and blame them (what P. F. Strawson called "reactive attitudes").[7] I then argue, in the third section, that this theory entails that the fact that an act is wrong is indeed a further reason not to perform the action, and it tells us what this further reason consists in. It is the fact that the act is something we legitimately demand of one another and ourselves as representative persons or members of the moral community. In the final section, I discuss some light the theory sheds on whether there is (always) overriding or conclusive reason to act as we are morally obligated (all things considered) and not do moral wrong.

Normative Concepts, Attitudes, and Action

Although it is possible to hold a buck-passing theory of value on other grounds, one natural line of thought that leads to buck-passing is a *warranted attitude theory of normative*

---

[5] Again, to features that are wrong-making in the sense of providing normative grounds of an act's wrongness. This differs from any features that might be wrong-making in the sense of being what an action's being consists in metaphysically.

[6] See note 3 above.

[7] I defend this analysis in greater detail in Darwall 2006.

concepts in general.[8] It is plausible to suppose that what normative concepts all have in common is, as Allan Gibbard says, using a phrase of Wilfrid Sellars's, that they are "fraught with ought" (Gibbard 2003: 212). The basic idea derives from A. C. Ewing and ultimately from Henry Sidgwick (Ewing 1939; Sidgwick 1967). Sidgwick said that all "ethical judgments" include "the fundamental notion represented by the word 'ought'" (Sidgwick 1967: 25). "Ought" here has a "flavorless" sense, in Gibbard's term, of thin justification or warrant, distinct, for example, from more thickly qualified senses like "morally ought" or "prudentially ought" (Gibbard 1990: 7; McLeod 2001). According to warranted attitude theories, every normative concept is tied conceptually to some specific attitude or set of attitudes; each is the concept of being a warranted object of its distinctive attitude or attitudes (cf. Anderson 1990).

For example, the concept of the *desirable* is that of being a justified object of desire, of being such as there is normative reason to desire. The concept of the *estimable* is that of what is warrantedly esteemed. The concept of *dignity* is that of what warrants respect. And so on. Every normative concept can be represented in terms of its distinctive attitude or attitudes and the fundamental normative notion of warrant, justification, ought, or (normative) reason.

There is, however, a crucial qualification. As recent discussion of the "wrong kind of reasons" problem makes clear, not just any reason for having some attitude is a reason of the "right kind" to justify or warrant an attitude in the terms that are distinctively relevant to the normative concept that is conceptually tied to it (D'Arms and Jacobson 2000a, 2000b; Rabinowicz and Ronnøw-Rasmussen 2004). For example, instrumental or strategic reasons for having some attitude, say, a desire or an intention to drink a toxin if one will be rewarded for having either attitude, as in Kavka's famous "toxin puzzle," are reasons of the wrong kind to establish that drinking the toxin would itself be either desirable or choiceworthy.[9] Reasons of the right kind are "fittingness" reasons; they show that the attitude "fits" or is a fitting response to the object (D'Arms and Jacobson 2000b).

On what we might better call *fitting attitude theories* of normative concepts, therefore, every normative concept can be analyzed in terms of "fittingness" (that is, support by warrant or reasons of the right kind) and the attitude or set of attitudes that is distinctive of the concept. So the concept of the desirable is that of being a fitting object of desire, the estimable, that of being a fitting object of esteem, dignity, that of being a fitting object of respect, and so on for every normative concept.

---

[8] In my view, the warranted attitude theory (or, more specifically, the fitting attitude theory, which I shall discuss presently) is the most plausible approach to analyzing normative concepts. It is not necessary to the argument of this paper, however, that it actually succeeds. We shall simply assume that it does as the most plausible line of thought leading to the view that wrongness is not itself a reason for acting. My point will be that accepting a fitting attitude theory of wrongness would not commit us to this. To the contrary, on the fitting attitude theory of wrongness I shall propose, wrongness is indeed itself a practical reason.

[9] The "toxin puzzle" refers to a situation Gregory Kavka described in which there is an instrumental reason to form an intention to drink a toxin (e.g., that one would be rewarded if one did), but in which this apparently gives one no reason to act on the intention (Kavka 1983).

Now for fitting attitude theories to be plausible, there must be some way of distinguishing reasons of the right from the wrong kind that does not itself depend upon the relevant normative concept. If the only way of distinguishing the right from the wrong kind of reasons to desire, say, is that the former bear on an object's desirability, then any attempt to analyze the concept of desirability in terms of the right kind of reasons to desire will be circular.

In my view, various promising suggestions have been made. Rabinowicz and Ronnøw-Rasmussen have proposed that reasons of the right kind appear also in the object or content of the attitude they purport to support. In other words, what the reason is strictly for is not just some specific attitude, but a specific-attitude-toward-something-on-account-of-the-reason (Rabinowicz and Ronnøw-Rasmussen 2004).[10] Pamela Hieronymi has argued that every attitude has its distinctive deliberative question and that reasons of the right kind are those that bear on that question (Hieronymi 2005). And I have proposed that the right kind of reasons for an attitude are those that are capable of being *the subject's reason* for the attitude, that is, those *on account of which* someone can directly form the attitude (Darwall 2006: 66). Thus, it is not psychically possible for *an agent's own reason* for intending or desiring intrinsically to drink a toxin to be that she will win a reward if she intends or forms an intrinsic desire to drink it. She can desire to have an intrinsic desire to drink the toxin for this reason, but not desire intrinsically to drink the toxin for this reason. Just as if she were offered a reward were she to believe that the U.S. war in Iraq was an unqualified success in every respect, she could *desire* for that reason to believe that proposition, that fact could not be her reason for having the belief itself. It would be psychically impossible to form the belief *for that reason*. One cannot reason: "I will get a reward if I believe p; therefore, p," as one would have to were one to believe p for the reason that one will get a reward.

Perhaps none of these proposals is fully satisfactory, but we need not worry about that.[11] Since the most powerful line of thought leading to buck-passing is a fitting attitude approach to normative concepts of some kind, we can simply assume that a solution to the wrong kind of reasons problem can be found. What we want to know is whether *if* a fitting attitude account of wrongness were true, this would show that wrongness is not itself a reason for acting, that is, whether such an account would support being a buck-passer about wrongness with respect to reasons for acting.

This brings us to Scanlon's buck-passing theory of value. As I said, the "letter" of the buck-passing theory, that being good or valuable is not itself a reason to hold any relevant attitude toward the valuable thing or to promote it, does not require a warranted or fitting attitude theory of normative concepts. Some things Scanlon

---

[10] For example, not just for a desire to eat an apple, but for a desire to eat an apple on account of its taste (Rabinowicz and Ronnøw-Rasmussen 2004: 414). This is related to a suggestion of W. D. Falk's in Falk 1986: 117.

[11] See also Parfit's recent arguments that normative reasons for having some attitude cannot derive from "state-given" considerations concerning its being good or better to have the attitude (Parfit 2011: I, 50–1, 420–32).

says, however, suggest such a theory. For example, he says that "to claim that something is valu*able* (or that it is 'of value') is to claim that [one and] others have reason to value it" (Scanlon 1998: 95). This suggests a warranted or fitting attitude account of the valuable (in terms of warrant for some valuing attitude or other). So understood, value would be a generic evaluative concept, related conceptually to a set of valuing attitudes. Being desirable, estimable, having dignity, and so on, would then be distinct species of value.[12]

A buck-passing theory about value, at least with respect to the relevant valuing attitudes—that being valuable or good is not itself a reason to have the (valuing) attitude toward that thing—would then follow straight away. If being valuable just is there being reason to have one or another valuing attitude toward something, and how valuable that thing is depends on the weight and character of the reasons for valuing it, then the fact that something is valuable cannot be a further reason to value it. By creating a further reason, the exact value of something (say, A), would thereby make the thing more valuable ($A + B$ (where B is the increased value owing to the additional reason created by the thing's having value A)).[13] But that would seem to be absurd.[14]

Clearly, the reason why a fitting attitude theory of value apparently entails buck-passing about value is that the attitudes that are implicated in the concept of value and the attitudes with respect to which the question arises whether value does or does not provide a reason *are the very same attitudes*. If the concept of the desirable is the concept of what there is reason (of the right kind) to desire, then the fact that something is desirable cannot provide a (further) reason to desire it. According to a fitting attitude theory, something is exactly as desirable as the (right kind of) reasons for desiring make it. Its being desirable does not make it more desirable yet.

But does that mean that being valuable cannot itself provide a reason for *action*? Presently, I will argue that there are kinds of value that do indeed provide reasons for action, namely, where the relevant valuing attitude does not itself conceptually implicate choice, action, or some other agential disposition. With the desirable, however, there does seem to be a fairly tight conceptual connection. Some disposition to bring the desired state about seems part of the very concept of desire. But if that so, then a buck-passing theory of the desirable would arguably entail not just buck-passing about reasons for desire, but also about reasons to bring about desire's object.

Whether a fitting attitude theory of moral wrongness will entail buck-passing about reasons not to perform wrongful acts, therefore, will depend on precisely which

---

[12] For a defense of such a view, see Anderson 1990.

[13] See Zimmerman 2007 for a parallel argument against holding that wrongness creates an additional reason.

[14] For our purposes, we don't strictly need to suppose that a fitting attitude actually does entail buck-passing about value. The argument of this paper is that even if it were to support buck-passing about the relevant valuing attitudes in this way, a fitting attitude account of wrongness of the sort I will propose would not entail buck-passing about wrongness with respect to reasons for action. Here again, then, we can just assume that a fitting attitude theory of the value of the sort Scanlon gestures to entails buck-passing about value with respect to the relevant valuing attitudes. I am indebted here to discussion with Ruth Chang.

attitude or attitudes are conceptually implicated in the concept of moral wrong. We must therefore ask: If the concept of moral wrong is a normative concept, what attitude or attitudes is it normative for?

The proposal whose implications we shall consider is one I have defended at greater length elsewhere, namely, that the concepts of moral obligation and moral wrong are irreducibly second-personal concepts, since they conceptually implicate attitudes through which we implicitly address agents and hold them accountable.[15] This is a version of J. S. Mill's idea, taken up more recently by P. F. Strawson, Richard Brandt, Allan Gibbard, and others, that the concept of moral wrong is the concept of what would be *blameworthy*, that is, a warranted object of Strawsonian reactive attitudes including blame, were an agent to perform the act without some adequate excuse.[16] I follow what I take to be the thrust of Strawson's point by analyzing reactive attitudes as invariably involving *demands* that are implicitly *addressed* to their attitudes' objects second-personally, if only in imagination. Mill said that "we do not call anything wrong, unless we mean to imply that a person ought to be punished in some way or other for doing it; if not by law, by the opinion of his fellow creatures; if not by opinion, by the reproaches of his own conscience" (Mill 1998: Ch. V, ¶ 14). As I interpret Mill through Strawsonian lenses, "punishment" in this passage should be taken in the broad sense of holding someone responsible with a reactive attitude like indignation, blame, or guilt.[17] *Holding* someone accountable, in this way, is implicitly a second-personal relation, since it involves the (imagined, at least) address of a demand to its object. The connection between the concepts of moral obligation and wrong, on the one hand, and the reactive attitude of blame is then this. What is morally wrong is what is blameworthy, that is what is warrantedly blamed, if the action is done without adequate excuse.

If this is so, then the attitudes for which the concepts of moral obligation and moral wrong are conceptually normative are attitudes other than intention, choice, or any agential disposition like desire. The object of a reactive attitude is, in the first instance anyway, a person, and not some action or outcome as this might appear from an agent's

---

[15]   In Darwall 2006: 91–118. There I define a set of second-personal concepts, which conceptually involve the idea of claims and demands that can be *addressed* (to an addressee, second-personally) and argue that these include the concepts of moral obligation, wrong, rights, the dignity of persons, and the very concept of a moral person (as a subject of obligations). What is new in the present paper are the implications I here draw from this analysis of moral obligation for the question of whether an action's wrongness is in itself a reason not to perform the act.

[16]   Strawson 1968. Strawson uses the term "reactive attitude" to refer to a set of attitudes, which include indignation, resentment, guilt, and moral blame, that implicitly hold their objects responsible and so regard them in a distinctively interpersonal (as I put it, "second-personal" way). For ease of expression, I will sometimes speak of actions, and not agents, as blameworthy—strictly speaking, it is agent who is appropriately blamed for performing a "blameworthy action" (speaking loosely). See also Brandt 1979; Gibbard 1990.

[17]   I use "blame" throughout to refer to an attitude rather than any specific activity or speech act. It is thus possible to blame someone without ever saying anything to him or to anyone. Blame in this sense also differs from a belief or judgment that someone is blameworthy. "I know that she still blames me for what I did twenty-five years ago though we haven't talked in many years."

deliberative standpoint. If consequently, the concepts of moral obligation and moral wrong are normative for reactive attitudes, then the reasons for being a buck-passer about evaluative concepts like the desirable will not simply transfer directly to being a buck-passer about moral wrong with respect to reasons *for action*, specifically, for avoiding moral wrong. To be sure, if what is wrong is what is warrantedly blamed if done without adequate excuse, then, on the assumption that someone lacks such an excuse, the fact that he acted wrongly cannot provide a reason for holding him responsible through reactive attitudes and blaming him that is additional to those provided by the acts wrong-making features.[18] On the proposal we shall consider, the latter reasons (the wrong-making features) consist in whatever reasons (of the right kind) there are for the reactive attitudes through which one holds someone responsible for performing an act of that kind. By analogy with our earlier point about the desirable, something does not become more blameworthy than its wrong-making features make it by virtue of being morally wrong; its being wrong just *is* its being blameworthy if done without excuse to whatever degree its wrong-making features make it. Anyone who accepts the fitting attitude account of moral obligation and wrongness I propose should therefore be a buck-passer with respect to reasons for blaming and holding morally responsible. But that would not entail being a buck-passer with respect to reasons for *action*, specifically, for avoiding moral wrong. The fact that an action is wrong might still itself be, and I shall argue actually is, a reason, indeed a decisive reason, not to perform the act or to intend or choose to do so.

Before I sketch this proposal in more detail, I would like to note briefly some other normative concepts where buck-passing about the relevant reasons for action is not very plausible. The explanation for this is, as I will be arguing is also the case with moral wrong, that the attitudes that are conceptually implicated in the normative concept are other than intention and choice.

Consider, for example, the concepts of the estimable and its contrary, the contemptible. To be estimable is to be worthy of esteem, and if something is estimable, that will be on account of its estimable-making features.[19] These are all, and only, whatever reasons of the right kind there are for esteeming it. For now familiar reasons, something's being estimable cannot be a further reason for esteeming it. And *mutatis mutandis* for the contemptible. The features that make something contemptible are all, and only, reasons of the right kind that exist for having contempt for it. But the rationale for being a buck-passer about reasons for esteeming or contemning does not directly transfer to being a buck-passer about reasons for *acting* in some way or other with respect to the estimable or the contemptible. Even if esteeming some trait generally

---

[18] That is, it cannot on the assumption we have been making, namely, that a fitting attitude theory of a normative concept entails buck-passing with respect to reasons for the attitudes that the concept conceptually involves.

[19] Again, "estimable-making" in the sense of being normative *grounds* of its being estimable, not there being facts in which the thing's being estimable consists metaphysically.

gives rise, say, to some desire to acquire the trait, the desire doesn't seem to be *conceptually* implicated in the former. We might imagine beings who admire some trait while lacking any desire whatsoever to act in any particular way with respect to it. Whatever relation exists between esteem and the desire to acquire or emulate seems different from the conceptual connection between a desire for some outcome and a disposition to bring that outcome about.

For all that supports being a buck-passer about reasons for esteem and contempt, therefore, it could still be the case, and arguably is the case, that the fact that something is estimable is itself a reason to *act* in various ways regarding it, say, to promote the estimable trait or to acquire or realize it in one's own life. Thus when Aristotle advances the view that virtuous activity (chosen for its own sake as noble or estimable) is the final good for us human beings and so what we have most reason to seek, he is not simply mouthing an empty truth, such as that what we have reason to seek is what we have reason to seek (or an "almost empty" truth, such as that what we have reason to desire is what we have reason to bring about). He is making a substantive normative claim.

Or consider the concept of welfare or well-being. Most philosophers believe that this too is a normative concept. But if it is, the question arises, for what attitude or attitudes is it normative? It seems clear that, unlike that of the choiceworthy, the concept of well-being is not simply that of what a person herself has reason to choose, intend, or do, since whether or not we do in fact have reason to do anything other than promote our own welfare, it seems clear that no incoherence or conceptual confusion is involved in thinking we do, for example, in thinking that *others'* well-being, or moral considerations, or a whole host of other considerations give us reasons to act that are additional to those that concern our own well-being. But if that is so, then the concept of welfare cannot possibly be identical with the concept of what the person herself has reason to do. Nor can welfare simply be the concept of the desirable, for similar reasons. We often think that things that have nothing to do with us or our own well-being are desirable, such as the survival of the planet long after we ourselves are dead, the flourishing of our children in the further future, or whatever. And whether or not any of these thoughts are true, there is no doubt that they are coherent.

I have argued elsewhere that the most plausible account of well-being as a normative concept is that it is what is desirable for someone *for that person's sake*, that is, what there is reason to desire for someone out of care or sympathetic concern *for her* (Darwall 2002). A *rational care theory of welfare* understands the normativity of welfare to be for desires for someone (or for some being) for her (or its) sake, that is, from the perspective of care of concern for her (or it). In other words, this concept of welfare is the one we need and make use of when, in caring for someone, we face the normative question of what to want (what we should want) for her (Wolf 2006). In yet other words, a person's welfare is what there is reason to desire for someone, conditional on there being reason to care for her.

If some account in this general direction is correct, then the warranted attitude that is conceptually involved in welfare or well-being is actually quite complex and does not itself conceptually involve intention or choice. Granted, if one cares for someone and is thereby disposed to have desires, and thereby to act, for her sake, then any reasons why something would be good for her, welfare-making features, will automatically become reasons to bring that thing about. But so far as the concept of welfare goes, this does not entail that, if something, X, is a welfare-making feature for Y (i.e., X would contribute intrinsically to Y's welfare), then there is reason for anyone, whether Y or anyone else, to bring X about. It is conceptually coherent to hold that something would contribute intrinsically to someone's welfare (by realizing some welfare-making feature), but nonetheless hold that there is no reason whatsoever to bring that thing about. Y herself might coherently judge this. Y might not care for herself or think she is worth caring for and think therefore that considerations of her own welfare provide no reasons for acting, either for her or for anyone else. What is conceptually incoherent is caring for Y, or thinking one should care for her (for reasons of the right kind), and not taking welfare-making features as reasons to desire that these features be realized in Y's life for Y's sake.

I take it as evidence that something in this general neighborhood is correct that there is no attraction whatsoever to holding a buck-passing theory of welfare with respect to reasons for action. No philosopher I am aware of seems tempted to deny that the fact that something will promote an agent's welfare or well-being is itself a reason for her to realize or promote it. To the contrary, it is hard to think of a more widely held view in the history of ethics. If a fitting attitude approach to welfare is correct, something's being for someone's welfare must consist in there being reasons for some attitude or other toward that thing. And this would naturally lead to a buck-passing view *for that attitude or attitudes*. But a rational care theory of welfare illustrates the possibility of a fitting attitude theory of welfare that does not entail buck-passing for welfare with respect to reasons for action.

Moral Obligation, Moral Responsibility, and the Second-Person Standpoint

Even if a fitting attitude theory of a normative concept entails buck-passing with respect to reasons for the attitudes that concept analytically implicates, therefore, it may nonetheless not support buck-passing with respect to reasons for action. What, then, about the concept of moral wrong? As with other normative concepts, whether a fitting attitude theory of wrongness supports buck-passing about reasons for acting will depend on the attitude or attitudes that are distinctive of the concept.

In *SPS*, I argue that the concepts of moral obligation and moral wrong are irreducibly second personal in the sense that they conceptually involve *addressable* (and so second-personal) authoritative demands. When we violate moral obligations, we violate legitimate expectations and demands that we have and can make, in principle anyway, of one another and ourselves as representative persons or members of the moral community.[20] When we think that an action is wrong, as Richard Nixon might or might not have thought about subverting the Watergate investigation by paying hush money to Hunt, we are committed to thinking that not performing that action is something we warrantedly thus demand of ourselves and one another. My claim here is that, so understood, the fact that an act is wrong gives us a reason not so to act that is additional to reasons consisting of the act's wrong-making features (and that this reason is a *second-personal reason* owing to its conceptual connection to (second-personally) addressable demands).

The thesis that the ideas of moral obligation and moral wrong conceptually involve the notion of (second-personally addressable) legitimate demands is rooted in two further theses. The first is the one I mentioned before, namely, Mill's and Strawson's idea that moral obligation and wrong are conceptually related to warranted reactive attitudes. What is morally wrong is what one is warrantedly held accountable and blamed for (with reactive attitudes) if one so acts without adequate excuse. The second is that holding someone responsible with a reactive attitude has an implicitly second-personal character (which is why Strawson contrasts its role in interpersonal relationships with taking an "objective" or third-personal view toward someone).[21] It involves the putatively authoritative address of a demand, if only in imagination.

To prepare the way for considering this thesis and its implications, we need first to focus more precisely on the concepts of moral obligation and moral wrong in order to notice how they differ from other concepts with which they might be conflated. I take it as obvious, first, that "wrong" in the sense we are interested in refers to a narrower notion than the broader sense that is involved in just any kind of mistake, failure, or

---

[20] This does not mean that just anyone has standing to make the demand publicly, for example, in speech or to reproach others for violation. Like Strawson, I hold that the demand is implicit in reactive attitudes (Strawson 1968: 92–3). Also, by the "moral community," I mean no actual community, but a regulative ideal like Kant's "kingdom of ends." We could as well say that the authority is one we have *as representative persons*. I am indebted to David Velleman and Samuel Scheffler for discussion on this point.

[21] "What I want to contrast is the attitude (or range of attitudes) of involvement or participation in a human relationship, on the one hand, and what might be called the objective attitude (or range of attitudes) to another human being, on the other. . . . To adopt the objective attitude to another human being is to see him, perhaps, as an object of social policy; as a subject for what, in a wide range of sense, might be called treatment; as something certainly to be taken account, perhaps precautionary account, of; to be managed or handled or cured or trained; perhaps simply to be avoided, though this gerundive is not peculiar to cases of objectivity of attitude. The objective attitude may be emotionally toned in many ways, but not in all ways: it may include repulsion or fear, it may include pity or even love, though not all kinds of love. But it cannot include the range of reactive feelings and attitudes which belong to involvement or participation with others in inter-personal human relationships; it cannot include resentment, gratitude, forgiveness, anger, or the sort of love which two adults can sometimes be said to feel reciprocally, for each other. If your attitude towards someone is wholly objective, then though you may fight him, you cannot quarrel with him, and though you may talk to him, even negotiate with him, you cannot reason with him. You can at most pretend to quarrel, or to reason, with him" (Strawson 1968: 81).

incorrectness. If in doing a math problem, I make a mistake and get the wrong answer, I do no wrong in the sense with which we are concerned; I violate no moral obligation.

Neither is the idea of moral wrong in the current sense the same as that of acting against the balance of reasons, or even indeed, against the balance of moral reasons. This is shown by the fact that supererogation, an act's being morally recommended but not morally obligatory or required, is a conceptually coherent possibility. That does not mean that theories that deny supererogation, like act consequentialism, which hold that it is always wrong to do anything other than the morally best, optimific act are necessarily mistaken. It just means that whether they are or not, whether there is such a thing as supererogation, is a substantive normative question that is not settled by the concept of moral obligation itself. And if that is so, moral obligation must be a different concept than that of being most morally choiceworthy.[22]

This should already make us suspicious of taking a buck-passing view of moral wrongness in relation to reasons for acting. If the concept of moral obligation were simply that of an action that is best supported by moral reasons, or best supported by reasons period, then being wrong could not be an additional moral reason, or reason period, not to perform the act. Being morally wrong would already involve being supported by all the reasons, or all the moral reasons, there are for acting. But that is not the way we normally think of it. Anyone who takes seriously the debate about whether views like act consequentialism "demand too much," for example, must already take for granted that the ideas of moral obligation and wrong involve a notion of requirement or demand that differs conceptually from that of the balance of moral reasons. And when act utilitarians disagree, they must likewise make use of this concept to disagree.

But how are we to understand this notion? What is it for morality to demand something? Plainly the idea of demand or requirement extends more widely than the moral. We speak, for example, of the requirements of reason, say, the demand not to have contradictory beliefs or plans. Unlike demands of reason or logic, however, talk of moral demands is conceptually linked to *accountability*.[23] What we are morally obligated to do is, as a conceptual matter, what we are morally answerable for doing.

---

[22] But might the concepts of moral obligation and moral wrong be analyzed in terms of morally *conclusive* reasons—a moral obligation being something there is conclusive moral reason to do and being wrong being something there is conclusive moral reason not to do? But what is it for reasons to be morally conclusive? If we give this an epistemic sense, such that reasons are conclusive if they conclusively establish that a certain act is what morality most recommends, then this really adds nothing to the possibility just canvassed. On the other hand, if reasons are morally conclusive when they warrant a moral *requirement* or demand, then this possibility amounts to the one I go on to consider presently. In order for there to be some other possibility, we would have to have a notion of morally conclusive reason that we understand independently of the idea of moral requirement or demand, which we could then use to understand this latter idea. I doubt that this is so. I am indebted to Samuel Scheffler for discussion on these points.

[23] For this reason, I argue in *The Second-Person Standpoint* that the normativity of moral obligation is not adequately captured by the Kantian idea that moral demands are demands of reason. Of course, it could still be the case that what is morally demanded is also demanded by reason. I argue that the most promising line of argument supporting this, indeed, proceeds from a second-personal account of moral obligation's normativity.

There is thus an important difference between moral obligations and, for example, requirements that are imposed by logic. Moral obligation is tied to a distinctive kind of responsibility—accountability—*conceptually*. If I fail to act as I am morally required without adequate excuse, it simply follows straight away that reactive attitudes like blame and guilt are thereby warranted.[24] Responses like these seem appropriate to logical blunders, however, only in certain contexts, and even here what seems to be in question is a moral error of some kind (as when I have a special responsibility for reasoning properly).[25] Moreover, although a connection to accountability is intrinsic to the concept of moral obligation, it is obviously no part whatsoever of the idea of a logical requirement or demand of reason.

Mill seems on safe ground, then, in saying that our concept of wrongdoing is essentially related to accountability. Even if it is natural to think that a person falls short of full virtue if she does only what can be required of her in the sense of what she can be warrantedly *held to* through reactive attitudes like blame and guilt, she none-theless does no wrong. We do not impute wrongdoing unless we take ourselves to be in the range of the culpable, that is, unless the action is such that the agent is not just morally criticizable in some way or other, but aptly *blamed* or the object of some other form of accountability-seeking reactive attitude if she lacks an adequate excuse.

This aspect of the concept of moral wrong has been stressed by a number of contemporary writers. John Skorupski says that calling an act "morally wrong... amounts to blaming the agent" and that the idea of moral wrong can't be understood independently of that of blameworthiness (Skorupski 1999: 29, 142).[26] Allan Gibbard quite explicitly follows Mill's lead in proposing that "what a person does is *morally wrong* if and only if it is rational for him to feel guilty for having done it, and for others to be angry at him for having done it" (Gibbard 1990: 42). And we can find versions of this Millian idea in other writers also (Baier 1966; Brandt 1979; Shafer-Landau 2003). It is consistent with these views, of course, that there remains a distinction between the wrongness of acts and the blameworthiness of agents. Someone is not to blame for wrongdoing if he has an excuse.

This gives us half of what underlies my thesis that the ideas of moral obligation and moral wrong conceptually involve (second-personally) addressable legitimate demands. The other half concerns the second-personal character of the distinctive attitudes, Strawsonian reactive attitudes, whose warrant is conceptually implicated in the idea of moral wrong. Reactive attitudes invariably involve a kind of "demand," as Strawson himself says, that is imaginatively addressed to its object and that must, therefore presuppose the authority to address it (Strawson 1968: 92–3).

---

[24] Indeed, the very idea of an "excuse" is not internal to the rules of logic; it must be understood in relation to a broader context that includes other norms.

[25] I don't mean, of course, that logical errors aren't subject to criticism, or that we don't sometimes use words like "blame," as when a teacher says that he doesn't blame his student for a given error on a first try.

[26] This claim is, however, too strong, since one may not blame someone for acting wrongly if the person has some adequate excuse for doing so.

Consider indignation, for example. Indignation is an example of what Strawson calls an *impersonal* reactive attitude, since it is felt from an observer's perspective rather than from that of anyone involved in the situation to which one is responding. To feel indignation toward someone is to feel that he is to blame for some conduct and therefore appropriately held accountable for it, if only by being subject to reactive attitudes from himself (guilt) and others (blame or indignation). It is essential to Strawson's argument in "Freedom and Resentment" that indignation differs from its seeming to one that some sanction would be desirable or even that the sanction would make for a more valuable or fitting whole (that it would realize something like poetic justice). The feeling of indignation invariably includes a sense of legitimate or authoritative demand that may be absent from the thought that some sanction would be either desirable or fitting. We feel indignation only when we feel we can reasonably *expect* or demand of others that they act in certain ways. Indeed, Strawson says, "the making of the demand *is* the proneness to such attitudes" (Strawson 1968: 92–3).

Similar points hold for *personal* reactive attitudes, which are felt, unlike indignation or moral blame, not as if from the perspective of a disinterested third party, but as if from the victim's point of view or that of someone identified with her.[27] We resent what we take to be violations against ourselves or those with whom we identify. If you resent someone's treading on your foot, for example, or, even more, his rejecting your request or demand that he stop doing so, you feel as if he has violated your valid claim or demand and as if some claim-exacting or responsibility-seeking response by you, or on your behalf, is justified.

Strawson contrasts "the attitude (or range of attitudes) of involvement or participation in a human relationship" (taking a second-person stance, in my terms), on the one hand, with "the objective attitudes (or range of attitudes) to another human being, on the other" (Strawson 1968: 79). We take an "objective" attitude toward those we see as unfit for "ordinary adult human relationships," such as very young children and those with "deep-rooted psychological abnormality," and regard them as appropriately subject to "treatment" or "management" rather than to reactive attitudes and forms of interpersonal address that involve them (Strawson 1968: 81). What is distinctive about reactive attitudes, then, whether they are *impersonal* attitudes like indignation or blame, or *personal* attitudes like resentment, is that they are felt as if in second-personal relation with another—they involve an imagined *address* of a claim or demand *to* their objects that holds them answerable for compliance.[28]

---

[27] In addition to negative personal reactive attitudes, Strawson also mentions gratitude, which he regards as a (positive) personal reactive attitude, which in this case, is felt as if from the perspective of a beneficiary.

[28] Thus, an attitude can be second-personal in the requisite sense and be third-party or "impersonal" in Strawson's sense. And the phenomenon of guilt shows that it is possible to take a second-personal attitude toward oneself. What makes an attitude second-personal is its having an implicit *addressee*.

Moral Wrongness: A Second-Personal Reason to Act

I shall take it, therefore, that the fact that a certain action, say, stepping unbidden on someone's foot or subverting a criminal investigation, would be wrong amounts to the fact that it violates a legitimate demand we make of ourselves and one another as representative persons. My claim, then, is that this latter fact, the fact that an act violates such a demand, itself provides a reason not to perform the act that is additional to the act's wrong-making features. Because the notion of an *addressable* demand is itself part of this further reason, I call it a *second-personal reason*. Since it is impossible to make a demand of someone without addressing her in some way, the idea of second-personal address is built into the very ideas of moral obligation and moral wrong. If, consequently, the fact that an action would be wrong is a reason not to perform the act, it is a second-personal reason.

Wrong-making features, such as that an action would cause harm or subvert a criminal investigation, themselves entail nothing about legitimate demands and so are not second-personal reasons.[29] My claim, however, is that in believing that such features *are indeed wrong-making*, we are committed to thinking that these features nonetheless ground a legitimate demand not so to act and that this fact, the fact that the act would violate a legitimate moral demand and so be wrong, gives us a further reason not to perform the act.

One way to appreciate this is to consider the relation between the concepts of moral *rights* and moral wrong.[30] So far as I know, no one denies that the fact that an action would violate someone's rights is a reason not to perform the action. Since violating a right is itself a wrong-making feature, however, that may not seem to count against a buck-passing theory of moral wrong with respect to reasons for action. But there is an important difference between moral rights and most other wrong-making features. That violating someone's right is wrong, at least other things equal, is not just a substantive normative truth; it is a conceptual truth.[31] As we shall see presently, something doesn't count as a violation of someone's right, unless it is something we legitimately demand, other things being equal, that people not do to that person. So the fact that an act would violate someone's right is not itself independent of the fact that it would be wrong, at least other things being equal.

Suppose that I intentionally tromp on your foot to gain advantage in getting to the table with designer underwear on sale when I could easily have gone around and risked doing without a pair of Calvin Klein's. Here I clearly violate your right. But in what does this fact consist? What is it to have a right? A right of this sort is a "claim right" in

---

[29] Again, by wrong-making features, I mean features that provide *grounds* or normative reasons for something's being wrong, not the features, if any there be, in which something's being wrong might consist metaphysically.

[30] For convenience, I shall shorten "moral right" to "right."

[31] I take it that it would be incoherent to assert that one has a right to something but that someone would do no wrong, not even other things being equal, if she were to deprive one of it.

Hohfeld's sense (Hohfeld 1923). I follow Joel Feinberg in holding that it is "claiming that gives [such] rights their distinctive moral significance" (Feinberg 1980). Claiming is in its nature second-personal; we make claims on others by addressing them second-personally. "I'm sorry, but that's my foot you're stepping on," you might say to me as I'm on my way to the Calvin Klein's, implying that I am where I have no right to be and where you have every right to demand I vacate, apologize, and so on.

Such a demand would not be a *mere* demand, however, simply an imposition of your will on mine. It would be addressed as a legitimate demand, one you have the authority to make of me, and which authority it would be unreasonable of me not to recognize. It seems obvious, moreover, that the authoritative demand in which your right consists gives me a reason not to step on your feet that is additional to the facts that I would be causing you pain, suffering, inconvenience, and so on. Before the concept of human rights became established, people recognized the latter reasons of pain and so on, but not yet the former reason consisting in a right not to be gratuitously caused these things. When, however, we accept that we have rights we can legitimately claim of one another, that we all are, in Rawls's phrase, "self-originating source[s] of valid claims," we recognize an additional reason not to cause pain and suffering, namely, that this is something we legitimately claim from one another as our right (Rawls 1980: 546).

As Hohfeld points out, the concept of a claim right is conceptually related to that of a moral duty or *obligation to the right holder* (Hohfeld 1923: 65–75). Your right against me analytically entails that I have a moral duty or obligation *to* you. An obligation *to* someone is a "directed" or "bipolar" obligation.[32] If I violate such a duty to you, I *wrong you*. In so doing, I violate an authority *you* have, as an individual person, to demand that others not tread on *you*. Our moral rights are what we have the authority to demand of one another *as individuals*. You have a right against me only if you have the individual authority to demand that I not act in some way toward *you* and a standing others do not have to hold me answerable, as is shown by the fact that were I to violate the right you would have a distinctive authority to forgive me at your discretion. It is a reflection of this individual authority that you can consent to my acting in ways that would otherwise violate your right, that it is up to you whether to seek compensation (as is recognized in the law of torts), and so on.

When I step on your feet unbidden, I fail to respect and so violate this authority you have as an individual person and so violate and fail to respect *you*. And in so doing, moreover, I fail to appreciate a reason not to step on your feet that is additional to the fact that I am causing avoidable harm, namely, that it violates your right, that is, on the current analysis, your legitimate demand of me as an individual person.

As I say, it is uncontroversial that the fact that an action would violate someone's right and so wrong that person is a reason not to do it. What is in question is whether something would be wrong *period* is a reason that supplements wrong-making features

---

[32] For the first use, see Gilbert 2006: 40; and for the second, Thompson 2004. See also Darwall 2012.

of wrongful actions, including, perhaps, that it would violate someone's rights and so wrong that person. On the second-personal analysis we are considering, however, wrongs and moral obligations *period* are no less conceptually connected to legitimate demands, and hence to the idea of a second-personal reason, than are wrongings and bipolar moral obligations *to*.

Moral obligations *simpliciter* are what we have the authority to demand of one another, not as individuals, but as representative persons, as representatives, as we might say, of the moral community.[33] So wrongdoing also always involves a failure to respect legitimate demands and the authority to make them that is additional to the individual authorities that are involved in violations of rights and wrongings. It violates our authority as representative persons to demand that people not act in that way. And this means that it also involves a failure of respect (of this *representative authority*) and so a failure to appreciate a further reason not to perform the act that is additional to the act's wrong-making features, including indeed, even the fact that it might violate someone's right (her *individual authority* to demand that one not so treat *her*) and so wrong her.

You have an individual authority to make claims and demands of me regarding my treatment of you that others do not have. You have the authority to allow or forbid actions involving you and your body that others don't, and you also have a distinctive standing to object, to demand apology, to seek compensation, to forgive, and so on. If you want not to "make a scene" by objecting if I step on your foot, then others have a strong reason to respect your wishes. And it is up to you and not others whether, for example, to forgive my brutish treatment. It is a reflection of all this, that violations of rights, wrongs *to* someone, are, as Strawson points out, the object of warranted *personal* reactive attitudes like resentment (Strawson 1968: 72). A stranger cannot warrantedly, or even intelligibly, feel resentment when I step on your foot, although you (and others personally related to you) can.

But your individual authority is not the only relevant standing in the case, not even the only relevant one you have. Although it is up to you in the first instance whether or not to object or complain about my action, it is not distinctively up to you whether or not to feel indignation or blame. The latter is an *impersonal* reactive attitude and so is felt not as if from the victim's point of view, but as if from a disinterested or impartial perspective that abstracts from personal involvement (Strawson 1968: 84–5). Impersonal attitudes are the ones to which the concepts of moral obligation and moral wrong *period* are conceptually related. Something is wrong if it is blameworthy, lacking adequate excuse. But whether to blame someone, whether that person is *to blame*, is

---

[33] Again, "the moral community" refers here not to any actual social collectivity but to a regulative ideal like Kant's "kingdom of ends." And the authority to blame others does not entail a standing to reproach (publicly). What practices of public accountability are justified is a substantive normative question that is not established by the concept alone.

not distinctively a victim's question. It is a question we face as representative persons, not as someone personally involved.[34]

This difference between our individual authority to claim our rights, on the one hand, and our representative standing to hold one another and ourselves accountable through blame, on the other, is reflected in the difference between the civil and criminal law. Whether or not to seek compensation in bringing a tort action is up to the victim. The state legitimately does not proceed on its own to rectify wrongings; rather the law of torts gives individuals standing to bring cases on their own behalf. But it is not, or at least not always, up to the victim whether to prosecute a crime. That is a question for the people and their representatives. In this way, legal guilt is like moral guilt. Whether to blame someone, whether she is to blame, is a question we face as representative persons. This is reflected also in Locke's distinction between the authority everyone has in the state of nature to punish transgressions of the law of nature, on the one hand, and the authority that individuals have, "to seek reparations" for violations of their individual rights, on the other (Locke 1988: II, §7–11).

Because it would violate your right, I have a reason not to step unbidden on your feet that is additional to the facts that doing so will cause pain, suffering, and other things that are bad for you. Stepping on your feet does not simply harm you, it also disrespects your rights, and therefore you, as someone with the individual authority to demand that I not do that to you. And this gives me an additional reason not to step on your foot.

But if the fact that it would violate your right gives me reason, so also does the fact that stepping on your foot would be wrong *period*. A wrongful act violates another authority in addition, not one you have as an individual, but one we all have as representative persons. In being blameworthy unless excused the wrongfulness of my act consists in its being something representative persons legitimately demand of me, that anyone can, at least in principle demand (including me of myself) through reactive attitudes like blame (and the self-reactive attitude of guilt). Thus all wrongs involve a kind of disrespect that is additional to disrespect of any individual's authority. Any wrong violates the legitimate demands of those to whom we are morally responsible, namely, one another as representative persons; so any wrong involves a failure adequately to respect this authority. Because this is so, an act's wrongness provides additional reason not to perform it: that the act would violate a legitimate demand and so fail to respect our authority as representative persons. Since this reason is

---

[34] If, then, it is a conceptual truth that violations of rights, wrongings, are also, other things being equal, wrongs period—that violations of "bipolar" obligations *to* someone are also, other things being equal, violations of moral obligations period—then it follows that a personal reactive attitude, such as resentment, can be warranted, only if an impersonal reactive attitude would be, other things equal, at least. I believe this conceptual thesis is true, but notice that the claim that the fact that an action is wrong is a reason not to perform it (consisting in the fact that the act violates a legitimate demand we make of another as representative persons) does not strictly depend on this conceptual thesis. I am indebted here to discussion with Verity Harte and Jules Coleman.

conceptually tied to an authority to address demands, an act's wrongness is therefore a second-personal reason not to do it.

Another way of seeing that wrongness creates an additional reason is to see the way in which being wrong interacts with the idea of reasonable demand. Since avoiding your foot puts no unreasonable burden on me, it is something we can demand of one another both as individuals and as representative persons. But what if stepping on your foot is the only way I can avoid significant injury to myself? In such a case, it seems arguable that we and you cannot reasonably demand that I not step on your foot, and so it is neither wrong nor a violation of your right for me to do so.[35] There seems a continuum of cases, holding fixed the harm to the victim, from ones where the burden to the agent is very great, and so his action not wrong, to ones where the burden is very small, and so his action clearly wrong. Let us suppose there are two different cases, A and B, between which there exists some just noticeable difference in the burdens to the agent, such that in case A the burden is insufficient to make the act of stepping on someone's foot not wrong (so in case A, the agent's stepping on the other's foot would be wrong), whereas in case B, with a somewhat greater cost to the agent, the same act would not be wrong. If we consider just the wrong-making features of the act—the relative cost to agent and victim, these will of course create different and differently weighted reasons. That an agent could avoid stepping on someone else's foot at lesser cost in case A than he could in case B no doubt creates greater reason for the agent to absorb that cost in case A than in case B. But whatever reason the wrong-making features themselves create in these two cases seems not fully to capture the reasons that result from the further fact these features ground, namely, that we can legitimately demand that an agent absorb the cost involved in case A, but not in case B, in other words, that not absorbing the cost in case A amounts to wronging someone and thereby doing moral wrong (assuming there is no further justification).

A Conclusion Concerning Conclusive Reasons

Finally, it is an often-noted feature of the concepts of moral obligation and moral wrong that they purport to entail that an agent has not just *some* reason to act, but conclusive reason (or at least, as Scanlon says, reason that is "normally conclusive") (Scanlon 2007: 6). Obviously, this is no part whatsoever of the concepts involved in obligation- or wrong-making features themselves, for example, that stepping on your foot in the case we initially imagined would impose a considerable cost on you at little cost to me. That does not rule out a buck-passing theory of wrongness with respect to

---

[35] Or, alternatively, though it violates your right and *would* be wrong (period) if I lacked this further justification, it is not wrong because the justification exists. What violates someone's rights would be wrong to do lacking some justification, just as what is wrong would be blameworthy if done without adequate excuse. It follows that what violates someone's rights would be blameworthy if it were done without *either* a justification or an excuse.

reasons for acting by itself, however, since it might be that the concept of wrongness just is that of there existing conclusive moral reasons (or reasons period) for doing something, with the reasons being provided entirely by wrong-making features. But we have already effectively excluded these possibilities. If action supported by morally conclusive reasons (or reasons period) just means action recommended by the weightiest moral reasons (or reasons period), we have already seen that this is a different concept than that of morally obligatory or demanded conduct. So far as our concepts go, an act may be thus supported or recommended without being morally required or obligatory. It follows, therefore, that if being morally obligatory purports to entail the existence of conclusive or normally conclusive reasons, then that must be because the facts of moral obligation and wrongness purport to provide some reason that can guarantee overriding weight *themselves*.

In conclusion, I would like to indicate how the second-personal analysis of moral obligation and wrongness I have been discussing can explain the conclusive-reason-providing purport of moral obligation and moral wrong. The root of the explanation is moral obligation's conceptual tie to accountability and warranted blame. As Bernard Williams and others have noted, when we blame someone we imply that there was conclusive reason for her not to have done what we blame her for having done (Williams 1995: 40–4; Gibbard 1990: 299–300; Skorupski 1999: 42–3; Shafer-Landau 2003: 181–3). It makes no sense to blame someone for doing something and then add that she had, nonetheless, sufficient reason to do it, all things considered. Blame implies not just that the person shouldn't have done what she did "morally speaking," but that she shouldn't have done it period. A person who in one moment "admits" her guilt, but in the next, asserts that she had, nonetheless, good and sufficient reasons for doing what she did can hardly be said to have accepted responsibility for her action. Or to put the point the other way around, if someone can establish that she had sufficient reason to do what she did, then she will have accounted for herself, justified her conduct, and shown thereby that blame is unwarranted. The point is not that the fact that one blames someone entails the existence of conclusive reason. Rather in blaming someone one presupposes such reason exists.

When we think that an act is morally wrong, and therefore blameworthy if unexcused, we think that, lacking excuse, blame is the fitting attitude for anyone to take toward someone performing the act. When an agent takes such an attitude toward herself, and addresses a demand to herself through a self-reactive attitude like guilt, whether retrospectively or prospectively, she feels as though there is conclusive reason not to perform the act.[36] But if the facts that *make* an act morally wrong in the sense of grounding or providing normative reasons for its wrongness do not purport to be conclusive reasons themselves and the fact that an act is wrong is not *just* the fact that such conclusive reasons exist, then what we must be thinking when we take such an

---

[36] For valuable insights about the relevance of prospective guilt, I am indebted to the work of Howard Nye.

attitude toward one another and ourselves is that the fact that an act is morally wrong provides a reason itself not to perform the act that guarantees conclusive reason not to do so. I have tried to say in this essay what this additional reason consists in: that the act is something we legitimately demand that people not do.[37] If this is right, trying to do without this thought might leave us with one thought too few.[38]

---

[37] It should be clear that I am not saying that this is a wrong-making feature, in the sense of a ground or normative reason of an act's wrongness. I am saying that this is what being wrong consists in, and that this fact provides a reason not to perform the wrongful act that is additional to the act's wrong-making features (grounds of or normative reasons for its being wrong).

[38] In addition to the other authors in the volume who participated in the conference on "Moral Obligation" at the Center for Philosophy & Social Policy at Bowling Green University, I am very much indebted to audiences at Brown University, the Western Canadian Philosophical Association meetings at the University of Alberta, the Scots Philosophical Club meetings at the University of Stirling, the University of Maryland, the University of Leiden, Washington University, the University of Oslo, Bielefeld University, the Moral Philosophy Working Group at Yale University, and the Middle Atlantic Reading Group in Ethics. I am also indebted to Ellen Frankel Paul for editorial advice.

5

Morality and Principle

Jonathan Dancy is largely responsible for the recent vigorous discussion of the position known as "moral particularism" (Dancy 1993, 2004, 2009; Hooker and Little 2000; McKeever and Ridge 2005, 2006; Lance and Little 2006). In his original 1983 *Mind* article, Dancy dubbed the view he there defended "ethical particularism," but his focus was squarely on particularism about morality (Dancy 1983). As Dancy's thought has developed since then, however, it has mainly been driven by considerations about normative reasons in general, rather than anything specifically about morality.

In *Ethics Without Principles*, for example, although Dancy again defines particularism as the position that "moral thought and judgment" do not require "moral principles," what does the major work in his argument is a general view about normative reasons he calls "holism." Holism, as Dancy defines it, is the thesis that a consideration can be a normative reason for something in one case, while no reason at all, or even a reason against it, in another (2004: 7). Dancy's diagnosis is that "errors of generalism" (denying moral particularism) "can mostly be traced back to errors in the theory of reasons" (2004: 15). So Dancy first tries to show that normative reasons are holistic generally and then argues that, since there is no reason to think that moral reasons are any different, they are likely to be holistic also. Moral particularism is then claimed to follow more or less directly.

Dancy's arguments for holism are convincing and his observations about the complex relations between normative reasons persuasive. Not every consideration that is relevant to there being reason to have some attitude, or the attitude's being justified or one ought to have, is relevant in the same way. *Normative reasons* are considerations that count in favor of or against an attitude. But considerations can also *defeat* or *enable* normative reasons, and so affect what attitudes we have reason, or ought, to have without being normative reasons themselves. For example, something's looking red can be a reason to believe that it is red. When, however, it becomes apparent that it looks red because a red light is shining on it, there is no longer any reason to think it actually is red. The fact that a red light is shining on the object is not, however, a reason to believe that the object is not red, or even not to believe that it is red, that is, a reason that weighs against and outweighs the earlier reason. It rather defeats the earlier fact's claim to be a reason. It shows that the fact that the object looks red is not, in fact, any reason to think it is red, and so affects what one should believe in a different way.

It is not difficult to find similar cases with normative reasons for action. If I promise to peel you a grape, that gives me a reason to do so. Suppose that it is the only reason in the circumstances and therefore that peeling you a grape is what I ought overall to do. If you release me from my promise, then I no longer have reason to do what I promised. It is no longer true that peeling a grape is what I ought to do. But, usually anyway, that is not because your releasing me counts against my peeling you a grape, although there might be circumstances in which it would. It is rather because it defeats the earlier reason. It makes it the case that what was a reason in favor of an action is one no longer.

The existence of defeaters and enablers is sufficient to establish holism, as Dancy understands it. The fact that something looks red is sometimes, but not always, a reason to believe that it is red. The fact that one promised to do something is sometimes, but not always, a reason to do what one promised. Defeaters (and enablers) affect what attitude there is overall reason for one to have, but not by favoring or disfavoring attitudes or actions themselves. They are not themselves normative reasons, but help determine whether other considerations are.

Dancy canvasses other possibilities also. A fact might *intensify* a normative reason, give it more weight, without being itself a reason. Dancy gives the following example. The fact that someone needs help that I am in a position to give is a reason to help her. But the fact that I am the only person who can help seems to be, in itself, not so much a (n additional) reason to help as something that intensifies the weight of the first reason (Dancy 2004: 41). Likewise, if I am but one of a billion who can help, this seems not to be a reason not to help, but something that *attenuates* the weight of the reason to help consisting in the fact that someone needs help that I can give (Dancy 2004: 42).

Let us assume, therefore, that holism holds true in the theory of reasons. How does this bear on moral particularism? I believe we should also grant Dancy that holism holds true in the theory of *moral reasons* also, that is, reasons that favor or disfavor actions from the moral point of view and so bear on what one *morally ought* to do in the sense of being morally choiceworthy or best supported by moral reasons.[1] After all, all the examples of normative reasons for acting we have been considering seem to be moral reasons (Dancy 2004: 37).

It turns out, however that, as Sean McKeever and Michael Ridge have argued, holism about moral reasons does not establish moral particularism (2005, 2006). Dancy acknowledges this, moreover. We can see why with an example Dancy himself gives that he takes to be in the spirit of McKeever and Ridge's point. That one's promise was extracted under duress, like being released from one's promise, can defeat the normative reason to do something that would otherwise be provided by the fact of one's promise. But it is entirely consistent with that nonetheless that the following general moral principle exists (Dancy calls it "P1"): "If you have promised, then you morally

---

[1] Or, as Dancy puts it, what one "most morally ought" to do (2004: 31–7).

ought to do the promised act, unless your promise was given under duress" (Dancy 2004: 81). So holism about reasons, even holism about moral reasons, cannot entail moral particularism. As McKeever and Ridge point out, indeed, a general principle like P1 actually *presupposes* holism, as Dancy defines it. So moral reasons' being holistic in Dancy's sense can hardly be incompatible with moral generalism.

P1 is no doubt too simple as it stands. Any plausible general principle about keeping promises would have to be much more complicated, including, for example, the absence of other defeaters such as having been released from one's promise. Taken by itself, however, holism in the theory of reasons, even of moral reasons, cannot establish that some such plausible generalist principles do not exist, as Dancy himself acknowledges (2004: 81–2).

Despite this, Dancy claims that an "indirect" argument from holism to moral particularism can nonetheless be given (2004: 82f.). He grants that there are some areas, like mathematics, where we plausibly suppose that universal general principles hold despite the fact that there is a kind of holism there also: "dividing one number by another will not always yield a smaller number; sometimes it will, and sometimes it won't" (2004: 82). But there is nothing, he claims, that could explain a similar supposition with respect to morality.

Now, as I have noted, Dancy defines "particularism" and "generalism" in such a way that they only concern moral principles, oughts, and reasons. But we can define other versions. A more general *normative particularism* would hold that the possibility of *normative* thought does not depend on the existence of general normative principles. *Normative generalism* would deny this, holding that normative principles are indeed necessary. And we might similarly define generalist and particularist positions within different specific normative domains.

Thus *epistemological generalism* would hold that the possibility of "thought and judgment" about what there is reason to, or what one ought to, *believe* depends on the existence of general epistemic principles. And *epistemological particularism* would deny this. Similarly, *practical generalism* would hold that thinking or judging there to be things we have reason overall to *do*, and so ought overall to do, requires us to suppose that there exist general practical principles. And *practical particularism* would deny this. *Aesthetic generalism* would hold that aesthetic thought and judgment, say, that something has or lacks some aesthetic quality hence that there is reason, or that one ought, to have some aesthetic attitude toward that thing, requires us to think that there exist general aesthetic principles. *Aesthetic particularism* would deny this. And so on.

Now partly, I think, Dancy is relying on the fact that although his opponents deny moral particularism, they are much less likely to accept generalism about normative reasons across the board, that is, *normative generalism*, or generalism with respect to any practical reasons and oughts, *practical generalism*. He quotes Scanlon as saying that although principles have a "significant role" in morality, there "seems little work for principles to do" when it comes to thought and judgment about normative reasons generally (Dancy 2004: 132).

Dancy, however, denies that there is any relevant difference in this respect between morality and other normative domains. This is because he thinks that moral principles, were there any, would have to concern what we morally ought to do, or perhaps, what we morally ought most to do, in the sense mentioned earlier, namely, what moral reasons for action support, either *pro tanto* or all things considered. Moreover, he takes it, indeed argues, that oughts quite generally, and so moral oughts in particular, are better conceived in terms of normative reasons and moral reasons, respectively, than vice versa (2004: 31). If what we morally ought to do is what the balance of moral reasons favor, or most favor, and if we have no need of principles to understand what it is for normative reasons in general or for moral reasons more specifically to favor an action, either *pro tanto* or all things considered, then why, he asks, should we expect that principles are necessary for moral oughts? If moral oughts are no different from oughts of other kinds in their dependence on reasons, and principles are unnecessary for reasons, and therefore for oughts, of other kinds, wouldn't they also be unnecessary for moral oughts?

Dancy expresses some skepticism that the moral can relevantly be distinguished from the non-moral within the space of practical normative reasons (2004: 132). If that were so, then moral particularism would simply follow, or perhaps be indistinguishable, from practical particularism. But Dancy's argument does not depend on this. We, might, for example, simply identify moral reasons by other-regarding content or through some characterization of the moral point of view, and that would not affect anything Dancy wants to say. He could still put his challenge in the following terms: if *oughtness* consists, quite generally, in the weight and force of normative reasons, and if principles are not required for the latter, then why should they be required *either* for oughts in general or for *moral* oughts more specifically? Even if moral oughts can be distinguished from oughts of other kinds by the content of, or point of view from which we accept, their supporting normative reasons, that wouldn't distinguish their normative character, weight, or force. If the normativity of the moral ought does not differ fundamentally from that of other oughts, and if principles are unnecessary for other oughts, then why should they be necessary for moral oughts?

My aim in what follows is to show that even if one were to concede every bit of Dancy's case for particularism deriving from the theory of reasons, including *almost* all of what he says about moral reasons and the moral ought, there would nonetheless remain a substantial case for generalism left standing that would have to be considered before particularism about morality could be established.[2] I shall argue, first, that

---

[2] I concede that "morally ought" can be understood in terms of the weight of moral reasons, but I shall argue that moral obligation, moral duty, and moral wrong cannot. My argument will be that the latter have a special character and that there is reason to think that nothing having this character could exist without there being relevant general principles. If, as I shall argue, concepts with this special character, like that of moral obligation, are intrinsic to the concept of morality as we understand it, then moral particularism will follow. It will also then be true that general principles are necessary for there to be moral reasons as well, since there can be no moral reasons without morality; moral obligations are necessary for that, and these cannot exist without

Dancy's arguments leave untouched a powerful rationale for thinking, as Scanlon says, that principles have a "significant role" to play in morality. And second, I shall try to sketch that rationale, at least in broad outline. My conclusion will be that there is an important and promising line of thought leading to moral generalism that Dancy has failed to consider.

For purposes of my argument, we can simply stipulate that *normative particularism* and *practical particularism* are both true. So I shall assume that neither normative thought and judgment in general, nor thought about normative reasons for acting and so practical oughts more specifically, depend, respectively, upon *normative* principles in general or upon normative principles of *action* more specifically. And we can also stipulate that there is a *sense* of the moral "ought," the one I take Dancy to have in mind, that may not require principles either.[3] This is the sense I mentioned before, namely, the one in which to say that someone morally ought to do something is to say that that action is supported by moral reasons, either *pro tanto* or overall, that is, that the action is morally *choiceworthy* in that sense.

My contention will be that conceding all of this does not yet touch anything a moral generalist should be, or, I think, that moral generalists primarily have been, concerned about. This is because the major rationale for being a generalist about morality is the thought that general principles, indeed general principles that can be assumed to be publicly formulable and available, are necessary for moral *obligations*. The concept of moral obligation has a special character that distinguishes it from that of what moral reasons favor or recommend, either *pro tanto* or overall. My argument will be that general principles are plausibly thought necessary in order for anything having this special character to exist, whether or not they are necessary for reasons and oughts generally, or for all *moral* reasons or oughts, more specifically.

There are two main ideas underlying my approach. First, moral obligations are, as a conceptual matter, what we are morally responsible or *accountable* for doing. And second, when we hold people answerable for complying with moral demands, we have to assume that they can know that they are obligated, that they can regulate their conduct by this knowledge, *and* that this is all capable of being common public knowledge. I shall argue that this gives a role to publicly formulable principles in morality that principles need not have in other normative domains. Conditions like these seem to be no part whatsoever of the idea that a consideration is a reason for someone to do something. It seems to be enough that the consideration counts in favor of the action.

---

general principles. If so, then though I can concede to Dancy that general principles might be unnecessary for *some* (non-obligating) moral reasons, they will nonetheless be necessary for moral obligations and therefore for there to be moral oughts and reasons at all.

[3] That is, as per the preceding note, that its being the case that one morally ought to do P requires a general principle that in such and such circumstances, anyone morally ought to do P.

In this respect, morality, at least the part that concerns moral obligation, resembles law. Just as a connection to public reason and principle seems part of the very idea of law, so also, I shall argue, is this essential for moral obligation. We need not think, as we do with law, that moral obligations require the relevant public understandings actually to be in place, or that *de facto* attitudes and practices have the same power to constitute morality as they do to constitute law. Nonetheless, I shall argue, it is plausibly a constraint on moral obligation that the relevant public understandings at least be possible.

By contrast, it is clearly no part of the idea of normative reasons or oughts, whether moral or non-moral, that we are automatically answerable for complying with them. *P*'s being a reason to do *A* just consists in *p*'s counting in favor of *A*. And *A*'s being something one ought to do, either *pro tanto* or overall, just consists in *A*'s being supported by such reasons, either *pro tanto* or overall. Being answerable for doing *A* when *p* holds, if anyone *is* thus answerable, would seem to be an additional fact that is neither part of nor entailed by the simple fact that *A* is supported by the relevant reason, either *pro tanto* or overall. In many cases, in fact—for example, with garden-variety self-regarding reasons—we do not believe that people actually *are* answerable for complying with them. And in moral cases where the operative reasons support a moral obligation, the mere fact that moral reasons favor the choice, even overall, considered apart from the fact that they ground an action's being morally *obligatory*, neither involves nor entails answerability either.

Moral Obligation as Distinct From Being Favored by Moral Reasons

Sometimes philosophers speak as though "moral obligation" and "moral duty" are simply synonyms for "morally ought" in the sense of being an action moral reasons favor or favor most.[4] A moment's reflection is sufficient, however, to show that this is not so. By "moral obligation" or "moral duty," I mean here what we are morally *required* to do in the sense that failing so to act would be *morally wrong*. To see that being a moral obligation in this sense does not mean being favored, or favored most, by moral reasons, even by reasons that conclusively recommend the act from the moral point of view, all we need to notice is that whether there is such a thing as moral supererogation, that is an action's being "beyond the call of duty," and something it would not be morally wrong to omit, is a substantive normative issue rather than a conceptual one.

Suppose someone puts forward the view that a certain action, say rescuing someone from a burning building, although it is conclusively recommended by moral reasons and clearly the morally best thing the agent could do, nonetheless is not, owing to the risks involved, morally obligatory or something it would be wrong for the agent to fail

---

[4] Dancy's discussion in Dancy 2004: 31–7 suggests this.

to attempt. The idea is not that the risks would be foolhardy for the agent to take, where this could constitute a moral reason that could weigh against trying to rescue the fire victim. Neither is the idea that the risks to the agent constitute an excuse for wrongly failing to attempt the rescue. Rather, the view is that the risks to the agent make an action, failing to rescue someone, that would otherwise be obligatory and wrong not to do, not wrong in this case. And this, even though the risks do not defeat the moral reasons for attempting to rescue the person. Were the person to enter the building and attempt the rescue, we might well regard her as a moral "hero" in Urmson's sense, whether she was successful or not (Urmson 1958). But if she failed to do so, this would not be something she need excuse, since her failure would not have been wrong or the violation of a moral obligation.

Note also that the idea that the risks to the agent in this case defeat a moral obligation is not, or at least not just, that it defeats a moral obligation *overall* or all things considered. Rather, the thought is that the risks also defeat any *pro tanto* moral obligation that would otherwise exist, that is, if the risks to the agent were not so great.

Now whether any such view is true or not, it seems obvious that it is conceptually coherent. Someone could clearly hold such a view with full mastery of the concept of moral obligation and without contradicting herself in any way. If, however, the concept of moral obligation were the same as that of the moral ought in Dancy's sense, that is, what moral reasons favor or most favor, however conclusively, then such a view would simply be conceptually incoherent. It would be like saying, "Rescuing someone in such a situation is what moral reasons most favor, or favor conclusively, but such an action nonetheless would not be what moral reasons most favor, or favor conclusively." The possibility of supererogation would be ruled out on conceptual grounds.

It seems clear, however, that this is not the case and that whether there is such a thing as supererogation is a substantive normative question rather than one that can be settled on conceptual grounds alone. And if that is so, then moral obligation must be a distinct concept from that being favored most, or favored conclusively, by moral reasons.

Moral Obligation and Accountability

Moral obligations are what morality *requires* or *demands*, not just what there are moral reasons for doing, however weighty or conclusive these reasons might be. But what is it for morality to require or demand something?

Plainly the idea of demand or requirement extends more widely than the moral. We speak also of requirements of reason or logical demands, for example, the demand not to have contradictory or incoherent beliefs or plans. But unlike demands of reason or logic, talk of moral demands is linked to accountability *conceptually*. What we are morally obligated to do is, as a conceptual matter, what we are morally answerable for doing.

There is thus an important difference between moral obligations and, for example, requirements that are imposed by logic. If I fail to act as I am morally required without adequate excuse, it simply follows straight away that what Strawson called "reactive attitudes," like indignation, blame, and guilt, are thereby warranted (Strawson 1968). Responses like these seem appropriate to logical blunders, however, only in certain contexts, and even here what seems to be in question is a moral error of some kind (as when I have a special responsibility for reasoning properly). And though a connection to accountability is intrinsic to the concept of moral obligation, it is obviously no part whatsoever of the idea of a logical requirement or demand of reason.

Similarly, the idea of *excuse* is obviously also external to that of rational or logical requirements, though it is not to moral requirements or obligations. It is a conceptual truth that one is warrantedly blamed for failing to comply with moral obligations unless one has some (adequate) excuse, though not that unexcused logical blunders are blameworthy.

Mill articulates this conceptual point when he says that "we do not call an action wrong, unless we mean to imply that a person ought to be punished in some way or other for doing it" (Mill 1998: Ch. 5). "Punishment" may sound overly strong, but Mill includes under this heading blame and "the reproaches of [the agent's] own conscience." We do not impute wrongdoing unless we take ourselves to be in the range of the culpable, that is, unless the action is such that the agent is not just morally criticizable in some way or other, but aptly the object of some form of accountability-seeking reactive attitude such as moral blame if she lacks an adequate excuse. What it is, indeed, for an action to be morally obligatory and its omission morally wrong, just is for it to be an action the omission of which would warrant blame and feelings of guilt, were the agent to omit the action without excuse.[5]

In *SPS*, I defend this analysis of moral obligation as entailing accountability and argue that it reveals what I there call moral obligation's "second-personal" character. Moral demands, I argue, are what we legitimately *demand* of one another and ourselves, where making such demands is invariably a second-personal matter, even when their object (and so addressee) is oneself, as in the emotion of guilt. Following Strawson, I argue that reactive attitudes have an essentially interpersonal (or, as I call it, second-personal) character since they implicitly put forward or address putative legitimate demands to their objects and therefore presuppose, I argue, the authority to make them.

Because of this second-personal character, holding someone responsible through reactive attitudes inescapably involves what Gary Watson calls the "constraints on moral address" (Watson 1987: 263, 264). In addressing putatively legitimate demands

---

[5] This claim is echoed in Baier 1966; Brandt 1979; Gibbard 1990: 42; Shafer-Landau 2003; and Skorupski 1999: 29, 142. Note that this still admits a distinction between wrongness, the violation of moral obligation, on the one hand, and blameworthiness, on the other. An action may be wrong, but not blameworthy, if the agent has an adequate excuse.

to someone, both addresser and addressee are committed to certain presuppositions as conditions of the reciprocal intelligibility of their interaction as second-personal address. Among these, I argue, is the addressee's competence to hold himself responsible by acknowledging the legitimacy of the demand and regulating his conduct by it.

My object here will be to argue that these presuppositions can be met only if what we hold people accountable for, moral obligations, are accessible to all, hence to those held accountable, as shared public knowledge. And practices of accountability must be able to be public also. Interpersonal answerability is public in its nature; justifying oneself to others is possible at all only within a shared space of public reasons. Since, moreover, people within a culture of mutual accountability must also be able to question claims of wrongdoing, much as participants in a legal order can contest charges of illegality, due process constraints would seem to be built into the very idea of a mutually accountable moral order no less than they are into that of a genuine legal order. And this, I shall argue, can give general principles a role in moral accountability, hence in moral obligation, that is similar to the role that rules and legal principles have in a valid system of law. It will follow that if the idea of moral obligation is essential to our concept of morality, as I shall argue it is, then morality will indeed depend upon general principles, and particularism about morality will be false.

It would be hubris to suppose that a fully convincing case for these claims can be offered in the space available here. I will be able to give only the barest sketch of an argument for general principles in morality that is broadly akin to one that is more familiar for principles in law. My hope, however, is to convince the reader that, when it comes to moral obligation, and therefore to morality, there are considerations that are relevant to whether principles have a "critical role," in Scanlon's words, that simply are not present with respect to normative reasons and oughts more generally, including practical reasons or oughts, or even just any normative *moral* reason, that is, any consideration that might favor an action from the moral point of view. We are not, in these latter cases, forced by the very nature of our concepts to suppose that people to whom normative reasons and oughts apply are *accountable* for acting as the reasons recommend and therefore that the reasons and oughts must be able to be practically available as part of a shared public culture.

Accountability and "Constraints on Moral Address"

Before I begin to make this argument, I need first to say something about the Strawsonian picture of accountability and second-personal address on which my argument will draw.[6] In "Freedom and Resentment," Strawson argues that consequentialist justifications for moral responsibility cannot provide "the right sort of basis, for these practices as we understand them" (Strawson 1968). Whether holding

---

[6] For a fuller development and defense see Darwall 2006.

someone responsible would be desirable or promote goods of any kind—whether personal or impersonal, moral or non-moral—is one thing; but whether the person's action was *culpable* and therefore warrants blame is quite another.

"Strawson's Point," as I call it, is an example of what philosophers call the "wrong kind of reason problem" (see, e.g., Darwall 2006; Hieronymi 2005; Rabinowicz and Ronnøw-Rasmussen 2004). For example, although there is perhaps a sense in which the fact that one will get a reward for believing *p* is a reason to believe *p*, this cannot possibly bear on whether *p* is *credible*. It is not a "reason of the right kind" to believe *p* in the sense we usually have in mind. Similarly, the fact that holding someone responsible for an action would have good consequences, or even indeed that it would instantiate an intrinsically valuable state of affairs, though these can provide some reason *to desire* to hold him responsible and blame him, it cannot provide a reason of the right kind for our practices of accountability "as we understand them," since it does not bear on the blameworthiness of his action.

To be a reason of the right kind a consideration must properly justify a *reactive attitude*. Strawson coined "reactive attitudes" in "Freedom and Resentment" to refer to mental states through which we hold people responsible, whether another person, as with indignation, resentment, or moral blame, or oneself, as in the emotion of guilt. Strawson didn't give a formal definition of these attitudes, but their central features are clear from the role they play in his argument about moral responsibility and freedom of the will. Strawson's central idea is that reactive attitudes involve a way of regarding the individuals who are their objects that commits the holder of the attitude to certain assumptions about the object individual and her capacities to regulate her will. Unlike "objective attitudes," like disdain, disgust, and annoyance, reactive attitudes are essentially characterized by "involvement or participation with others in interpersonal human relationships" (Strawson 1968). There is always an essentially "interpersonal" or, as I prefer to put it, "second-personal" element to reactive attitudes. Through the attitude we *hold* its object to something and thereby implicitly make a demand *of* (and so implicitly address it *to*) him or her (as it were, second-personally). As Strawson puts it, "the making of the demand is the proneness to such attitudes" (Strawson 1968). The reason that reactive attitudes distinctively implicate freedom of the will, then, is that we can intelligibly address a demand to someone to regulate her will appropriately only if we suppose that she can so regulate it as a result of recognizing our demand's legitimacy. The supposition is a "constraint on moral address" (Watson 1987: 263, 264).

Consider the difference between disdain expressed by a put-down, like "He's as thick as a post," and an attitude of indignation or moral blame. Unlike the latter, the former is unfettered by any constraints of address that inevitably arise when we take a second-person perspective toward someone. Disdain is not standardly addressed to its object at all; if it has an addressee, it is likelier to be others we think capable of appreciating why its object is a worthy target. When we blame someone for something, however, we implicitly make a demand *of him* to act differently and, if he has not, to take responsibility for not having done so, where taking responsibility is essentially an *interpersonal* matter (holding himself answerable to us (and, indeed, to himself) as representative persons). In so regarding him, we perforce see him as intelligibly so regarded, as someone who is *competent* to take such an attitude toward himself and guide himself by it. We see him as capable of entering into reciprocal human relationships of mutual accountability.

Disdain involves no such assumptions. One can hardly imagine the disdainer in our example, believing his disdain's object to be too thick to appreciate how thick he is and unable to change his thickheadedness, withdrawing the put-down as not expressing a fully intelligible attitude. To the contrary, to such a person, such further "thickness" would only seem to confirm the fittingness of the disdain. Moral blame, on the other hand, holds its object to a demanded standard and to its object's holding himself to that standard by making himself answerable for compliance. So it is not fully intelligible, or, at least, it is unwarranted in its own terms and not just unfair, when its object is someone who is known to lack the psychic capacities or knowledge necessary to do this. It just doesn't make sense to blame someone for dull-wittedness, unless one is under some illusion about the human ability to take responsibility for mental endowments. But no matter how regrettable or unfair, disdain for dull-wittedness is obviously an intelligible attitude.

Strawson makes an important distinction *within* reactive attitudes between "personal" and "impersonal" ones. This can be confusing, since it is possible to lose track of the fact that Strawson holds that *all* reactive attitudes, even impersonal ones, are "interpersonal" (or second personal). "Personal" reactive attitudes are those, like resentment and guilt, that are felt as if from the perspective of a participant in the events that give rise to it, whereas "impersonal" reactive attitudes, like indignation or moral blame, are felt as if from a third party's point of view. One cannot resent or forgive injuries to people with whom one lacks some personal connection, but this is no impediment to moral blame or disapproval. Nonetheless, however "impersonal" blame is in Strawson's sense, it is not an attitude he characterizes as "objective." It is just as interpersonal or second personal as personal reactive attitudes like resentment or guilt.[7] Thus although impersonal reactive attitudes are as if from the perspective of a third party, they are not third-personal attitudes in the usual sense; they involve the same second-personal element of implicit address as do personal ones, only as if from the perspective of a representative person rather than any individual's standpoint.[8]

The difference between *warranted* personal and impersonal reactive attitudes tracks a distinction between an *individual authority* we presuppose when we implicitly address putatively legitimate "personal" demands that others not treat *us* in certain ways and a

---

[7] "The same abnormal light which shows the agent to us as one in respect of whom the personal attitudes, the personal demand, are to be suspended, shows him to us also as one in respect of whom the impersonal attitudes, the generalized demand, are to be suspended" (Strawson 1968: 87).

[8] Similarly, *second personal* does not imply *second party*. Guilt, like any reactive attitude is second personal, since it involves implicit address, but it clearly is not a second-party attitude. In feeling guilt, one implicitly addresses a demand to oneself. Finally, any second-personal attitude is also first personal. Address, whether implicit or explicit is always from someone (an individual (I) or a collective (we)).

representative authority we assume when we implicitly address "impersonal" demands as representative persons in moral blame. Personal reactive attitudes and individual authority are conceptually implicated in moral claim *rights* and correlative "bipolar" obligations that those against whom the right is held have *to* the right holder. For example, a right not to be harmed or coerced entails a correlative obligation others have *to him* not to harm him. And this involves, as a conceptual matter, others being distinctively accountable *to him* for respecting the right and his individual authority to hold them thus accountable, or, indeed not to, at his discretion. Thus in U.S. civil law, for example, it is up to victims whether or not to seek compensation for a violation of their rights, as it is morally, whether to forgive or to resent. Only the victim, or perhaps those personally related to him, has or have the standing to do either.

When, however, it comes to the responsibility involved in moral obligations *period*, as we might call them (that is, wrongful conduct rather than the wronging *of someone* that consists in the violation of a bipolar obligation *to him*),[9] accountability is not distinctively to the victim, but to everyone, including the victim *and* the violator, as representative persons. It is, again, a conceptual truth that violations of moral obligation warrant the impersonal reactive attitude of moral blame when they are unexcused. It is a reflection of this that whereas it is up to the victim to seek compensation for violations of rights through the law of torts, it is up to the people and its representatives, e.g., public prosecutors, to decide whether and how to hold people responsible for violations of criminal law.

The line of thought I wish to consider for moral generalism derives from the second-personal character of moral accountability, and hence, moral obligation. When we address a moral demand to someone, whether others or ourselves, we take up a second-person standpoint with respect to them. We "regard" them, as Strawson says, "inter-personal[ly]." And this makes us subject to "constraints on moral address," namely presuppositions of the intelligibility of so understanding ourselves (Watson 1987: 263–4). In *SPS* I sum these into what I call "Pufendorf's Point": We can intelligibly hold someone responsible only if we regard her as capable of holding herself responsible. Genuinely to conceive ourselves as under *obligation*, rather than just obliged by force or having incentives to avoid unwelcome sanctions, we must be capable of blaming ourselves for failing to comply.[10] A being subject to obligation must be capable of being "forced," not externally, but "of itself to weigh its own actions, and to judge itself worthy of some censure unless it conforms to a prescribed rule" (Pufendorf 1934: 91). As I would put the point, we can intelligibly regard someone as under a moral obligation and hold her accountable, only if we regard her as able to take up the impartial (Strawson's "impersonal") second-person standpoint of a representative person on herself, recognize the legitimacy of the moral demand, and make the demand of herself from this perspective.

---

[9] Of course, these may be the very same action.

[10] See also Hart's distinction between being obligated and being obliged (Hart 1961: 6–8).

General Principles and Accountability, Legal and Moral

It is uncontroversial that generally formulable rules or principles are intrinsic to the rule of law in a way they are not, say, to rule by decree. This is common ground between legal positivists and their critics; the main issue between them is whether the existence of rule-structured practices, including perhaps second-order rules, such as Hart's "rule of recognition," is sufficient for a legal order, as the positivists suppose, or whether, as Dworkin argues, appeal to general moral principles is also necessary (Hart 1961; Dworkin 1978: 23ff.).[11] Whether conventional rules are sufficient, or whether these must be supplemented by moral principles, it has seemed more or less obvious to philosophers of law that it is part of the very idea of a legal order that it involves regulation by standards that can be formulated in a general way and are not irreducibly particularistic. It is consistent with this, of course, that legal standards will involve concepts that take judgment to apply and that may not be able to be readily operationalized in empirical terms. For example, uses of force otherwise proscribed by law are permitted in self-defense when they are "reasonably" believed necessary to repel a threat to which they are "proportionate" (Black 1999). Even so, it just seems essential to the rule of law that laws must be formulable in general terms that those subject to them can be expected to understand and regulate themselves by, despite differences in values, taste, and expertise.

It is widely accepted that law claims *authority* over and *obligates* those subject to it, thereby making them accountable for compliance (e.g., Raz 1979). I take it that a central attraction of the rule of law, as opposed to rule by decree, is that a legal order's claims to obligate have a substantially better chance of actually being legitimate and obligating than would comparable claims of a regime that did not govern by rules and principles that can be formulated in general terms and that anyone subject to them can be expected to know, understand, and regulate themselves by.

There are certainly many areas of human life where we live happily and appropriately by particularistic judgments, for example, regarding aesthetic matters. Judgments about art, food, décor, music, and so on, seem irreducibly particularistic, and it would be foolhardy to try to systematize them, or even worse, to attempt to ground them, in general rules and principles. We need not think of these areas as any less serious or even, indeed, less objective, though general agreement or even understanding cannot be expected. As Louis Armstrong is reputed to have said about jazz music, "if you have to ask what jazz is, you'll never know." But the aesthetic differs from law and morality in not purporting to impose obligations. Artists may sensibly take themselves to be obligated to pursue their art in certain ways and not in others, of course. And outsiders may make these or similar judgments also. But the point remains that obligation-imposing purport is not intrinsic to aesthetic standards in the way it is to moral and legal requirements.

---

[11] Such as, "no person should profit from wrongdoing," which, Dworkin argues, the U.S. Supreme Court appealed to in deciding law in *Riggs v. Palmer.*

Because the aesthetic seems particularistic, and because law, by its nature, purports to obligate, legal requirements seeking to impose aesthetic standards would be not simply unjust, but downright ridiculous. Imagine a city ordinance outlawing kitsch, schlock, or the banal, even with restricted scope, say, in literature. What would make such a law ridiculous, I take it, is the manifest absurdity of purporting to hold people answerable for something they cannot be expected to be able to hold themselves to in their own judgment, that is, the obvious violation of "Pufendorf's Point."

The difference between law and morality is that whereas legal requirements *purport* to obligate, moral requirements necessarily actually do. Clearly, laws can exist that do not impose genuine, that is, *de jure* obligations. Law necessarily *claims de jure* authority, and arguably it must have *de facto* authority to exist at all. But law need not actually have the *de jure* authority it claims in order to exist *de facto*. However, this cannot be true of moral obligations, at least as we are currently thinking of them. These are *de jure* in their nature; if they don't have the authority they claim, then they simply do not exist. They are merely putative and not actual moral obligations. "Legal obligation," by contrast, can refer to something that has only *de facto* authority and none *de jure*.

If what we have said so far about the absurdity of legally mandating the aesthetic is correct, it follows even more strongly that morality could not include any such requirements either. "Pufendorf's Point" implies that *de jure* obligations cannot possibly exist unless those subject to them can intelligibly be held answerable for complying with them.

We cannot, however, conclude moral generalism, or even moral-obligation generalism, straight away from this. The example of the aesthetic combines two different features: its particularistic character, one the one hand, and its relation to *expert* or even *esoteric* particularistic judgment, on the other. A putatively obligating standard that would require a particularistic expertise that only some can be expected ever to acquire would violate "Pufendorf's Point," but that might be owing simply to its esoteric quality. Might moral judgment be particularistic but nonetheless sufficiently widely shareable to impose obligation?

The moral particularist can admit that *legal* obligation cannot be particularistic, since formulability as general rules and principles is part of the very idea of law. But why couldn't the moral order, even an order of moral obligations, differ from that of law in precisely this respect? Even if "No law without general rules and principles" expresses a central truth about the law, why suppose that "No morality without general rules and principles" expresses a core theorem of morality?

The reason why generally formulable rules and principles are essential to the idea of law is that nothing counts as a legal order unless there is something publicly formulable and specifiable with which subjects are held responsible for complying. Locking someone up cannot count as holding him responsible for and enforcing compliance unless there is something that is publicly accessible to enforcer and enforced alike to which the enforcement can refer—for example, that one is not to do an action of kind A in circumstances C. Both "A" and "C" may be quite complicated, but not so complicated that no one could intelligibly expect those subject to the putative standard to understand and be able to regulate themselves by it.

But why must the same thing hold with morality? Might the truth about moral obligation be particularistic even if law cannot be? A particularistic moral order would not be fit to be a legal order, but perhaps it might become one by establishing legal institutions and promulgating the single law: "Comply with your moral obligations." Such a law would seem to be universal and general, even if the moral obligations with which citizens were legally obligated to comply were themselves particularistic. So even if law has to take a universal general form in order to impose obligations, it might be that morality and moral obligations do not.

While this seems right as far as it goes, it underrates accountability's role in morality. We can see this by considering some things Dancy says about the idea that morality is tied to the social or interpersonal in a similar, but nonetheless crucially different, way. Dancy considers the possibility that a rationale for moral generalism might be found in the thought that "morality is essentially a system of social constraints" that is necessary to fix expectations in a socially beneficial way (2004: 83). He evidently has in mind a kind of indirect or rule-consequentialist approach like Brad Hooker's (Hooker 2000). Dancy's reply is that such a view "is a description of something like a set of traffic regulations" (Dancy 2004: 83). "Morality," Dancy continues, "was not invented by a group of experts in council to serve the purposes of social control" (Dancy 2004: 83). Nor is morality necessary to fix expectation, since "people are quite capable of judging how to behave case by case, in a way that would enable us to predict what they will in fact do" (Dancy 2004: 83).

Dancy is of course right that morality, unlike legal orders, is not invented. So *a fortiori* it is not invented for any purpose: not social control, not fixing expectations, nor any other. And as far as the point I currently want to make goes, we could even allow Dancy that it is frequently true that people are competent to judge "how to behave case by case" in a way that enables us to predict what they are likely to do. Of course, this would not yet enable us to *fix* expectations as we can through the rule-structured practices, like promising, that rule consequentialists frequently discuss. But the roles that rule- and principled-structured practices, like those in which legal systems consist or the more informal "moral" practices of indirect consequentialism, play in bringing about various beneficial consequences, like stable expectations, are actually quite different from the kinds of considerations to which I have been adverting.

According to morality as accountability, rules and principles are essential not to bringing about valuable consequences, even of mutual accountability itself. Rather they must be in play in order for us to be morally accountable to one another, and to ourselves, as representative persons in the first place. The idea is not that general principles are somehow prior to moral accountability, or vice versa. Rather they come together as a package deal. Moral obligations entail moral accountability conceptually, and agents can intelligibly be held accountable only if there exist general rules and principles that are accessible to all who are morally bound as a matter of common public knowledge.

Above we considered the conceptual point that the very idea of enforcing law and holding people (legally) responsible for complying with it entails that there must be something publicly formulable and recognizable in which law itself consists. When someone is charged with breaking the law, there must be some way of formulating the law he is charged with breaking. It is no good to say just that he acted illegally; there must be a formulable rule or principle that he can be charged with breaking.

When we think about the conceptual relation between moral obligation and accountability, we can see that something similar must hold in the moral domain also. When we blame someone for having acted wrongly, ourselves or others, we assume the burden of characterizing the putatively wrongful act in some way that goes beyond the judgment that the particular act's features simply combined holistically in the circumstances to make up a wrongful act. As with the law, there must be some more specific *charge*. Moreover, when we hold someone accountable, we put him in the position of *justifying* himself to us, either to us as individuals, as in the case of rights violations, or to us (and himself) as representative persons, as in moral blame. This means that any charge of wrongdoing has to be publicly contestable; it must be able to be put in terms that, in principle, anyone can assess, criticize, and emend. Moral blame must be embeddable in a shared public culture of accountability.

Consider: you are walking with a friend at dusk in the winter woods, and he falls and badly sprains his ankle, making it impossible for the two of you to get to warmth and safety before nightfall. There is a locked cabin with a fireplace nearby and wood stacked beside. You deliberate about what to do and decide to break in and start a fire in the fireplace so that you and your friend can be safe overnight before trying to get back to town the next day. Have you done wrong?

Note, first, that if anyone, including you yourself, were to charge you with wrongdoing, this charge would have to be put in some more specific way, like, "You acted wrongly because you trespassed; you broke into someone else's property." It is no good just to say: "What you did Tuesday night at 5:30 p.m. in the woods was wrong." Or even: "The properties of your action on Tuesday night at 5:30 p.m. taken holistically amount to moral wrong." To intelligibly hold you accountable, the person must be able to levee some more specific charge like, "You broke into someone else's property, and that is wrong," implicitly assuming a general principle. It is then of course open to you to say, "Yes, often, maybe usually, maybe even almost always, that is wrong, but not when it is necessary for safety and survival." In so doing, you implicitly emend the proposed principle, "It is wrong to trespass, except when this is necessary for safety and survival."

A particularist might well reply that there is no reason to suppose that this emended principle holds without exception. No doubt, a fully acceptable principle would have to be significantly more complicated. But, however complicated, two points would nonetheless remain. First, it seems essential to interpersonal accountability (and, indeed to intrapersonal accountability) that criticism, because it is essentially second personal, must be able to be put in terms that the person to whom it is addressed can understand, respond to, and contest. This means, second, that obligation- and wrong-making features are not just normative grounds (which might admit, as such, of being irreducibly holistic and particularistic). Any features that could make an action morally obligatory or wrong have to be able to mediate second-personal accountability. They must be able to be formulated in terms that can mediate a publicly sharable discussion about whether the conduct warrants accountability-seeking reactive attitudes, specifically, moral blame.[12] And if this is right, when it comes to moral obligation, particularism seems to be ruled out on conceptual grounds.

Moral Generalism

The foregoing reflections are obviously too cursory to be fully convincing. I hope, however, that they show that there is a potential line of argument for generalism, and against particularism, regarding moral *obligation*, with which Dancy has yet to deal. In this last section, I wish briefly to indicate why, if this argument were to go through, generalism, and the denial of particularism, as Dancy understands these, would thereby be established.

In a well-known chapter of *Ethics and the Limits of Philosophy*, Bernard Williams dubbed morality "the peculiar institution" (Williams 1985). Williams's rhetorical point was to associate morality with a kind of slavery, their "peculiar institution" being the terms in which whites in the antebellum South used to refer to the enslavement of African-Americans. What makes morality "peculiar," in Williams's view, in other words, what is distinctive about it, is its characteristic notion of obligation (Williams 1985: 174–5). Williams's ambition there was neo-Nietzschean, to argue that the "morality system" with its distinctive concept of moral obligation was an unhealthy set of concepts to live with, since it shackles individuals' pursuits of cherished projects from which they derive their very integrity and identity.

Though I certainly reject Williams's rhetorical and philosophical agenda, I accept his view that moral obligation is an ineliminable aspect of the concept of morality as it developed in early modern philosophy in the West from the seventeenth century on. The idea that obligation is central to the idea of morality, at least as it has been conceived in the modern period, is also the core of Elizabeth Anscombe's critique of "modern moral philosophy" as essentially incoherent (Anscombe 1998). The only way morality could be a coherent concept, Anscombe argued, is if its putative obligations could derive from God's supremely authoritative command, but only few moderns accept the divine command theory.

---

[12] I do not mean, of course, that the discussion or consideration must actually be public. More often than not, it will not be. The point is that its terms must be publicizable.

Obviously, this is not the place to try to respond to Anscombe's critique.[13] My point here is that if she is right, as I think she and Williams are, in characterizing its target—the centrality of moral obligation to morality—then generalism about morality will follow from generalism regarding moral obligation. Assume, then, that there would be no such thing as morality unless there were moral obligations. And assume, as the argument of the last section attempted to conclude, that moral obligations depend upon general principles. It follows from these two assumptions together that there can be such a thing as morality only if there are valid, obligation-creating general principles. So it would follow that particularism as Dancy defines it is false.

What, then, about the possibility of holistic moral oughts and reasons, and therefore, of particularism about these? I said above that I can concede that there is a sense in which there might be non-obligating moral reasons and oughts that are particularistic. However, if what we have just said is correct, then there is also a sense in which the very existence of *moral* reasons and oughts depends on general principles too. Any non-obligating normative moral reason or ought need not itself depend on a general principle. However, a reason or ought can be a *moral* reason or ought only if there is such a thing as morality. And there can be such a thing as morality only if there are moral obligations. And *these* require, if the argument of the last section is correct, that valid general principles be in place. So there can be moral normative reasons and moral oughts at all, and any specific normative reason or ought can be a *moral* reason or ought, only if there are valid general principles.

I put forward this argument, again, not so much to establish its conclusion as to show that there is an argument for generalism that Dancy's formidable case for holism about normative reasons and oughts simply does not touch. If this argument is correct, though there are senses of "ethics" in which "ethics without principles" is clearly possible, "morality without principles" is not.

---

[13] I attempt to do so in Darwall 2006.

II

Autonomy

6

"Because I Want It"

How can an agent's desire or will give him reasons for acting? Not long ago, this might have seemed a silly question, since it was widely believed that any normative reason for acting must be based in the agent's desires.[1] The interesting question, it seemed, was not how what an agent wants could give him reasons, but how anything else could. In recent years, however, this earlier orthodoxy has increasingly appeared wrongheaded as a growing number of philosophers have come to stress the action-guiding role of reasons in deliberation from the agent's point of view.[2] What a deliberating agent has in view is rarely his own will or desires as such, even if taking something as a reason is intimately tied to desire.[3] Someone who wants to escape a burning building doesn't evaluate her options by considering which is likeliest to realize what she wants or wills. She is focused, rather, on her desire's object: getting out alive. The fact that a successful route would realize something she wants is apt to strike her as beside the point or, at best, as a trivial bonus.

This point is sometimes put by saying that desires are in the "background," rather than the foreground, of the practical scene a deliberating agent faces (Pettit and Smith 1990). The metaphor is somewhat misleading, however, since an agent's desires are normally not so much in the background of her deliberative field as outside of it altogether.[4] If we must locate them spatially, a better place might be within or behind the standpoint from which the agent views her alternatives rather than toward the back of the scene she views. Sometimes desires shape the way an agent sees things, as in the burning building just mentioned. In other cases, desires seem shaped themselves by what the agent takes as reasons, as in Nagel's category of "motivated desires" (Nagel 1970: 29–30). Here, that the agent has a certain desire may "simply *follow*" from the fact that she takes certain considerations as reason giving.[5] In either case, it can seem puzzling why the fact that an agent desires or wills something (as opposed to facts

---

[1] Where "desire" is understood in the broad sense as any disposition an agent might have to bring something about. I shall generally follow this usage.

[2] For earlier criticisms of this view, see Nagel 1970; Bond 1983; and Darwall 1983. For more recent critiques, see Pettit and Smith 1990; Quinn 1993; and Scanlon 1998.

[3] On this latter point, see Scanlon 1998: 39–41.

[4] I take the term "deliberative field" from Herman 1993: 193–207.

[5] Nagel argues that this is true, for example, of moral and prudential reasons (Nagel 1970: 29).

about *what* she wants or wills) should give her a practical reason, that is, a consideration bearing intrinsically on what she should do.

Despite this, "because I want it" can sometimes give one a reason for acting that is additional to the reasons for which one wants or wills. Consider, for example, what we might say to someone seeking advice about what to do. Although we might well begin by pointing to reasons for wanting to do this or that, we could suggest as well that what, in light of these, she (that is, the agent) wants is also relevant, perhaps decisively so. Appreciating the backgrounding of desire from the agent's point of view makes it difficult, however, to see why this should be so. In what follows, I shall suggest what may seem a surprising explanation of why it is, namely, our standing as one free and rational person among others, able to address claims *to* each other *as* free and rational. To make a claim is, necessarily, to express one's will. In claiming, therefore, we commit ourselves to the reason-giving character of the will. Ultimately, I shall argue, we can justify claims we make on others as free and rational only by acknowledging an equal standing all free and rational agents have to make such claims. Moreover, I shall argue, our epistemic access to this status comes through such "second-personal" claim making. The point will not be that the reason-giving character of the will depends on any actual claim we make on others or that they make on us. Rather, the thought will be that in addressing such reasons to each other, second-personally, we commit ourselves a priori to the standing of free and rational persons to make such claims and thereby to the reason-giving character of the will. Ironically, it will turn out, what explains why an agent's own will can give *him* reasons is inextricably linked to why his will can give them also to others.

Theoretical and Practical Reason: A Preliminary Comparison

The basic idea can be glimpsed by reflecting on a disanalogy between theoretical and practical reason to which we shall return later. Belief, by its very nature, aims to represent the world and so is appropriately regulated by it. Correct representation is belief's "constitutive aim," so it is guaranteed by what beliefs are that we ought to believe truths and disbelieve falsehoods.[6] The idea is not just that beliefs are mental states that picture the world as being some way, say, that p. That is as true of supposing

---

[6] Or, at least, it is guaranteed that we ought to believe the truth on some matter if we have any beliefs on it at all. For discussion of the idea that belief has this "constitutive aim," and of whether desire does, see Velleman 1996. A problem with this view might be that, even if belief's constitutive aim is correct representation, it can't follow directly that we ought to believe truths (or not believe falsehoods) because such an "ought" would have to be categorical and for that to follow it would also have to be true that belief's aim is one we ought to have. An alternative picture might be to treat it as a conceptual truth that beliefs ought to be regulated by the truth (or the world), since, from the first-person point of view, deliberation about what to believe is no different from inquiry into what is true. Whatever the details, however, what seems clear is that it is of the nature of belief that it is regulated by something (truth, or the world) that is what it is independently of norms for belief. I am indebted here to some work by, and discussion with, Nishiten Shah.

or pretending that p as it is of believing that p. If p is not the case, a supposition that p is false no less than is a belief that p. Rather, the thought is that, unlike pretense and supposition, belief aims to represent the world *correctly*. Truth is regulative for any state of mind we will count as a belief. If a mental state represents the world as being that p, but is insufficiently responsive to evidence of p's truth, we will count it, not as a belief that p, but as some other kind of representative state.[7]

We might think of the set of a person's beliefs as defining her subjective theoretical standpoint. But this simply means: her standpoint on the world—how the world seems to her or the world-as-she-believes-it-be. Suppose we ask how the fact that one person believes something can give another person a reason to believe it. It follows from the nature of belief that it can do so only insofar as it can give the other person evidence.[8] Even if someone's belief that p is reasonable, in the sense of being supported by evidence available to her, it may give us no reason to believe p whatsoever if our evidence explains away hers as misleading. A similar consequence follows concerning the relation of an individual's own subjective theoretical standpoint to what she has reason to believe herself. Only if her believing that p gives her some evidence that p is true, as it might, for example, if she has some evidence about the reliability of her beliefs, can it give her some reason to maintain her belief that p.

Compare now practical reason. What, if anything, plays the role in practical reasoning that the world does in theoretical reasoning? (We can ignore for the present the difference between desire and willing something as an end and use "desire" to refer to both.) It has become common to treat desire and belief as having contrasting functions given by complementary "directions of fit."[9] In a slogan, beliefs aim to fit the world, whereas desires aim for the world to fit them. This difference between desire and belief need not entail the Humean thesis that, since desires lack the representative function of beliefs, they are regulated by nothing, so that, strictly speaking, there are no normative reasons for desire or action. Desires might be regulated by norms for desire and action, whatever these might be, and normative practical reasons ultimately grounded in these. The point is that norms for desire and action must be given in some other way than they are for belief. We cannot read them off a representative function, since desires have none.

Suppose, however, that there were something to which desires aim to be responsive in some broader sense, if not to represent it. Call this "value." Desires would then be regulated by value, just as beliefs are regulated by the world. Not "*just* as," of course,

---

[7] As David Velleman puts it, "When someone believes a proposition . . . his acceptance of it is regulated in ways designed to promote acceptance of the truth," whereas, for example, when "someone assumes a proposition, he or his cognitive faculties are disposed to regulate his acceptance of it in ways designed to promote the ends of argument or inquiry," and so on (Velleman 1992: 14).

[8] It is consistent with this that testimony, telling someone that p, might give reasons that are more "second personal."

[9] See, for example Smith 1994: 111–19. Smith cites Platts 1979: 256–7, who attributes the idea to Anscombe 1957.

since the way beliefs are regulated follows from their representative function, and desires have none. Desires would not aim to *represent* value. Nonetheless, we might try out the idea that in some broader way desires are mistaken when they are out of proportion to value. It will now follow from the nature of desire that we ought not desire what lacks value, we ought not desire one thing more than another when there is no difference in value, and so on.[10]

By analogy with what we said about belief and an individual's subjective theoretical standpoint, we can define an individual's subjective practical standpoint by the set of her desires.[11] Since, however, desire lacks a representative function, we shouldn't say that a person's practical point of view is simply the way value seems to her. Her desires or will are not simply value-as-she-sees-it. Nonetheless, since we are taking desires to be, intrinsically, regulated by value, our tentative picture will have it that the relation of an individual's subjective practical standpoint to what others have reason to desire and do (and for what she has reason to desire and do herself) is the same as that we noted above concerning an individual's subjective theoretical standpoint. If an individual's desire does not track value, it will give another no reason for acting whatsoever, even if the person's desire is reasonable in the sense of responding to value as she sees it, or to value as it would be on her view of the (non-evaluative) world, or to value as it would be on a subjectively reasonable view of the world, and so on.[12] Similarly, the fact that she desires something will give *her* a reason for acting only if she has some reason for regarding her desires as reliable indicators of value.

In theoretical reasoning, an individual point of view is simply one perspective on the world—an appearance—and it can be discounted as mere appearance if we have some reason to think it is illusory. Similarly, on our tentative picture, an individual's practical perspective is, if not discountable as mere appearance, discountable all the same if it fails to track real value. If an agent's desires fail to track value, then they fail to give *anyone* reasons for acting, the agent *or* others, regardless of how strongly held or how rational the desires might be in subjective terms.[13] However much something matters *to* someone, unless its mattering to her is evidence that it matters *period*, the fact that it matters to her will give no reason to others *or* to her, either to do, or to forbear doing,

---

[10] Not "agent-relative value" (that is, not value *to the agent*—either value as the agent sees it, or value from the agent's point of view, *or* benefit to the agent (the agent's good)), but what is called "agent-neutral value" or value *period*. For the distinction between agent-relative and agent-neutral generally, see Nagel 1970; Parfit 1984; Scheffler 1982; and McNaughton and Rawling 1995. For the relevance of this distinction to value in particular, see Sen 1983.

[11] Using "desire" in the broad functionalist sense given by its direction of fit. So understood, desires will include many things that could usefully be distinguished in a more fine-grained analysis: intention, norm acceptance, emotion, and so on.

[12] Unless, of course, the satisfaction of desire has value in itself, but, as I discuss further in the next section, that seems implausible when we reflect on desire's direction of fit. By a "subjectively reasonable" view of the world, I mean whatever beliefs are supported by evidence available to the person.

[13] That is, they fail to give anyone what we might call *objective* reasons. They would still give anyone who reasonably thought they tracked real value *subjective* reasons (that is, evidence of objective reasons).

anything.[14] On the current picture, the only way a person's values can give *anyone* reasons is by reflecting, or providing evidence of, value.

To contemplate such a picture is, I think, to find it both questionable and repellent.[15] It is questionable because it assumes that desire and the will have, like belief, a constitutive aim that is *substantive* in the sense of being able to be formulated independently of norms for the attitude.[16] Our concepts of the world (what is the case) and truth are distinct concepts from the concept of what we ought to believe, so the constitutive aim of belief (truth) is substantive in this sense.[17] When we say that belief is regulated by truth, we are not simply making the tautologous claim that we ought to believe what we ought to believe. We are making a substantive claim, albeit one that is guaranteed by the nature of belief. It is constitutive of belief that it aims at, and is responsible to, something that is independent of compliance with norms for belief from which these norms can be derived. It is not obvious, however, that there exists a defensible concept of value that is independent of the concept of what we ought to desire, esteem, and choose which could serve as a substantive constitutive aim for desire and the will in the way that truth does for belief. It is not obvious, in other words, that desire is, in its nature, responsible to anything independent of norms for desire from which such norms can be derived (in the way they can for belief). If that were so, we would be making a substantive, rather than merely formal, claim when we say that we ought to desire the desirable (or that value is desirable) or when we say that we ought to choose the choiceworthy (or that value is choiceworthy).

Now one way this *could* be so is if we accepted a Moorean conception of intrinsic value. According to Moore, for something to have intrinsic value is for it to be the case that it "ought to exist for its own sake."[18] If we were to accept this meaning, we could claim something substantive by saying that we ought to desire what is intrinsically good, since it is a substantive claim that we ought to desire (choose, bring about) what ought to exist. As I shall discuss further in the next section, moreover, this substantive claim might seem defensible in a way that is analogous to the normativity of truth for belief. Truth is normative for belief because, as it is sometimes said, belief is the "holding true" attitude.[19] If desire is, as it is also said, the "making true" attitude, then it

---

[14] Unless, of course, it matters period that it matters to him (or, to someone). I discuss this case four paragraphs below.

[15] For an important discussion of these matters in a more general context, see Nagel 1986.

[16] For discussion of this distinction between "substantive" and merely "formal" aims in relation to belief and desire, see Velleman 1996: 714–15.

[17] In Velleman 1992, Velleman suggests that the "attainable" might provide a substantive constitutive aim for desire; however, that would provide no help in this context.

[18] Since Moore can be read as giving special emphasis to the irreducible normativity of value (cf. his famous "open question" argument), it might seem odd that his views could underwrite the picture we are currently considering. The reason they might, as is now explained in the text, is that Moore's idea appears to be that value is normative, not for choice, desire, or action in the first instance, but for states of affairs (Moore 1993: 34).

[19] Actually, this is insufficient, since assuming p also is a way of holding p true. What makes truth normative for belief is that it is the kind of holding true that responds to truth (or evidence of it) in its distinctive way.

might be natural to think that what we should *make* true (desire) is what should *be* true.[20]

To think this, however, we would have to think it possible for it to be true that a state of the world ought to exist (for its own sake) quite independently of any truths about what anyone should desire, feel, esteem, aim at, or do. I shall argue that we cannot defensibly think this. Oughts gain their sense through their role in normative guidance, so only what can be normatively guided can be subject to a norm. But if that is so, then we lack a defensible idea of what ought to *be* that is independent of the notions of what anyone, actual or hypothetical, ought to esteem, desire, feel, or do in the way required to provide a substantive rather than merely formal constitutive aim for desire (as truth does for belief). The practical realm seems different from the theoretical realm in that practical normative reasons are not grounded in any aim that is itself independent of practical norms. The aims of practical reason seem (practically) normative all the way down.

Second, we are repelled by the thought that we should hesitate to interfere with a person's pursuit of projects to which he is deeply and passionately committed, or to further projects of one's own about which one cares deeply, only to the extent that these projects track genuine value. To the contrary, we are apt to believe that persons have some claim to pursue their own projects, so long as these do not pose threats to others. On this alternative picture, a person's desires create, within these limits, *agent-relative* reasons whether or not his desires reflect the (agent-neutral) value of any state of the world.[21] One's own desire or will can, within limits, create a reason for one to act, and that of others can create a reason for one not to interfere. And these agent-relative reasons are not reducible to the (agent-neutral) value of people pursuing their own projects or of their being allowed to do so. An agent-relative reason not to interfere *oneself* differs from any (agent-neutral) reason to promote non-interference, since the agent-relative reason counsels not interfering oneself even when not interfering would bring it about that another person interferes in an exactly similar case. Rather, we find it natural to think that we have a reason to *respect* others' pursuits that is additional to and independent of any we might have to promote them. Here we take it that we have reasons that derive from an agent-relative *norm of action* (the norm of respect) that does not itself derive from the value of any state of the world. A similar logic applies for the agent-relative reason to do what *one* wants or wills.

Viewed this way, an individual's practical standpoint is not merely a perspective *on* some external thing, called value; it is the perspective *of* a free and rational agent. And because it is, it can ground a claim to respect that cannot be reduced to any agent-neutral value it might have more or less adequately in view. The perspective of a free

---

[20] As Velleman puts it, "desire takes its propositional object as representing *facienda*—things that aren't the case but are to be brought about," whereas "belief takes its propositional object as representing *facta*—things that are the case and in virtue of which the proposition is true" (Velleman 1996: 707).

[21] For this distinction, see the references in note 10.

rational agent can never be discounted as mere appearance. Of course, to bring out this Kantian aspect of the alternative picture is not yet to defend it. My present purpose is simply to point to how we might see practical reasons and reasoning as fundamentally different from reasoning about belief and to suggest that we might find in this difference a way of grounding the reason-giving character of an agent's desire (and will) for herself that is similar to the way it can ground its reason-grounding character for others. What underlies both, I shall argue, is our standing in rational *inter*action to make claims *as* free and rational agents on others. And what gives us epistemic access to this status is our participation in such second-personal rational activity.

First, however, I want to show how other attempts to ground the reason-giving character of desires fail and to illustrate how puzzling desire's (or the will's) reason-giving character should seem if we view deliberation solely from within a single agent's first-person point of view, neglecting the second-personal character of certain forms of rational thought, deliberation, and discourse. I will begin with the common, but I believe mistaken, idea that instrumental reasoning entails or presupposes that an agent's desires or ends give him reasons for acting.

Instrumental Reasoning

There is an utterly uncontroversial form of instrumental reasoning that agents engage in from their desires or ends. So don't agents, in reasoning instrumentally, take their desires as reasons for acting, specifically, as reasons to take the means necessary to achieving their desired ends?[22] Furthermore, since instrumental reasoning is uncontroversially rational, doesn't it also follow that an agent's desires actually *are* such reasons? It takes some care to see what is or should be uncontroversial here. To see this, however, is to see why neither consequence follows. Consider the two following patterns of reasoning, one theoretical, the other practical:

I. p	II. A is to (should) be done
If p, then q	A will be done, only if B is done
Therefore, q	Therefore, B is to (should) be done

Suppose someone believes the premises of argument I. There is then an obvious sense in which these beliefs will give him reason to believe q (support his believing that q).

---

[22] Again, we will be ignoring the difference between desiring something and adopting or willing it as an end. In doing this we will be simplifying even more than we have to this point since the instrumental reasoning we will be considering only holds, strictly speaking, for the case of willing something as an end, and not for the general case of desire. This will not affect the argument of this section, however. If we can show that the validity of instrumental reasoning doesn't entail that the fact that one wills an end is a reason to take the means to achieving it, we will be able to conclude *a fortiori* that it doesn't entail that the fact that one desires something is a reason to take steps to realize what one desires.

This obvious sense, however, is only that *what he believes* (that is, p and if p, then q) gives him reason to believe q, not that *his believing* these propositions does. After all, he may have no reason to believe either of these premises, no reason to believe both, or, worse, reasons to disbelieve both or either of them. To take the worst case, suppose that he ought not to believe either premise. It will be hard to see in this case how the fact that he does have these beliefs can give him any reason whatsoever to believe q. This does not mean, of course, that nothing follows from his believing these premises concerning what he has reason to, or ought to, believe. It follows that he ought either to believe q or to give up one of his beliefs that p or that if p, then q. This much is demanded by the requirement of consistency in belief. Finally, if he ought (has reason) to believe both p and if p, then q, it will follow that he ought to believe q. By virtue of the validity of argument I, reasons for believing its premises become reasons for believing the conclusion. And reasons for disbelieving its conclusion become reasons for disbelieving the conjunction of the premises.

The situation is exactly analogous in the practical case. To simplify, suppose that someone who wills A accepts that A is to be done and vice versa. Consider now someone who accepts both premises of argument II: she wills that A (adopts A as end) and believes that A will be done only if B is done. Here also, there is an obvious sense in which her belief and end give her reason to do B (accept that B is to be done). But again, the relevant sense is that *what she accepts* gives her these reasons. Correct reasoning from her belief and end, in this sense, leads to the conclusion that she should will B. Analogously, however, the facts that she has this belief and end may give her no reason at all to will B. Maybe she has no reason to have either or both of these commitments, or, worse, reasons not to have both or either of them. In the worst case, in which she has reason not to have A as end and not to believe that A will be done only if B is, the fact that she has this desire and belief may give her no reason whatsoever to will B. If, however, she does have this end and belief, then something does follow about what she ought to do: she ought either to will B or to give up either her end of doing A or her belief that B is necessary to doing A. We might think of this requirement as a demand of *practical* consistency that is analogous to the requirement of consistency in belief in theoretical reasoning. Finally, if she does have reasons for willing A and for believing that A will be achieved only if B is, then it will follow that she ought to will B. Reasons for accepting these premises of argument II become reasons for accepting the conclusion. And reasons for rejecting the conclusion become reasons for rejecting one of the premises.[23]

---

[23] I discuss this point in Darwall 1983: 15–17. For more extensive discussion see Broome 1999. More recently, there has been a vigorous debate involving Broome, Niko Kolodny, Michael Bratman, Joseph Raz and others concerning whether there exist any free-standing norms of practical coherence or just truths about normative reasons for acting. Since I am arguing that even if a norm of practical consistency exists, it would not follow that desires provide reasons, nothing I want to say here depends on the outcome of this debate. I will therefore proceed in the text as though there is a valid norm of practical coherence.

It is a familiar thought that instrumental reasoning issues in "hypothetical" rather than categorical imperatives. But care is required in interpreting this idea. On the basis of the last two paragraphs, what we should say is that the imperatives or prescriptions that follow from instrumental reasoning are imperatives of practical consistency that tell the agent either to take the means or to give up the end or the belief that the means in question is the only means. They do *not* tell the agent, if A is your end, and B the only means, then you should do B. There is a sense in which they do recommend B *hypothetically*, but that is: conditionally on a "hypothesis" the agent is committed to assuming *in having* A as her end, namely, that A is to be done. They do not recommend doing B simply on the condition that the agent *has* A as end.[24] In this way, they are just like hypothetical theoretical reasoning: *assuming* that p, and if p, then q, then q. Theoretical reasoning of this kind gives a person no reason to believe q simply on the condition that he believes p and if p, then q. It only gives him a reason to believe q on the hypotheses he accepts in having those beliefs. Likewise, instrumental practical reasoning gives an agent no reason to take the means to his end simply on the condition that he has the end and the belief about the means to it. Rather, it gives him a reason to take the necessary means on the hypotheses he accepts in having the relevant end and belief.

An analogous line of thought applies to formal theories of decision, which assume some ranking of preferences (utilities) and subjective probabilities.[25] Here, too, the uncontroversial kernel of such theories can be seen in terms of hypothetical reasoning and the demand for practical consistency, extended now to the more complex case in which agents must deal with potentially conflicting ends and preferences. The rational force of the principle of maximizing expected utility (preference-satisfaction), like that of instrumental reasoning, is that of a consistency demand requiring that an agent *either* choose the utility-maximizing act or change her preferences or probability estimates. In particular, the formal theory of decision does *not* entail that an agent's preferences give her reasons for acting. As with instrumental reasoning, it says which action is most highly recommended, conditionally or hypothetically—conditionally, however, not on the agent's having the preferences and beliefs she does, but on what she is committed to assuming in having those preferences and beliefs.

Direction of Fit, Standards, and the Phenomenology of Desire

If, however, the idea that an agent's desires gives her reasons is unsupported by instrumental reasoning, it also finds no apparent support when we reflect on what it is to have a desire from the agent's point of view. Consider, again, the familiar view that

---

[24] On this point see Greenspan 1975 and Hare 1971.
[25] I discuss this at greater length in Chapter 6 of Darwall 1983.

belief and desire are functional states that are defined by complementary directions of fit. It is intrinsic to belief that it must fit the world. And desire, as Michael Smith puts it, is "a state with which the world must fit" (Smith 1994: 116). In neither case, of course, is the "must" a logical "must." The point is not that it is logically impossible to believe what is false or for the world not to be as desired. Rather, the intended sense is that of a normative requirement or standard. The world provides a standard of correctness and regulation for beliefs. In complementary fashion, it is said, desires provide a standard of correctness and regulation to the world.

What can this talk mean, though, when it comes to desire? In the case of belief, the situation seems straightforward enough. It follows from the nature of belief that we ought to believe what is true. However, in what sense must the world fit or be regulated by desires? An obvious problem in interpreting this idea is that the world provides a single, consistent standard for beliefs, but desires provide no such standard for the world. If beliefs are in conflict, the world rules on which, if either, is correct. But if desires exist for contradictory states, as they plainly can either intersubjectively or intrasubjectively, what can it mean to say that the world "must fit" these conflicting desires?

Now, ultimately our goal is to understand the relation between desire and normative reasons for acting, and a normative reason is something that can count in favor of an action in deliberation from the agent's point of view. So we might consider whether there is a natural interpretation of desire's claimed direction of fit that is, as it were, phenomenological, from the agents' point of view. We have already seen problems inherent in the very idea that desires can provide standards to which the world must fit. This is false, moreover, to the phenomenology of desire. To the person who desires that p it is not as if *her desire* somehow grounds or creates a standard that the world should be such that p. For instance, to the person who wants to escape a burning building it is not as if she must find a way out because this is what she wants. It is more like she must escape because she must live. We might try the following, therefore. To the person with a desire that p it is *as if the world should be that p*. From the perspective of the desire, as it were, it is as if there is this standard the world should fit.[26] If I desire the relief of a child's suffering, then it is to me as if the world should be such that child's suffering is relieved. Or if I spy a juicy apple and want to eat it, then it is to me as if the world should contain my eating the apple, as if that should be true of the world.

On this interpretation, the claim about desire's direction of fit would then be a claim about how things seem from the perspective of the agent who has the desire, or perhaps better, how the agent sees things insofar as he has the desire.[27] If we interpret the claim

---

[26] Although this interpretation marks a gain in coherence, it may not mark a gain in clarity. Talk of the phenomenology of, say, color experience may be thought to have a clear sense that is lacking here. How, exactly, do things seem when it seems as if there is a standard to which the world must fit?

[27] Note that the agent might simultaneously have a conflicting desire, say, that not *p*, from which perspective it will seem that the world should be that not *p*. It is also possible for him to have the desire that *p*, but regard it as entirely discreditable. In this case, although the desire presents him with a kind of

about desire's direction of fit in this way, the claim would not be, again, that from the agent's perspective it is as if *his desires* provide standards (or "reasons") for the world. An observer explaining the agent's conduct by his beliefs and desires (perhaps, the agent himself as self-observer) might identify his desiring that p with his *holding* the standard to the world that p be true. However, this would be a psychological rather a normative hypothesis: a claim about how things are in the head rather than about how things should be, or what anyone should do, in the world. From the deliberative standpoint, an agent who desires that p will take it that p should be true *simpliciter*, not that p should be true *because he desires it*, or that the world should be as he desires it to be. The latter is the way things would seem to someone with the second-order desire for the satisfaction of his first-order desires *whatever they might be*.[28]

This way of projecting direction of fit into the phenomenology of desire is a further reflection of the thought that, from the agent's point of view, desire is "backgrounded." Just as a belief that p is an attitude toward p, and not toward any attitude toward p, so, similarly, is a desire. The desire that p is also an attitude toward p, and not toward an attitude toward p. However, it is a different attitude than belief. Whereas believing p is its being to one *as if p is true*, desiring p is its being to one *as if p is to be (or should be) true*. To appreciate the backgrounding phenomenon, consider unconscious desires. To someone with the unconscious desire for approval it is not as if *his desire* for approval is a standard for the world, since he is not even aware of having this desire. It is to him as if things should be such that he is approved of by others. Alternatively, think of someone who consciously wants approval but has low self-esteem. To suggest that it is to him as if the world should be such that others approve of him because this is what he wants would seem a cruel joke.

How do action and, ultimately, reasons for acting get into this picture? On the standard model, desires are for states of affairs, say, that the world be such that p. Such a state of affairs might include an action. If I desire to keep a promise, for example, then it is to me as if things should be such that I keep the promise. In other cases, the state of affairs might not itself include an action but be something that will obtain only if action is taken. I want someone's pain to stop and that will happen only if I can find her some pain-relieving medication. If I reason instrumentally from my desire that her pain stop (that is, from the "appearance" my desire give me), I will be led to a state in which it is to me as if I should find her some medication (if this is possible). Now, perhaps I am not in a position to find any and you are. Instrumental reasoning with this premise will lead me from my original desire to a desire that you find the medication. It will then be to me as if the world should be such that you find the medication.

"appearance" that the world ought to be such that *p* is true, like a knowledgeable viewer of the Müller-Lyer illusion, he gives this appearance no weight at all in his overall judgment of how the world should be.

[28] The italicized portion is important. The mere having of a second-order desire for the satisfaction of one's desire that p would not necessarily involve its being to one as if it ought to be that p because one desires that p.

This brings out two important consequences of interpreting direction of fit phenomenologically. First, if desire involves an appearance of a standard for world-states, it involves an appearance of a standard of action only in an unusual sense, namely, as a constituent of some such states. In the first example, wanting to keep my promise is wanting that my promise be kept. And this involves its being to me as if the world should be such that I keep my promise. It is important to note that this, though, is different from its being to me *as if I should keep my promise*. The latter appearance involves a standard *for action* (and, perhaps derivatively, a standard for desire), not a standard for what actions the world should contain. On our current picture, however, to an agent with a desire (apparent) standards for action only get into the picture via standards for world-states of which actions are constituents.

The second consequence is implicit in what we have just noted, since any standard for states of the world is, of necessity, agent-neutral. A standard according to which the world (intrinsically or non-derivatively) ought to be that p will not be sensitive to whether an act that would bring p about is done by the agent or by someone else. To the agent who desires that p, and to whom it is as if the world should be that p, it is, *so far* anyway, a matter of indifference whether p is brought about by her, by someone else, or by some non-agential cause. It will be to her as if the world should contain a bringing about of p *period*.[29] Of course, p might be something self-referential. An agent might desire that she tie her own shoes. On the current picture, this would lead by instrumental reasoning to a desire that what is necessary to bring about her tying her shoes take place. The point is that, as a logical matter, the means that figure in the object of the derived desire could, in principle, as easily include acts by someone else as by the agent herself *and* that, just insofar as the agent desired the *state* of her tying her shoes, she would be indifferent between whether these means were taken by her or by someone else, assuming that they were equally effective in producing this state.[30]

We have had two goals in reflecting on desire's direction of fit in this section. One has been to argue that, contrary to what formulations such as "Desire is a 'state with which the world must fit'" might suggest, it is actually quite puzzling how an agent's desires or will could give her practical reasons when we think about desire's direction of fit from the agent's point of view. To an agent with a desire that p, it will seem much more like the world should be that p than that the world should be as she desires, or that it should be that p because she desires it. A second goal, however, is to begin to debunk the view of practical reasons that the picture we have been considering suggests. If desire involves an appearance of a standard for a state of the world, then this standard can give us practical reasons only if we can credit this appearance. We give weight to our beliefs in considering what to believe because we take our beliefs to be formed with a view toward getting things right. We frequently take them, moreover,

---

[29] Unless, of course, she desires that p occur uncaused.

[30] Obviously, some means necessary for *this* state of affairs could not, as a logical matter, be taken by anyone except her.

to be formed in response to an engagement with the very states of the world to which they aim to respond. For something similar to be true of desire, we would have to take our desires to bear some similar relation to the normative standards for world-states of which desires seem to be appearances. Whatever practical reasons our desires would then give us would be owing to their more or less reliable responsiveness to independent facts about what states of the world ought to exist ("for their own sake," as Moore said).[31]

On reflection, however, such a picture is quite incredible. Even disregarding the problem of what processes might underlie epistemic access to such standards, the very idea that it could non-derivatively be the case that a state of affairs ought to exist, independently of any fact concerning what any person, actual or hypothetical, ought to desire, feel, or do, seems incoherent. If someone ought to believe, feel, or do something, then there is a valid norm that requires or recommends that action or attitude. For example, believers ought (must) not believe both of two contradictory propositions since there is a norm of consistency of belief requiring this. And agents ought (must) not adopt something as an end, believe that something else is a means necessary to it, but fail to intend (or worse, intend not) to take the means owing to a valid norm of instrumental practical reasoning. And similarly, in general, for any truth about what someone ought to believe, do, feel, care about, fear, esteem, and so on. Any sensible "ought" claim, it seems, must make implicit reference to some norm. But how could there be norms for states of affairs? By their very nature, norms can hold only where normative guidance is possible—only, that is, where it is possible that they be complied with or violated, followed or flouted. A state of affairs can't comply with or violate anything.[32]

Desire and Taking as a Reason

Alternatively, we might relate the phenomenology of desire, not to norms for states of the world, but more directly to normative reasons for action and attitudes.[33] To desire something, we might think, is to be disposed to take certain things *as* reasons for acting. To a person who wants to get out of a burning building, it is as if she has reason to flee. Her attention is "directed insistently," as Scanlon puts it, to the fact that she will burn to death if she remains inside, a fact that "presents" itself as a reason to get out.

On this picture, desire involves the appearance, not of a norm for a state of the world, but of a reason for acting. To someone with the desire to survive, the fact that

---

[31] Such a view would be an instance of "substantive realism," as Christine Korsgaard calls it. For Korsgaard's discussion, see Korsgaard 1996b: 35–7.

[32] Sometimes we say things like "It shouldn't happen that children go to bed hungry," even when there is nothing we can do that could prevent it. However, such talk can be understood in terms of norms for attitudes, if not for actions ("It is lamentable [undesirable, shameful, etc.] that children go to bed hungry").

[33] Something like this is suggested by Scanlon's discussion of desire in the "directed-attention sense" (Scanlon 1998: 39).

survival can be achieved only by jumping out of a window presents itself as a reason to jump. The idea here is not that the appearance of this reason is its seeming as if one's survival is a state that ought to exist for its own sake, giving anyone equally a reason to promote it. The necessity of jumping to survival can present itself as a reason for *one* to jump without its appearing that others have reason to help one survive. (This does not mean, of course, that it appears that they do not have such a reason.)

The idea that an agent's desire or will can give him reasons for acting is nevertheless equally puzzling on this view. To have a desire is to be disposed to take certain facts about the desire's *object* as reasons, not the fact that one has the desire. On this picture, desire is more like a mode of access to practical reasons—that through which practical reasons appear—than it is a reason for acting itself, or a ground on which practical reasons might depend. In this respect, the current alternative is structurally analogous to the position we considered previously. Whether desire involves appearances of standards for states of affairs or practical reasons directly, on either alternative, its role seems to be epistemic rather than that of a practical reason or of a ground of practical reasons.

One advantage the current picture has over that discussed previously is that it has no need of the Moorean notion of a state of affairs' oughting to exist for its own sake. Nonetheless, like the previous alternative, it analogizes the epistemological structure of practical reason to that of theoretical reason. If desire involves an appearance of practical reasons, as ordinary perceptual beliefs involve appearances of the world, then we should credit these practical reasons only if we should credit the appearances that desire provides us. Respectable empirical and philosophical theories support this on the theoretical side, since they warrant us in believing that beliefs involving world-appearances can be related to the world in some reliable way. Here we seem to have a metaphysically respectable conception of an independent reality to which our beliefs are responsible and to which our perceptual apparatus and other belief-forming mechanisms may become well tuned. It is far from obvious, however, that we have in the practical realm any comparably defensible picture of freestanding facts of practical reason to which desires (or practical experience of some other kind) respond and give us epistemic access.[34] All there is, one is inclined to say, are norms of practical reason, not an independent order of fact to which desire is in its nature responsible and from which norms for desire can be derived.[35]

Giving Practical Reasons, Will, Freedom, and Authority

The moral of our story so far has been twofold. First, so long as we think of practical reason on the model of theoretical reason, it will be puzzling how an agent's will or

---

[34] This is, of course, the problem that Gilbert Harman raised in Harman 1977: 3–10.
[35] I think Scanlon does not sufficiently appreciate this difficulty in Scanlon 1998: 55–72, and, in any case, that the considerations adduced in the next section provide a better account of how considerations of "the reasonable" can provide reasons for acting.

desires could give her reasons to act (and, as well, how they might give others reasons to help or even to allow her to act on them). Second, however, we have found grounds for skepticism about this analogy between theoretical and practical reason. In this section, I want to consider a specific disanalogy between theoretical and practical reason with an eye toward locating desire- or will-based practical reasons in the standing of free and rational agents to make claims on one another as free and rational.

Consider, first, how one person can give another person a reason for belief. If someone says that p, that will give you a reason to think that p only to the extent that it gives you evidence of p. The clearest case is where what the person says is evidence. You want to know whether to believe the party is to be this Saturday or next, for example, and someone says that it is unlikely to be next Saturday because everyone will be leaving for vacation next Friday. It is also possible for someone to give you a reason to believe that p just by asserting p. Even in this case, however, although what the person says isn't evidence, her saying it must be. If you have no reason to treat what someone says or her saying it as evidence of the truth of what she says, she can give you no reason to believe it.[36]

Consider now the practical case. In particular, consider cases where one person attempts to give another a reason for acting, not by expressing his belief (even his beliefs about practical reasons), but by expressing his desire or will. Here we recognize a variety of cases where one person (or collective body) can give others reasons that are not similarly parasitic on the relation between the addresser's desire or will and something independent to which the addressees take the desires to be appropriately responsive and from which they take the reasons ultimately to emanate. Unlike the theoretical case, in these instances the reason seems to depend entirely on the relationship of addresser to addressee, specifically, on the *authority* the addresser has to give the addressee a reason in this way.

Think about orders, for example. When a sergeant tells her platoon to fall in, her charges do not take it that the reason she gives them derives from the value of a state of affairs, their falling in, that she has revealed to them by her order. The reason depends, rather, on the nature of their relationship, on the sergeant's authority to demand that her platoon act in this way. Something similar holds for decrees, legislative acts, requests, demands, and claims more generally. When a legislature expresses its legislative will, it is understood to give citizens a reason to comply that derives not from the independent value of some state that is its will's object (citizens paying a tax, say), but

---

[36] It is consistent with this that in *telling* someone something, addressing him second-personally, the addresser may be able to give the addressee a reason for believing what the addresser says that that the addressee would not have had if the addresser's saying it were considered only third-personally, as a mere assertion. A relation of trust between addresser and addressee might explain why telling something to someone may give the addressee reasons for belief he would not have had but for this second-personal address (Hinchman 2005). Even if it is possible for one person to give another a distinctive "fiduciary" reason second-personally this reason is ultimately parasitic on evidence in the usual way. If the addressee has no reason to think that the addresser's beliefs have *some* reliable relation to the truth, nothing the addresser could tell the addressee could give him reason to believe anything.

from the authority such legislative bodies have with respect to citizens. (Of course, various conditions must be satisfied for this authority to exist in the first place, and neither a sergeant nor a legislature can require, or even request, that a person do just anything.) Similarly, if a subject makes a request of the king, or if one person simply asks another for the time of day, these too are thought to give their addressees reasons because of the standing the relevant individuals have to express their will to relevant others in these ways and thereby to give them, if not (in these cases) reasons for compliance, at least reasons to *consider* complying. Finally, if one person demands certain treatment from another as an equal with the same dignity as he, she attempts to give the other a reason by presuming on their equal standing as one person among others.

Call expressions of will that purport to be reason giving in this way *claims*. Claims have several important features that are worth remarking. First, by definition, claims purport to give those to whom they are addressed reasons for acting. Second, these reasons are agent-relative. They are addressed to the agent himself, purporting to be a reason for compliance that cannot be reduced to the value of any state, even the state of agents' complying with this and equally worthy claims. When, for example, the sergeant orders her platoon, the platoon members do not thereby acquire a reason to most effectively promote some valuable state of affairs, say, that of military discipline; they simply have a reason to fall in themselves. Third, because the reason purports to be independent of the value of any state, including any such value to the addressee, it purports to be unconditional on the addressees' desires. A claim therefore advances a reason that is putatively *categorical*, that is, a reason that is not hypothetical *either* in the sense of depending on the desire of the addressee for any state *or* in the sense of depending on the truth of any appearance to which the addressee is subject (any "hypothesis" the addressee accepts) *in* having any such desire. Fourth, claims are implicitly presented as valid or, at least, as *reasonable* in the sense of warranting the consideration of those to whom they are addressed. And fifth, in addressing claims, addressers implicitly regard addressees as having the requisite authority and capacity to consider, recognize, and act on the reasons they purport thereby to give them.

This last feature is of particular importance. It is at the heart of Fichte's thesis that agents can acquire a conception of themselves as free and rational only when they entertain a claim or "summons" (*Aufforderung*) that is addressed to them by another agent.[37] Claims purport to give agents reasons that are independent of the agents' desires, and to do so, moreover, not by inducing a desire for any state of affairs, but through the agent's recognition of the addresser's authority to make the claim. To address a claim is, therefore, implicitly to address someone as free and rational in this sense. To see oneself as the addressee of a claim, consequently, is to *see oneself being seen*

---

[37] Fichte 2000: 29–52. For further discussion see Darwall 2005 and 2006.

as free and rational, thereby gaining a second-personal perspective on oneself. One sees oneself, not as viewed "third-personally" in an "objectifying" way, but as summoned in a reciprocally recognizing rational interaction. In recognizing this view of oneself and responding, one implicitly identifies with and thereby recognizes the other by reflecting the other's view of oneself back to him or her. Even in hearing and seriously entertaining a claim, and gaining a second-personal perspective on that through reciprocal recognition with another, one gains an awareness of oneself as "self-active" (Fichte 2000: 32).[38] In the second-personal addressing and entertaining of claims, agents reciprocally recognize each other as free and rational.

To appreciate properly the point Fichte is making, we need to think of a pure case of claim making. Any actual case, of course, may involve a mixture of various "non-rational" elements like intimidation, coercion, manipulation, or seduction, or other rational elements such as trying to get the addressee to appreciate reasons in the neighborhood of the claim but distinct from it. A's foot, let us suppose, is squarely on B's gouty toe, causing B pain he wishes to be rid of. Suppose that B requests or demands that A remove his foot. B might do this in a variety of ways, however, that mix other elements with a pure claim. B might look threateningly at A, attempting to induce either fright or a rational calculation of costs and benefits. Or B might try to induce a sympathetic desire in A so that A will take B's pain as a reason to remove his foot regardless of any claim B might have to A's doing so. Or B might look at A with his best Charlie Chaplin grin, hoping to charm A and curry favor.[39] In a pure case, however, B addresses a claim not to be hurt to A that purports to give A a reason to remove his foot from B's toe that is independent of any reason A might appreciate through sympathy or a desire for any state (say, the relief of B's pain), and, therefore, that is independent of the value of any state. Moreover, B attempts to influence A rationally rather than by such non-rational influences as intimidation, charm, and fear.

Theological voluntarists, like Pufendorf, argue that moral reasons are created in this fashion by divine command. In commanding us not to harm each other, for example, God addresses us as free and rational agents and thereby gives us a reason not to harm that cannot be reduced to any good that complying with this command can achieve. Pufendorf believed, of course, that the validity of these reasons depends on an assumption of God's superior authority over us.[40] But he also thought that moral reasons being created in this way depends on the possibility of *internal* acceptance of this authority by those God addresses so that ultimately they can hold themselves accountable second-personally by making the same demands of themselves that God makes of

---

[38] Christine Korsgaard makes a similar point in Korsgaard 1996b: 139–43.

[39] Compare here Adam Smith's contrast between the distinctively human capacity for independent, second-personal "exchange" as opposed to the attempts of animals to gain the good will "by every servile and fawning attention" (Smith 1976: I, 26).

[40] Pufendorf 1934: I.i.§§2–6, pp. 4–7; I.vi.§4, p. 89. I discuss this aspect of Pufendorf's views in Darwall 2003.

them.[41] The problem that Pufendorf faced, however, was that although he believed that God's commands can create reasons for any free and rational agent to whom they are addressed *and* that His commands can create these reasons only through free and rational agents' recognition of God's superior authority, he had no good argument for why a free and rational agent would necessarily recognize this authority. He took this relationship for granted and assumed that any other free and rational being would do so as well.[42]

What authority, however, is a free and rational agent bound to recognize? Only, it would seem, whatever authority one is committed to in making and considering claims in the first place. To make or entertain claims at all is to be in a second-personal relation in which each reciprocally recognizes the other as free and rational.[43] Even to consider seriously a claim is to reflect back to the addresser a recognition of the addresser's authority to submit claims for consideration (which is itself a kind of claim). And to make a claim is to put it forward as something it would be reasonable for the addressee to consider and accept. It seems implicit in the very idea of one free and rational will making a claim on another (as free and rational) that the former must take the latter to be capable of accepting this claim and being guided by it, thereby being accountable to the other by holding himself accountable. Further, the addresser of the claim must apparently also take the addressee to share (or to be capable of sharing) this understanding. The possibility of such a shared understanding seems a presupposition of any such claim.

---

[41] This claim is implicit in Pufendorf's distinction between coercion and being under an obligation. Many things can "influence the will to turn to one side" or the other, but other evils "bear down the will as by some natural weight, and on their removal [the will] returns of itself to its former indifference." Obligation, however, "affects the will morally," so that it "is forced of itself to weigh its own actions, and to judge itself worthy of some censure, unless it conforms to a prescribed rule." In effect, Pufendorf here invokes a notion of *internal* blame or censure, that is, accepting blame as justified (blaming oneself in authorizing the view of the other who blames one (Pufendorf 1934: I.vi.§5, p. 91)).

[42] This is not quite right since Pufendorf argues, like Locke, that God's authority can be grounded in a debt of gratitude owed to God for His creation (Darwall 2006: 110–11).

[43] There may seem to be many obvious counterexamples to this claim. Most vividly, what about orders to children or to slaves? It is important to distinguish, again, the pure claim from any attempt simply to cause a certain action or response. Claims are issued with the aim of getting a certain response *in virtue of a recognition that the validity of the claim* creates a reason so to respond. Thus, a pure order is issued to gain a response by virtue of a recognition that the validity of the order (one's authority to issue such an order) gives a reason. By their very nature, then, claims are issued to beings who are implicitly regarded as competent to recognize their valid, reason-giving character and to freely act on them. Of course, one can do this even if one doesn't *believe* that the addressee is thus competent. The point is that one regards or treats him as though he were. And frequently, of course, for example, with children, this is done to insinuate proleptically the very recognition on the addressee's part that is necessary for the claim to "come off."

Still, the suggestion that participants in any second-personal claim-making implicitly regard *each other* as (equally) free and rational may seem implausible. What, again, about masters and slaves? Here we should recall Hegel on "lordship and bondage." Hegel claims that there is a contradiction in the master's second-personal address since he asserts a superiority that is belied by the recognition he seeks from the slave (Hegel 1977: 111–19). Any pure order presupposes a free recognition of the validity of the order. If, of course, the master can expect the slave will freely respect the authority his order presupposes, then no contradiction need be involved. However, see the next paragraph.

What claims might one free and rational will make on another and reasonably expect reciprocation? The very logic of the question suggests a line of response that is developed in different ways in Kant and post-Kantian German idealism, especially in Fichte and Hegel (and before that, I would argue in Adam Smith), and, in our own time, in, among others, Rawls and Scanlon. If we take no particular moral relationship for granted and simply ask what demands one free and rational will might make on another and reasonably expect reciprocation, a natural answer would seem to be: whatever demands *any* free and rational being would make on any other, since it will be reasonable to make the demand only if it would be reasonable to accept it. And it will be reasonable to accept it only if one would reasonably make it also oneself.

Our ultimate goal in considering claim-based reasons and their relation to reciprocally recognizing second-personal reason-giving is to find there some basis for the idea that an agent's will can be a source of reasons, both for herself and for others. To that end, consider the parable of A and B. A and B both contemplate the same juicy apple with the same desire. A desires that he have the apple and forms the end of getting it for himself. He sees the state of his having the apple as something to be brought about and sees the juiciness of the apple as a reason for him to get it. For her part, B desires that she have the apple and adopts the end of getting it for herself. She sees the state of her having the apple as something to be brought about and sees its juiciness as a reason for her to get it. Suppose that A and B each become aware of the other and the other's desire. To simplify, suppose that neither is moved to sympathy and that their desires remain as before.

At this point, neither A nor B treats his or her desire for the apple as a source of reasons or value. Their desires are, from their respective practical perspectives, "backgrounded." Each sees his or her having the apple as a state that should be brought about. Similarly, each sees the other's having the apple as having no value, as not being a state to be brought about. From the practical perspective of each, the other's agency is simply a potential instrument or obstacle to a valuable state. Indeed, so far anyway, the same is true of A and B's view of themselves. From the perspective of their respective desires for these states, *their own* rational activity (and will) figures practically only to the extent of its usefulness in bringing about this valuable state.

Suppose, however, that A turns to B and attempts to give B a reason to let him, A, have the apple. We might imagine A to begin by expressing his desire, saying that his (A's) having the apple is a state of affairs that should be brought about, while B's having the apple is not. Of course, this cannot succeed, except by accident, since from B's perspective, there is nothing to be said for A's having the apple and everything to be said for B's. B has no reason to trust A's judgment that A should have the apple since, from B's perspective A's judgment is illusory, a mere expression of A's desire. Any such attempt of A's to give B a reason would not differ structurally from theoretical reason giving. It could succeed only to the extent that B has reason to think there exists some reliable relation between A's judgment and what it purports to be of. It would not yet be an instance of claim making.

At the same time, however, A's expression of his desire might give B pause in the credit she accords her own desires' appearances as evidence of reasons. From a first-person perspective, corrected only by further appearances that come with better informed desires and unchallenged by another's will, B could comfortably credit the epistemological access she apparently got to reasons through her own desires. Now, though, here is A, and his desires appear to him to give him access to reasons no less than B's do for her. Moreover, and this is the critical point, B can provide no explanation of why her desires' appearances (or A's, for that matter), should be correct. Not only does she lack an account of the sort she could give of why she credits her experiential beliefs—namely, that she has reason to take her having them to be best explained by the facts her experiences make apparent to her. In addition, seeing herself as a free and rational agent addressed by another puts her into a position to see why there couldn't be such an account. She sees herself as free to accept a source of categorical reasons that is utterly independent of anything of which desires could be an appearance.

Suppose now that A attempts to make a claim on B. "I would have the apple," A says. "So you, B, should let me have it." For the first time, B feels the force of A's will as an attempted claim, *as purporting to be reason giving for her*. And, for the first time, in response, she feels the force of *her* will as no less a reasonable basis for such a claim. "I, too, would have the apple," she might say, and say something further that could bear the following philosophical translation: "Neither of us can assume any antecedent authority over the other, so it would be unreasonable for you to expect me to just let you have the apple. Neither can I reasonably make such a claim of you." Suppose she continues, making use of philosophical materials to which we recently alluded: "We are already implicitly reciprocally recognizing each other's authority to propose and consider claims, by addressing these claims and considerations to each other as free and rational." "So," she concludes, quoting now a famous philosopher, "we are already implicitly recognizing each other as 'self-originating sources of valid claims'."[44] A and B might then agree, on that basis, that each could make a reasonable claim, say, to half of the apple, and divide the apple between them, with one cutting and the other choosing.

When an agent acts solely on desires from his own practical perspective, he takes the reasons his desires present him with for granted, that is, as reasons grounded, not in his desires, but in the desirable features of their objects, as he views them under his desires' influence. It is only when an agent is addressed in a way that makes him aware, simultaneously, of a potential source of reasons in the will of another rational and free agent *and* in his own rational will, that he becomes aware of reasons anchored in the rational authority of *a free rational agent*, himself or some other. What enables the agent to authorize the reasons generated within his own practical standpoint—to say

---

[44] Rawls 1980: 543.

that what he cares about gives him reasons because, on reflection, *he* cares about it—simultaneously de-centers his practical view. It makes him aware that he is one person, occupying one practical standpoint, among others and commits him to reasons that transcend his practical perspective and commits him, as well, to his freedom to act on them.

It follows that the reason why an agent's practical perspective—her desires, values, concerns, and so on—can give her reasons beyond those to which her perspective responds—those that ground the desirability, value, and worthiness of what she desires, values, and cares about—is because she is one person among others who is no less entitled to respect than anyone else. It is a familiar thought that the fact that someone else cares about or wants something is a reason to let them have it, or at least not to interfere with their getting it, that can be to some extent independent of whether they have reason to care about or want it (Jaworska 2007). To refuse to give weight to others' desires and cares when they have little or no reason for them is a form of disrespect for them as persons. But if others' desires can make legitimate claims on us in this way, so also can our own. Just as the fact that one wants something can weigh appropriately in others' deliberations so also can it weigh appropriately in one's own.

A vivid way of seeing this is to imagine someone who manifests a kind of self-effacing servility (Hill 1973). Though she defers to others' wishes, she gives short shrift to her own concerns and desires. We can easily imagine saying to such a person that she is no less entitled to her respect than others are, and that she could just as appropriately take the fact that *she* wants to do something as a reason also.

The irony of the resulting position will not, perhaps, have been lost on the reader. According to the old orthodoxy, the normative practical force of an agent's own desires and will is straightforward and by default, whereas whatever normativity morality and respect for persons might have is problematic and to be argued for from that starting point. According to the line of thought I have sketched here, however, this is almost the reverse of the truth. The reason-giving power of an agent's own will is grounded in the equal authority of free and rational persons.[45]

[45] An earlier draft of this paper was presented at a conference on practical reason at the University of Rome (La Sapienza). I am indebted to members of the audience, especially to Jonathan Dancy, Carla Bagnoli, Allan Gibbard, and Tito Magri. I also owe much to participants in the Moral Epistemology conference, organized by the Center for Philosophy and Social Philosophy. Finally, I am indebted to Nishiten Shah for very helpful discussion.

7

The Value of Autonomy and Autonomy of the Will

It is a commonplace that "autonomy" has several different senses in contemporary moral and political discussion. The term's original meaning was political: a right of states to determine their own affairs. It was not until the nineteenth century that "autonomy" came (in English) to refer also to the conduct of individuals, and even then there were, as now, different meanings.[1] Odd as it may seem from our perspective, one that was in play from the beginning was Kant's notion of "autonomy of the will"[2]—as Kant defined it, "the property of the will by which it is a law to itself independently of any property of the objects of volition" (4:440). That's a mouthful, to say the least. And interpreting what Kant meant, or should have meant, by it is a complex exegetical and philosophical task. On any reasonable interpretation, however, it can be hard to see how Kantian autonomy of the will is related to any kind of autonomy that is at issue in current debate (or, for that matter, autonomy's original political sense). What can the value of someone's making her own choices and leading her own life, or her right to do so, have to do with autonomy of the will as Kant understood it?

In what follows, I shall argue that there is, indeed, a deep connection between these. More specifically, I shall maintain that the idea of a right or *claim* to autonomy actually presupposes autonomy of the will, at least, that it does when the latter is given the interpretation I shall propose. (I shall call the former idea: *autonomy as claim or demand*.)[3]

---

[1] The *Oxford English Dictionary* lists two relevant earliest uses: "b. Liberty to follow one's will, personal freedom (1803 W. TAYLOR in *Ann. Rev.* I. 384 The customers of a banker can desert to a rival at will, and thus retain an autonomy of conduct); c. *Metaph.* Freedom (of the will); the Kantian doctrine of the Will giving itself its own law, apart from any object willed; opposed to *heteronomy* (1817 COLERIDGE *Biog. Lit.* 70 Kant . . . was permitted to assume a higher ground (the autonomy of the will) as a postulate deducible from the unconditional command . . . of the conscience; a1871 GROTE *Eth. Fragm.* ii. (1876) 45 Kant . . . means by Autonomy, that there are in this case no considerations of pleasure or pain influencing the will)." *OED Online*.

[2] To which Coleridge referred in his early use of "autonomy" in *Biographia Literaria* (see note 1).

[3] Here I draw on Joel Feinberg's thesis that the "moral significance" of rights depends on the possibility of *claiming* them, or, as I shall put it, the *second-personal authority* to address claims and demands. "Having rights, of course, makes claiming possible; but it is claiming that gives rights their special moral significance. This feature of rights is connected in a way with the customary rhetoric about what it is to be a human being. Having rights enables us to 'stand up like men,' to look others in the eye, and to feel in some fundamental way the equal of anyone" (Feinberg 1980: 151).

To make a claim to anything, hence to autonomy, is to take up a *second-person standpoint*. It is to *address* a claim or demand *to* someone *as* a free and rational agent. It is a presupposition of this standpoint, I shall argue, that addresser and addressee alike can accept and act on reasons that are grounded, not in the value of anything that might be an object of their desire or volition (that is, neither in any outcome nor in any act considered in itself), but in an *authority* each has as a free and rational will. Autonomy *as demand* makes sense only in second-personal terms, and the second-person standpoint presupposes autonomy of the will as I propose to interpret it. It assumes a capacity persons have to make demands that are grounded in the authority of free and rational wills as such, and thus in no value outside the will. Because that is so, laying claim to our autonomy commits us to assuming autonomy of the will.

Before we begin, it will be useful to distinguish briefly other senses of "autonomy" that are in use in contemporary ethical theory. All are kinds of self-rule, an agent's determining her own conduct for herself. Heteronomy, by contrast, is interference with self-determination, either by others (more or less successfully) substituting their will for the agent's, making her choices for her, or by internal psychic barriers interfering so that she does not, or perhaps cannot, properly decide for herself. Here we might distinguish the following:

Personal autonomy	The agent's determining his conduct by his own most highly cherished values.
Moral autonomy	The agent's choosing in accord with his own moral convictions or principles.[4]
Rational autonomy	The agent's acting on what he believes to be the weightiest reasons.
Agential autonomy	The agent's behavior being a genuine action and so attributable to him as an agent.

In each of these cases, moreover, we can distinguish between an agent's having the *capacity* to determine his conduct in any of these ways and his successfully *exercising* this capacity.

Autonomy as Benefit and Autonomy as Demand

In this section and the next, I shall explore how *autonomy as claim or demand* contrasts with other ways in which autonomy (of various kinds) may be valued, specifically, as a *benefit* or part of well-being, as a *personal value*, or as a *moral value* of the sort that, say,

---

[4] Autonomy of the will is also a kind of moral autonomy, according to Kant, since he believes that it is both necessary and sufficient for the moral law. I argue that this Kantian thesis can be defended when autonomy of the will is given the interpretation I advance here (*second-personal competence*) in Darwall 2006.

Kant, Butler, or Richard Price upheld as a paradigm of morally good action—an agent's determining her conduct by her own conscientious judgments.

Consider, for example, how personal autonomy can enter as a value within a utilitarian moral theory. For a *Benthamite* utilitarian, autonomy of any sort has only instrumental value. If the only intrinsically valuable outcome is well-being or happiness and happiness consists in pleasant feeling, then none of the kinds of autonomy just mentioned (personal, moral, or rational), nor the social recognition of a claim or right to autonomy, will have any intrinsic value. Of course, any or all of these may have significant instrumental value. As Mill argues in *On Liberty*, individuals may be the best judges of what will bring them pleasure; so a right to autonomy and exercising the capacity for personal autonomy may both bring substantial instrumental hedonic benefits. It is consistent also with a Benthamite approach that exercising autonomy is itself enjoyable and so a direct source of pleasurable feeling. Still, in any of these cases, the value consists in the benefit and the benefit, in pleasant feeling, to which autonomy in any of its guises is no more than instrumental. Neither the value nor the benefit depends upon the fact that the pleasant feeling results from autonomy in any way.

Alternatively, a utilitarian can take the position that Mill seems to take, that personal autonomy is intrinsically beneficial to a person, that it is a constituent or "ingredient" of well-being or happiness.[5] This makes autonomy intrinsic to that which is intrinsically morally desirable, happiness or welfare, but not yet intrinsically morally worth promoting in itself (that is, regardless of whether it is a constituent of happiness). What makes an outcome intrinsically worth promoting from the moral point of view is still happiness or well-being; it is just that Mill believes that autonomy is an intrinsic part of that.

Since there is an obvious sense in which personal autonomy gives a kind of priority to the agent's preferences, something like Mill's idea may lie behind some preference-based forms of utilitarianism. However, as important as autonomy is to human happiness and welfare, it nevertheless seems clear that what someone wants, or even what she would want were she autonomous, whether personally, rationally, or morally, can diverge from what would actually make her happy or benefit *her*. Elsewhere I have argued that there is an important difference between what someone *takes an interest in* and prefers, even were she personally or rationally autonomous, on the one hand, and what is *in someone's interest*, in the sense of what promotes her welfare or benefits *her*, on the other (unless, of course, these terms are defined to guarantee a coincidence) (Darwall 2002). People can care, indeed care rationally and autonomously, about a wide range of things, including the future of the planet long after they are dead, where it is hard to see how the realization of what they care about would benefit them, at least, benefit them to the degree of their concern (or rational concern).

---

[5] And also, Mill believes, a distinctive kind of pleasure. I have in mind here Mill's doctrine of *quality* of pleasure and his remarks about the "sense of dignity" in Chapters II and IV of *Utilitarianism* (see esp., paragraph 6 of Chapter II of Mill 1998) and about "the interests of man as a progressive being" in Chapter I (paragraph 11) of *On Liberty* (Mill 1989).

What is for someone's well-being or good, I have argued, is not necessarily what the person herself wants, whether actually or rationally, but what it would be rational for someone (including she herself) to want for her *for her sake*, that is, out of sympathetic concern *for her* (Darwall 2002). Here I will simply assume that, even if autonomy is intrinsic to the welfare and happiness of mature human beings, preference-based accounts are implausible as theories of happiness or well-being.

If, however, it is implausible to think that happiness or welfare varies with preference, it is worth asking why the idea that moral and political choice should respond to people's preferences nonetheless has such an appeal (and why, also, preference-based versions of utilitarianism are so common). I believe that this idea does appeal, but that what makes it appealing is not the notion of autonomy as benefit, but rather that of autonomy *as claim or demand*. I conjecture that what lay behind the increasing shift from hedonistic to preference-based forms utilitarianism during the last century and that continues today (for example, within the theory of social choice or in cost/benefit analyses of public policy) has been less a change in view about what really makes people happy or benefits them, or positivist scruples about evidence of our inner lives, than the idea that people have a claim to decide for themselves or to exercise a kind of "vote" in matters that concern them. If so, it would be truer to this idea to speak in terms, not of autonomy's role in welfare, but of a justified claim or demand for autonomy. What is in question seems less what we should want for people insofar as we *care* for them (benevolently, with sympathetic concern),[6] than how to *respect* one another's wishes and legitimate claims to autonomy.

To see the difference, consider the relations between parents and children. Parents appropriately relate to their children with love and sympathetic concern throughout their lives, but their children come to have a standing to make claims on them of a very different kind as they mature. For example, parents may legitimately give relatively little, or perhaps no, *intrinsic* weight to a very young child's protest against eating a healthful food, although they should, of course, take account of its bearing on the child's welfare, for example, the likelihood that eating it will be unpleasant, the long-term effects of insisting that she eat it, and so on. At this stage, parents may properly be guided by the child's welfare alone.[7] When, however, their daughter returns to her parents' home in middle age, to take an extreme case, the situation is obviously much changed. For parents not to take a middle-aged daughter's preferences and will as having intrinsic weight, indeed, as governing in such a case would clearly be disrespectful: paternalism in the pejorative sense.[8] Even to urge her to eat "her broccoli" at this point would be objectionable.

---

[6] See Chapter 3 of Darwall 2002.

[7] Except, of course, to the extent that giving second-personal standing proleptically to children who don't yet have it can help them to acquire it.

[8] For a very insightful account of paternalism that is especially illuminating in this connection, see Shiffrin 2000.

The point is not just that when we reach maturity autonomy plays a greater role in well-being. That is, of course, true. Even out of concern for their daughter and her welfare alone, her parents should want to give her space to make her own decisions. Suppose, however, that they take all this into account and come to the conclusion that however important autonomy is to her well-being, so also is diet, and that since she would be better off in the long run if she ate her green vegetables, they should press them on her. Whether they would be mistaken or not, their practical reasoning would already seem to involve one thought too many. Paternalism is objectionable not just because those who seek to benefit us against our wishes are likely to be wrong about what really benefits us. Paternalism is not just misdirected care. It is, rather, a failure of respect—a failure to recognize the authority persons have to demand that they be allowed to make their own choices, at least within certain limits.

Although autonomy as demand contrasts with autonomy as benefit, it can nonetheless be considered a value in the broad sense in which the dignity of persons is sometimes called a kind of value. In *SPS*, I argue that rights such as the right to autonomy can be grounded in a shared basic second-personal authority—the authority all persons have to make claims of one another and hold one another accountable (Darwall 2006). In my view, this is what the dignity of persons is, or, at least, it is its second-personal aspect. Seana Shiffrin points out that the most problematic feature of paternalism is not that it aims to restrict freedom in the person's own interest, but that it seeks to substitute a would-be trustee's judgment or practical reason for the other's and so fails to value and respect the other as an equal person or rational agent (Shiffrin 2000).

Other Dimensions of the Value of Autonomy

In the next section, I shall begin my argument that any claim to autonomy must presuppose autonomy of the will. In this section, I canvass further differences between the kind of value or dignity that Kantians believe persons have as ends in themselves, which includes or entails the authority to demand respect for their autonomy, and other kinds of value with which autonomy, in its various guises, may be involved.

We have already seen how autonomy as demand differs from autonomy as benefit. It differs also from the idea that autonomy is a constituent of intrinsically valuable *outcomes*, as this idea might enter into a consequentialist moral theory that is neither utilitarian nor welfarist. Here the thought would be that realizing autonomy of some kind is a good outcome in itself, regardless of its relation to welfare. A crucial difference between this notion and autonomy as demand is that the former involves *agent-neutral* reasons for anyone to promote the relevant outcomes whereas the latter involves *agent-relative* reasons flowing from "deontological constraints" that are placed on us by anyone's right to autonomy.[9]

To take a kind of case that is frequently used to make this distinction, suppose that you are in a position in which the shocking spectacle of your interfering with A's autonomy would lead B to forgo interfering with C's autonomy in an exactly similar way. So far as the agent-neutral intrinsic value of the occurrence of autonomy, or disvalue of interference, goes, there would be no reason, on balance, for you to respect rather than to disrespect, and so interfere with, A's autonomy yourself. Whether you interfere or not there would still be exactly one disvaluable interference and one valuable instance of autonomy. A warranted demand for autonomy, by contrast, entails a reason for an agent not to interfere with, that is, not to violate, others' autonomy *himself*. It would therefore give you a reason not to interfere with A's autonomy yourself that is not simply balanced by the fact that this would lead to an exactly similar interference by someone else. Authoritative claims or demands entail deontological constraints that can be stated only in an agent-centered or agent-relative way: "Do not do X if X would involve you (the agent) interfering with someone's autonomy." In this way, they contrast with the agent-neutral: "Do not do X if X would bring about a greater balance of disvaluable interferences with autonomy."[10,11]

Yet another kind of value that autonomy can have is *personal value*, that is, value *to* someone of a kind (sometimes called "agent-relative value") that can diverge from what benefits him or is part of his well-being. (This was implicit above, when we noted that preference satisfaction and welfare can come apart.) We devote ourselves to all sorts of aims and projects that matter and have value *to us*. To be sure, the success of our projects bears substantially on our well-being. But personal value and well-being are nonetheless distinct concepts. Many environmentalists, for example, act tirelessly to produce hoped-for effects that may not occur until long after their deaths. And even if they can be benefited after their death, it is hard to believe that the benefit can equal the value these future hoped-for consequences had *to them* while they were alive.

More important than autonomy's personal value is its significance for the very concept of personal value. The reason we have this category at all is to signal that the

[9] I mean agent-neutral in a "positional" sense, that is, that the reason does not derive, most fundamentally, from a normative fact concerning the *agent's* position in relation to others. A reason for acting is agent-relative rather than agent-neutral if it cannot be formulated without essential reference to the agent, as such: e.g., that it would be in his (the agent's) interest, that it would relieve his pain, that it would relieve someone else's (someone other than the agent's) pain, that it would relieve pain he caused, that it would keep his promise, etc. The following would thus be agent-neutral reasons: that it would relieve pain, that it would promote relief of pain by someone who caused pain, etc. On the distinction between agent-relative (or agent-centered) and agent-neutral reasons, principles, values, etc., see Scheffler 1982; Parfit 1984; Nagel 1986; and McNaughton and Rawling 1995.

[10] These can both be read as *pro tanto* injunctions.

[11] Note that "agent-relative" in this positional sense can differ from other senses of "agent-relative," according to which a principle, norm, or value is agent-relative if it depends on the agent's own values or preferences, or on the intensity of these. Throughout this essay, I mean to be referring to agent-relativity in the former, positional senses. I am grateful to John Deigh for pressing me to clarify this point.

fact that someone values, wants, cares about, or is devoted to something can be a source of reasons that add weight to whatever reasons there might be for him to value it—that is, to the object's value independently of his valuing it, whether in terms of well-being or values of other kinds. To be sure, in being devoted to my children, I naturally take them and their welfare to have a value that is independent of their value to me.[12] This is an agent-neutral value that entails an agent-neutral reason for anyone to promote my children's welfare, myself included. In addition, there is the (agent-relative) reason I have to promote my children's welfare that derives from my parental obligation to provide form my children. On top of both of these, however, it seems clear that I have additional reasons to promote my children's welfare, adding further weight, that come from the *personal* value my children have for me, my devotion to them, and my children's role in central aims and projects that give meaning to my life. These latter reasons are agent-relative.[13]

Although other people have the same agent-neutral reason, deriving from the agent-neutral value of my children's welfare, to promote their welfare that I do, I have agent-relative reasons to do so that derive from my agent-relative obligations *and* from my children's personal value to me. And this affects the reasons that other people have as well. Others plainly don't have the same agent-relative reasons to promote my children's welfare coming from my children's value to me. But others do have, in addition to any agent-neutral reasons bearing on the situation that come from the agent-neutral value of my children's welfare, agent-relative reasons *not to interfere* with my acting for my children's sake because of my children's personal value to me and perhaps even to help me.[14] What makes these latter reasons agent-relative, again, is that they can be stated only in an agent-centered or agent-relative way: "Don't interfere with others' pursuit of personal value (and in this way with their autonomy)."[15]

Since our normal way of valuing things involves seeing them as valuable in themselves, that is, as having features that warrant our valuing them (irrespectively of whether we do in fact value them), there is a puzzle about how the fact that something has personal value (that one actually values it) can acquire independent weight as a reason. I have argued elsewhere that the reason it does derives from the equal dignity of persons (and, I here add, from the authority we have as persons to demand respect for our autonomy).[16] This is perhaps clearest when we are considering our conduct toward others. In the case of the broccoli-pushing parents we considered earlier, it seems clear

---

[12] On this point, see Darwall 2002: 69–72.

[13] In the same positional sense noted above in notes 9 and 11.

[14] Thanks to John Deigh for asking me to clarify these points.

[15] See notes 9 and 11 above.

[16] I defend this claim in Darwall 2001. The claim is too crude as it stands, since we certainly think we owe respect, including of their wishes, to beings that lack the full capacities necessary for autonomy of the will (or what I shall call "second-personal competence" later in this paper), including humans with mental disabilities, children, and other animals. Christie Hartley has argued that the claims of the disabled can be accounted for within a broadly contractualist moral theory that is congenial to the present framework in Hartley 2009. I am grateful to her for discussion on these points and to Martha Nussbaum for pushing me to clarify them.

that their daughter's values, preferences, and wishes give her parents reasons that are additional to (and partly independent of) any reasons that might exist for their daughter to want to avoid or to eat broccoli. For them to fail to heed these reasons grounded in her preferences and personal values just *is* for them to fail to respect her autonomy and her dignity as an equal person. Moreover, we can fail to respect ourselves in these ways no less than we can others. Giving little weight to one's own wishes and values, by being inappropriately deferential to those of others, can be no less a failure to respect oneself.[17]

If this is right, autonomy's role in the equal dignity of persons, that is, as claim or demand, is central to the significance of personal value. It partly reflects this fact, I believe, that *personal autonomy* (the agent's determining herself by her own values) is a kind of autonomy frequently under discussion in contemporary moral philosophy. Of course, someone might identify autonomy of this kind with *rational autonomy*, acting on what one believes to be the weightiest reasons. But I doubt that those who champion personal autonomy have anything this formal in mind. For personal autonomy to be linked in the ways it frequently is to self-actualization, identity, and the expression of oneself *as an individual*, it must be understood in relation to personal values, that is, to valuings that can be a source of reasons additional to any reasons that warrant them. It follows, I believe, that if we give weight to personal value, then autonomy must itself have personal value for us also *and* that we must credit autonomy as demand.

Finally, we can distinguish autonomy as claim or demand from any role that *moral autonomy* might play in an ideal of moral character or morally good (or morally right) action. For example, it is important to the accounts of moral virtue we find in Butler, Price, and Kant that there is a distinctive moral goodness that can be achieved only by a morally autonomous agent, one who self-reflectively governs herself *as* a moral agent by her own moral convictions. This is an important element of their views, which distinguishes them, not just from virtue ethics like Aristotle's, but also from other more explicitly moral virtue ethics, like Francis Hutcheson's (and to some extent, Hume's), which see moral goodness as residing primarily in motivations, like benevolence, whose content is not, however, explicitly moral.[18] I cannot pursue the point here, but I believe there to be deep affinities between the idea that morally good character involves moral autonomy and the thought that autonomy as claim or demand is inherent in the dignity of persons. These are, however, different ideas. Although Butler, Kant, and Price can all be interpreted as having versions of both, the two ideas can clearly diverge.

---

[17] Think, for example, of the deferential wife in Hill 1973.
[18] For discussion of Hume and Hutcheson, see Darwall 1995.

Autonomy as Demand and the Second-Person Standpoint

In this section, I want to bring out the way in which authority as demand involves the addressing of a distinctive kind of reason for acting from a second-person standpoint. To see the contrast between *second-personal reasons* and reasons for acting of other kinds, consider two different ways a middle-aged daughter might try to convince her parents to stop urging her to eat broccoli. One would be to persuade them that that would best promote her welfare. In caring for their daughter, her parents want her well-being. If they could be convinced that it would actually be better for her in welfare terms to be free to make her own dietary choices, then they would see themselves as having a reason to bring that about. This reason, we should note again, would present itself as agent-neutral.[19] From the perspective of their benevolent concern for her, their daughter's welfare, including her autonomy in a case like this, would seem to them to have a value that creates a reason for any agent who can to bring it about.[20]

Alternatively, the daughter might lay a claim to her autonomy. She might say something that expresses or implies a demand that they back off and let her make her choices for herself. She might demand this as the person whose autonomy they would otherwise violate, or as a representative person or member of the moral community, whose members understand themselves as demanding that people not interfere with one another's autonomy,[21] or as both. In either case, she would be presupposing an authority to make the demand and, consequently, that her parents have reason to comply with it, indeed, that they are *answerable* for doing so. In addressing this claim, moreover, the reason she would be giving them would not be agent-neutral, like one that comes simply from her well-being itself. Rather, she would be giving them an agent-relative reason grounded in her authority to demand respect for herself as a person and, hence, for her claim to autonomy.[22] The reason would be for them to respect her autonomy themselves, not for them to bring about an agent-neutrally valuable respecting of autonomy as individuals who are especially well situated to do so.

But neither would she just be pointing to an agent-relative constraint. In claiming or demanding her autonomy second-personally, she would be presupposing the authority to claim or demand it, including the authority to hold her parents accountable (if only, to complain) if they fail to comply. Again, she might make this claim on her own

---

[19]   Again, in a "positional" sense. That Sarah, let us say, would be better off, will seem to them to be a reason having *some* force, at any rate, for anyone. In this way, it would differ from the fact that Sarah is their daughter, etc.

[20]   "A" or "some" reason. Such a reason might, of course, be overridden.

[21]   As Strawson points out, the making of this second demand (as a member of the moral community) might consist simply in a disposition to reactive attitudes like indignation or blame that implicitly address demands: "the making of the demand *is* the proneness to such attitudes" (Strawson 1968: 92–3).

[22]   In the same positional sense. There is a difference between the agent-neutral, "Bring it about that the autonomy of people is respected," and the agent-relative "Respect the autonomy (of others)."

behalf, or simply as a member of the moral community with the standing to hold one another accountable for complying with moral demands, or both.[23] Whichever, the reason she would thereby address would be second personal in the sense that it presupposes an authority for second-personal address.

Unlike *non*-second-personal reasons, such as those deriving directly from someone's welfare, a second-personal reason depends for its very existence upon an authority to *address* the reason second-personally and on the reason's conceptual connection to (second-personal) practices of responsibility or accountability, that is, to *holding* people responsible. Reasons of agent-neutral value or well-being exist whether or not anyone can address them second-personally.[24] Even if it were impossible to claim or hold anyone to account for promoting well-being (and autonomy insofar as it is a part of that), there would still be a reason for people to promote it. Moreover, it is possible for one person to give another such a non-second-personal reason, as in advice, without making any direct claim on his conduct and so, in that sense, without addressing him directly as an agent. The claim would rather be on him as a cognizer of, and on his beliefs about, reasons for acting.[25] Although they pertain to conduct, any claims addressed in advice are, in a broad sense, epistemic.

But this is not true with reasons that derive from warranted claims and demands on our wills or conduct. Whatever reasons stand behind or justify her authority, the fact that their daughter *has* the authority to demand that her parents not interfere with her choices in this kind of case, or that others can make this demand and hold the parents responsible as members of the moral community, is an additional reason that simply would not exist but for the possibility of addressing the reason person-to-person. Acknowledging such a reason, moreover, is acknowledging someone's standing to address it. If consequently, her parents acknowledge that their daughter has a warranted claim to autonomy, they implicitly acknowledge her authority to address this claim to them (second-personally) and to hold them to account.

Second-personal reasons are invariably tied to *respect* (in the sense of recognition or acknowledgment)[26] of a distinctive kind of *practical authority*: the authority to make a demand or claim. Making a claim or putting forward a demand as valid always presupposes the authority to make it and that the duly authorized claim creates a distinctive reason for compliance (a second-personal reason). The relevant authority consists in the standing *to* claim or demand, which creates a reason of this distinctive

---

[23] In Darwall 2006, I argue that moral obligation is conceptually related to moral responsibility (accountability), which must itself be understood in terms of members of the moral community's authority to address moral demands to one another and hold one another responsible.

[24] So also do reasons grounded in agent-relative norms that are not, unlike those of moral obligation, tied to second-personal responsibility (for example, dictates of prudence).

[25] Compare: "I'm not tell you to do anything; I'm simply giving advice." This is Hobbes's distinction between "command" and "counsel" (Hobbes 1994: xxv, ¶1).

[26] On this sense of "respect" in general (recognition respect) and the distinction between it a kind of esteem we also call respect (appraisal respect), see Chapter 6 of Darwall 2006.

kind. And a second-personal reason just is one that derives from an authoritative claim or demand.

These three notions—practical authority of this kind, the claims or demands it enables one to make, and second-personal reasons—bring a fourth in their wake: the idea of responsibility or accountability *to* others. The authority to demand implies, not just a reason for the addressee to comply (of whatever weight or priority), but also his being accountable for doing so. Conversely, accountability implies the authority to hold accountable, which implies the authority to claim or demand, which is the standing to address second-personal reasons. These four interdefinable notions thus form a cluster: practical authority of this distinctive kind, claim or demand, second-personal reason, and accountability. Each of the four notions implies the other three.

The very idea of a claim to autonomy thus implies the authority to make the claim second-personally. And if we see this claim as inherent in the equal dignity of persons, we are consequently committed to accepting that dignity includes or entails a second-personal authority, specifically, the authority to demand respect for autonomy and to hold one another accountable for complying with this demand. We must see ourselves as accountable to one another as members of the moral community for respecting each other's autonomy, and as distinctively accountable to those whose autonomy we threaten or violate.

Thus Rawls's famous remark that persons are "self-originating sources of valid claims" can be seen to involve two distinct elements (Rawls 1980: 546). Partly, Rawls is saying that persons, by their nature, have a claim on our deliberative attention in the sense that they are morally considerable or, more strongly, that their nature sets constraints on permissible actions with respect to them, including, on interfering with their autonomy. But I interpret Rawls as also saying something more, namely, that persons have, by their nature, the authority or standing *to* claim or demand that these constraints be complied with, and hence, to demand that their autonomy not be subject to interference. The idea is not simply the conceptual truth that any being capable of claiming (or of being subject to a claim) must be a person. That would be true even if no one had the authority validly to claim anything. It is the normative thesis that persons, as such, *do* have standing to claim certain treatment, and to demand respect for this second-personal standing. The dignity of persons, our being self-originating sources of claims in this sense, is our having the authority to demand compliance with the mandatory norms that express respect for us as equal free and rational persons. And if we accept that persons have, as such, a claim to autonomy, we must think that the dignity of persons includes the authority to demand respect for this claim, hence, that we are accountable to one another for allowing each other to make our own choices.

The idea that persons have, as such, a right or claim to autonomy brings in a second-person standpoint, then, in two different ways. First, the notions of moral obligation and moral wrong are themselves conceptually related to that of moral responsibility, and this implies a second-personal authority to address claims and demands in holding people responsible. As Mill put it, "we do not call anything wrong, unless we mean to imply that a person ought to be punished in some way or other for doing it; if not by law, by the opinion of his fellow-creatures; if not by opinion, by the reproaches of his own conscience" (Mill 1998: Ch. V, ¶14) "Punishment" no doubt seems too heavy-handed in many cases, but Mill's central idea is still sound. Our moral obligations are what we are appropriately held, and hold ourselves, responsible for doing. In supposing, therefore, that the dignity of persons makes it wrong to interfere with autonomy, we are committed to thinking also that we are responsible to one another as members of the moral community not to interfere. In this sense, anyone, and not just their daughter, has in principle the standing to hold the parents responsible, if only through Strawsonian "reactive attitudes," such as blame, moral disapproval, and indignation, that, as Strawson pointed out, implicitly make a demand, if only in imagination (Strawson 1968: 92–3; see also Watson 1987 and Wallace 1994). If we blame the parents for their paternalism, we implicitly address a demand to them to stop, if only in imagination. And if their daughter blames them, she does so also, not as the specific person they disrespect, but as a member of the moral community to whom all are accountable. Any such demand presupposes the *representative authority* of any person or member of the moral community.

If, however, she invokes a claim or *right* to autonomy that she herself has, then she implicitly claims an additional, *individual authority* to address demands to them (or that others might have to do so on her behalf) concerning their conduct of *her*. Her parents might recognize this second authority by apologizing to her for their disrespect. The difference between these two different authorities echoes that between the right of punishment and the right of compensation in the state of nature as Locke describes these in the *Second Treatise* (Locke 1988: 273–4). Everyone has the authority to punish violations of the "law of nature," but only victims and their representatives can exact compensation. Both punishment and compensation involve second-person reasons, since both presuppose the authority to claim or demand and that involves the address of a second-person reason.

Second-Personal Reasons and Free Agency

In this section, I shall illustrate how the second-person standpoint reveals a fundamental difference between theoretical and practical reason.[27] When we address or acknowledge a claim or (purportedly valid) demand on someone's will, we presuppose a kind of freedom in the practical realm that lacks an apparent analogue in theoretical reasoning. In the next section, I shall connect this species of practical freedom to Kant's doctrine of autonomy of the will.

---

[27] I argue for this at greater length in Chapters 10 and 11 of Darwall 2006.

When we reason about what to believe, you and I aim to construct representations of an independent world, and our respective perspectives are simply the way that world is, according to each of us, respectively. Fitting the world is belief's internal aim, so a belief is mistaken or incorrect, and not just inaccurate or false in the way a counterfactual hypothesis is, when the world is not as the belief represents it (Velleman 1996; Shah 2003). Granted, we presuppose a kind of freedom in theoretical reasoning also— we must assume that our reasoning is free of various alien influences—but reasons on the basis of which it is possible to form beliefs ultimately are responsible to and defeasible by their relations to this independent realm they purport to represent so far as we can discern it.

It is a consequence of this that, although there can be second-personal reasons for belief, as when one person gives testimony or makes some other sort of epistemic claim on another, these reasons ultimately depend upon or are, at least, defeasible by third-personal considerations, for example, by the person's reliability as a witness. No reasons for belief seem to be second personal all the way down.

Consider now what practical reasoning would be like if it were structurally analogous to theoretical reasoning in these ways. A good analogy is the picture we find in Moore's *Principia Ethica*, according to which reasoning about what to do is simply figuring out the relative value of all possible outcomes or states of the world, along with the feasibility and costs of realizing these, in order to determine which act, of those one can do, would bring about the most valuable states (Moore 1993). We might think of an agent's ranking of possible states as given in his preferences or desires. The idea wouldn't be that the agent thinks these states good because, that is, for the reason that, he desires or prefers them. Rather in preferring them, he thinks them good (to whatever degree, in whatever order).

On this picture, action, like belief, would be governed by its relation to a (putatively) independent order. Just as it is part of the very idea of belief that we appropriately aim to believe only what is true, so also would it be intrinsic to action, on this picture, that it aims to realize valuable (or the most valuable) feasible outcomes or possible states of the world. In other words, just as theoretical reasoning is regulated by the truth of the world as it is, so also would practical reasoning, on this picture, be governed by the world as it ought to be (the value of possible outcomes) and can be made in light of how it is. Moreover, our freedom of choice would be constrained similarly to the way in which our freedom is restricted in forming beliefs. It is only possible to believe something on the basis of, that is, for reasons that are appropriately related to, the world as it is, so far as we can discern these. For example, it is simply psychically impossible, in reasoning about what to believe, to come to believe p on the grounds that it would be desirable to believe p. What is required are epistemic reasons appropriately related to whether p is true. Similarly, on the Moorean picture, the only reasons on the basis of which it would be possible freely to choose to act would be those that are responsive to and defeasible by their relation to actual world states and to the value of possible world states (the world as it should be and can be made in light of how it is) so far as the agent can discern these. If this picture were true, it would simply be psychically impossible to decide to do something for reasons other than that action would bring about valuable, or the best, *outcomes* or states of the world.

When we make claims and demands on one another from a second-person stand-point, however, we see that this picture cannot be right. When you make a claim or demand on me, you must presuppose that I *can* act on the demand simply by accepting your authority and, consequently, the second-personal reason you address, which reason is itself, again, irreducible to the value of any outcome. This possibility is simply a presupposition of the intelligibility of your addressing the claim and putative second-personal reason *to* me (and implicitly holding me responsible for acting on it).[28] And if I consider such a claim from you, I must likewise presuppose the possibility of my finding it valid and acting on it, again, independently of the value of outcomes. Indeed, in even considering your claim I am already acknowledging that you have a kind of authority, namely, to present a claim for my consideration. So in considering the claim, I am already acting on a second-personal reason grounded in this authority.

A claim or demand for autonomy addresses a second-personal reason. And second-personal reasons consist, or are grounded, not in the value of outcomes or possible states of the world, but in authority relations we assume to obtain between us when we address them.[29] Unlike reasons for belief of any sort, second-personal reasons for action are second personal all the way down. So when you and I presuppose that I can act on the second-personal reason you address in your claim, we both assume that I have a freedom of choice that apparently finds no analogue in theoretical reasoning or in practical reasoning on the Moorean picture. Similarly, when a middle-aged daughter asks her parents to stop treating her like a child, she addresses a second-personal reason to them that is grounded in her claim to autonomy, hence, in her authority to demand it, not in the value of a hoped-for outcome considered as a possible state of the world. The latter could only give her parents a reason to bring about a valuable state, not a reason to respect the autonomy *of someone who is addressing an authoritative demand to them.*

"There is," as Dewey put it, "an intrinsic difference, in both origin and mode of operation between objects which present themselves as satisfactory to desire and hence good, and objects which come to one as making demands upon his conduct which should be recognized. Neither can be reduced to the other."[30] The value of a hoped-for outcome considered as a possible state of the world is a reason to desire that state. In

---

[28] The capacity to act on the proffered reasons is thus not just a presupposition of *moral* address, as Gary Watson has noted in connection with moral responsibility, but of the address of any demand or claim (Watson 1987: 263–4).

[29] Of course, any such assumption of authority might be mistaken. In Darwall 2006, however, I argue that to take up the second-person perspective at all is to be committed to an equal second-personal authority that free and rational agents have to make claims and demands of one another. And I attempt also to show how second-personal reasons grounded in this authority can be fit within an overall theory of practical reason.

[30] By "demands" here, Dewey means something second-personal: "Men who live together inevitably make demands on one another" (Dewey 1998: 319). I am indebted to Elizabeth Anderson for this reference.

caring for their daughter, her parents take themselves to have a reason to bring her welfare about owing to the value of that possible state (as it seems to them from the perspective of their concern for her). That their daughter has a valid claim to her autonomy, however, is a reason for them, not, in the first instance, to desire any state,[31] but to *respect her claim* and so act as she warrantedly demands, and for her to hold them accountable if they don't. Consequently, the daughter must assume as a condition of the intelligibility of her addressing the claim to them that her parents can act on a reason that is irreducibly second-personal and, consequently, that they and she have a kind of freedom to act on reasons that are rooted, not in the objects of any desire (the value of a possible state of the world), but in claims she has the authority to make as a free and rational will.

When we make practical, rather than epistemic, claims on one another (including within the latter, an adviser's claims on her advisee's beliefs about choiceworthy actions), we presuppose the freedom to act on reasons that are grounded, not in our respective relations to an order we purport to represent, but in irreducibly second-personal authority relations that hold between us. It follows that in practical reason, our respective perspectives are not simply standpoints *on* an independent something, say, a ranking of the value of possible states of the world, together with facts of the actual world. So practical claims are not discountable when they reflect any such evaluative order poorly. This is why paternalism and other violations of autonomy can be objectionable even if they realize more valuable states. Even when your ends are badly supported by independent reasons, I have some reason not to interfere with, and perhaps to further, your pursuit of them. The fact that your ends have value *to you*, or that mine have value *to me*, is itself a source of reasons for both of us. The perspectives from which we make practical claims on one another are the standpoints *from* which we lead our lives as free and independent rational agents and relate to one another on terms that presuppose and respect this very status. It is our ability to take a second-personal standpoint that enables us to respect one another's dignity and to hold one another responsible for doing so.

Autonomy of the Will

We are now in a position to see why autonomy as demand presupposes autonomy of the will. Kant defines autonomy, again, as "the property of the will by which it is a law to itself independently of any property of the objects of volition" (4:440). But what does Kant mean by an "object of volition"? "Desire," he tells us, "is the faculty to be, by means of one's representations, the cause of the objects of these representations" (6:211; see also 5:9). Both desire and belief involve a representation of a possible state of the world. Belief is the "faculty" to be, by means of the world, the cause of one's

---

[31] In the first instance. It is, of course, a reason to desire the state of their respecting her autonomy as a consequence of the reason to respect her autonomy.

representations' fitting the world. And desire is the faculty to be, by means of one's representations, the cause of the world's fitting one's representations.[32] The object of desire is the represented outcome, the possible state of the world that the faculty of desire enables us to make actual.

But not all behavior that results from beliefs and desires involves the will, which Kant defines as "the capacity to act in accordance with the representation of laws" or "principles" (4:412). Neither, however, does an act's resulting from a desire preclude it from being an instance of autonomy. When, in non-rational beings, desire is "deter-mined only by *inclination*" or "sensible impulse," it involves "animal choice (*arbitrium brutum*)" (6:213). Rational human agents are subject to inclinations also, but although "affected," they are not "determined" by them (6:213). To will an action to which she is inclined, an agent must incorporate or "take up" her inclination into some normative representation or principle that gives *her reason* for acting (Kant 1999: 24). If, however, the principle is itself "precede[d]" by a desire that furnishes "the condition of its becoming a principle," then the principle is "empirical." It is "unable to furnish a practical law," and the will is heteronomous (5:21, 33). Autonomy of the will, pure reason's being "of itself practical," occurs only insofar as "reason can determine the faculty of desire as such" (6:213).

All actions result from desire. But not all desires are, in Rawls's helpful terms, "object-dependent"; some are "principle-dependent" (Rawls 2000: 150–1). If a motivating desire is object-dependent (that is, if it depends ultimately on properties of the object of desire), then the action it motivates is heteronomous. Autonomy is realized only if the motivating desire is principle-dependent rather than object-de-pendent.[33] So autonomy of the will requires an agent's accepting and acting on normative principles and reasons *independently of her regard for any object or possible state of the world*, that is, on principles and reasons whose validity she regards as independent of the value of possible states.[34] Most obviously, she must be able to act independently of her inclinations toward object states (object-dependent desires). Less obviously, but no less importantly, she must be able to act on principles and reasons that are independ-ent also of any putative evaluation of some state (like a Moorean intuition that it is intrinsically good).

Although the capacity to accept and act on norms, including agent-relative deonto-logical constraints, is necessary for autonomy of the will, it is not, however, sufficient. We can see why by comparing a deontological intuitionist picture of the sort associated with W. D. Ross and Richard Price with Kant's. According to deontological intuition-ists, acts are morally obligatory, right or wrong, at least "*prima facie*" or *pro tanto*,[35] in

---

[32] On "direction of fit" see, for example, Smith 1994: 111–19.

[33] N.B., not "if, and only if." Being principle-dependent is necessary for a motivating desire to be consistent with autonomy of the will. I will discuss why it is not sufficient in the next paragraph.

[34] For an insightful analysis of the psychology of norm acceptance, see Gibbard 1990: 68–82.

[35] For the idea of "prima facie duties," see Ross 1930.

virtue of their intrinsic nature, their being the kind of act they are. There is an obvious sense, then, in which, although deontological intuitionism does not suppose moral obligations to depend on the objects of *desire*, if we take these to be possible states of the world or outcomes,[36] it does nonetheless take them to depend on "features of the objects of *volition*." What we choose or intend directly is acts, not outcomes, and deontological intuitionists do believe that the moral law depends on features that are intrinsic to these.

Kant's picture by contrast is that the moral law comes from what Kant calls the "form" of the will rather than from its content or objects. What Allison calls Kant's "reciprocity thesis" is Kant's claim that the moral law, and its fundamental formula, the Categorical Imperative (CI), are equivalent to autonomy of the will (Allison 1986). It follows from this thesis that there can be a moral law only if its fundamental principle is a formal one (like the CI) that entails autonomy of the will, and that the will can be a "law to itself" only if the CI, and hence the moral law, is valid. But what reason, other than the CI's independent plausibility as a moral principle, is there for thinking that what most deeply underlies moral obligations must be a formal principle like the CI ("Act in accordance with that maxim through which you can at the same time will that it become a universal law" (4:421)). What is it that links the very idea of moral obligation to a formal principle of the will (and thus to autonomy of the will)? No deontological intuitionist, it seems, should accept that, and nothing has yet been said that undermines their position.

In my view, the deep idea underlying the thought that moral obligation must bottom out in a formal principle of the will like the CI, is that otherwise we cannot adequately account for moral obligation's conceptual tie to responsibility. If persons are subject to moral obligations by virtue of being free and rational agents, then these capacities for determining their wills must include whatever it takes to hold themselves responsible for complying with them. In holding her parents responsible for not violating their daughter's autonomy, we (and their daughter) must assume, not just that there are weighty or even conclusive reasons for her parents not to do so. That could be true even if they didn't know of these reasons, were in no position to know them, or knew of them but were unable, for whatever reason, to act on them. When we make demands of people and hold them responsible, we are subject to what Gary Watson calls "constraints on moral address" (Watson 1987: 263–4). The very intelligibility of addressing a demand to someone depends upon the addresser's assuming that the addressee has what it takes to accept the addresser's authority and regulate his conduct by the legitimacy of his demand. To hold someone morally responsible for something, consequently, we must think that he is in a position to hold himself responsible also.

---

[36] Recall that this seems to be Kant's view also.

When, therefore, we hold people responsible for not violating others' autonomy, even when no one is demanding this of them explicitly and directly, we are committed to assuming that they have, in being subject to this obligation, a way of determining this for themselves and acting on this determination. The CI is Kant's proposal for the requisite reasoning process—in effect, the form that moral reasoning would have to take if it is to lead us to conclusions that we can intelligibly be held responsible for reaching. And autonomy of the will follows as a corollary. If, as autonomy as claim or demand supposes, we are responsible to one another for not violating each other's autonomy as a matter of moral obligation and moral right, then it must be the case that in being subject to this obligation and constrained by this right, we have what it takes to hold ourselves responsible and comply with them for the requisite second-personal reasons, as we must assume when we hold one another responsible for doing so.

Consequently, if being a free and rational will is what makes us subject to the moral law and to the demand for autonomy, then this law and demand must be grounded in what makes us thus subject. Being free and rational wills must enable us simultaneously to determine demands to which we are subject as such, including the demand not to violate one another's autonomy, and to determine ourselves to comply with these demands.

In my view, it is our capacity to take up a second-person standpoint and address and acknowledge claims and demands to and from one another, and to and from ourselves, that makes us morally accountable beings, hence subject to the moral law and to the valid demand for autonomy. Indeed, as I see it, being "second-personally competent" in this sense is ultimately how "free" in the formula "free and rational" should be understood. Only because we can assume that we each can take up the standpoint of one among others, determine what demands it makes sense to hold one another to from this perspective, and then address these demands to one another and to ourselves, can we sensibly actually hold each other to these demands.[37]

When you and I make a claim to autonomy that we take to be rooted in the dignity of persons, therefore, we presuppose that we are bound by practical laws and reasons that are valid, not by virtue of any "object" of volition, whether the value of any outcome or of any act considered in itself. We must assume that we are thus bound by virtue of an authority we have to make demands of one another as free and rational wills, a second-personal authority that we can recognize only from a second-person standpoint. Whatever value autonomy has as part of well-being or as a constituent of valuable outcomes, we also claim or demand autonomy as part of respect for the dignity of persons. And when we do, we must assume autonomy of the will as well.[38]

---

[37] I argue for these claims in Darwall 2006.

[38] A previous version of this paper was presented to a conference on autonomy and well-being held at the University of Toronto in April, 2004. I am indebted to other participants in the conference, including especially Samantha Brennan, Marilyn Friedman, Jennifer Hawkins, Tom Hurka, and L. Wayne Sumner for their helpful comments. I am also indebted to two anonymous referees for *Ethics* and Martha Nussbaum and John Deigh for their criticisms and suggestions.

III

Authority and Law

8

Authority and Second-Personal Reasons for Acting

In *SPS*,[1] I argue that a distinctive kind of reason for acting, a *second-personal reason*, is an ineliminable aspect of many central moral categories, including rights, moral responsibility, moral obligation, respect for and the dignity of persons, and the very concept of moral agent or person itself. Second-personal reasons are distinguished from reasons of other kinds by their conceptual relations to authoritative claims and demands that must be able to be *addressed to* those to whom they apply (second-personally, as it were). I have argued, more specifically, that there are four interdefinable, irreducibly second-personal notions: the authority to make a claim or demand, a valid (authoritative) claim or demand, accountability or responsibility *to* someone (with the relevant authority), and a second-personal reason for acting (that is, for complying with an authoritative claim or legitimate demand and so discharging the responsibility). Each one of these notions entails the other three, and no proposition that does not already involve one of these four concepts can entail any that does.

Call the authority I am concerned with *practical authority* to distinguish it from various forms of epistemic authority or expertise, including the kind of authority on practical matters a trusted adviser might have. A challenge that can be posed to my irreducibility thesis is that it is possible to establish claims to practical authority by invoking solely non-second-personal reasons. In what follows, I consider Joseph Raz's influential *normal justification thesis* according to which claims to practical authority can be established by showing that an "alleged subject" is likely to comply better with reasons that apply to him independently already if he accepts the directives of an alleged authority as binding and tries to follow them than he would if he were to act on his own assessment of independent reasons (Raz 1986: 53). I shall argue that the normal justification thesis does not hold for practical authority as I propose to understand it;[2] moreover, that the correct diagnosis of why it does not shows that both practical authority and reasons that are conceptually related to it are irreducibly second personal.

---

[1] Darwall 2006.
[2] Or more cautiously, any cases where it may hold will be by virtue of recourse to reasons that are themselves already within the circle of second-personal concepts (i.e., second-personal reasons).

Let me try to get the intuitive idea of a second-personal reason across with an example. Compare, first, two different ways in which you might try to give someone a reason to stop causing you pain, say, to remove his foot from on top of yours.

One would be to get him to have sympathetic concern for you in your plight and to want you to be free of pain. In desiring this, he would see relief of your pain as a better way for the world to be, a possible outcome or state that, as Moore put it, "ought to exist for its own sake" (Moore 1993: 34). And he would most naturally see his desire, not as the source of the reason, but as a kind of access to an *agent-neutral* (and *state-of-the-world-regarding*) reason for removing his foot that is there anyway.[3] The reason would not be essentially *for him* as the agent causing another person pain. It would apparently exist, most fundamentally, for anyone who is in a position to bring about the state of relief of your pain, and *therefore* for him, since he is well placed to do so.[4] Finally, in "giving" him the reason in this way, you might not need to address or relate to him in any way at all. Anything that would get him to see your being in pain as a bad thing, like an unaddressed grimace or whimper, might serve. In no sense, not even epistemic, need he be taking any reason to move his foot *on your authority*.

Alternatively, you might lay a claim or address a purportedly valid demand. You might say something that asserts or implies your authority *to* claim or demand that he move his foot and that simultaneously expresses this demand. You might demand this as the person whose foot he is stepping on, thereby claiming and exercising what you take to be a right against him. Or you might demand it as a representative of the moral community, whose members understand themselves as holding themselves and one another to a (moral) obligation or demand not to step on each other's feet. Or you might do both simultaneously. Whichever, the reason you would address would be agent-relative rather than agent-neutral. It would concern, most fundamentally, your

---

[3] On this point, see Darwall 1983; Bond 1983; Pettit and Smith 1990; Quinn 1993; Hampton 1998a; Scanlon 1998: 41–55; and Dancy 2000. Agent-neutral reasons contrast with agent-relative reasons, those whose formulation includes an ineliminable reference to the agent for whom they are reasons (like "that it will keep a promise I made," "that it will avoid harm to others, i.e., people other than me," and so on). Agent-neutral reasons can be stated without such a reference: "that it would prevent some pain from occurring to someone (or some being)." On the distinction between agent-relative (also called "subjective" or "agent-centered") and agent-neutral (also called "objective") reasons, principles, values, etc., see Nagel 1970; Scheffler 1982; Parfit 1984; Nagel 1986; Darwall 1986; McNaughton and Rawling 1991; and Ridge 2005.

I argue for the claim that sympathetic concern involves its seeming that there are agent-neutral reasons to further someone's welfare in Darwall 2002: 68–72. I do not deny, of course, that someone who already accepted various agent-relative norms might not be moved, through empathy and sympathy, to feel some special responsibility for relieving the pain. My point is that this would not come through sympathy alone.

[4] Roughly speaking, again, a reason is agent-neutral if it can be formulated without essential reference to the agent (as such); otherwise it is agent-relative. It should also be noted that superficially agent-relative reasons may be grounded more deeply in agent-neutral considerations and values, and/or vice versa. For example, rule-utilitarianism holds that rules of right conduct include agent-relative principles, for example, those defining rights of promise and contract, on grounds of overall agent-neutral value.

addressee's relations to others, in this case, that his keeping his foot on yours causes another person pain, causes inconvenience, and so on, and that this is something we can and do reasonably demand that people not do. The reason would not be addressed to him as someone who is simply in a position to alter a bad state. If he could stop, say, two others from causing an identical gratuitous pain by the shocking spectacle of keeping his foot firmly planted on yours, this second, claim-based reason would not recommend that he do so. The reason would be addressed to him as someone who is a person *causing* gratuitous pain to another person, something we persons normally assume we have the authority to demand that persons not do to others.

What is important for our purposes is that someone can sensibly accept this second reason for moving his foot, one embodied in your claim or demand, only if he also accepts your *authority to demand* this of him (second-personally). That is just what it is to accept something *as a valid claim or demand*. And if he accepts that you can demand that he move his foot, he must also accept that you will have grounds for complaint or some other form of accountability-seeking response if he does not. And that third parties will have grounds for moral blame. Unlike the first reason, this latter is second personal in the sense that although the first is conceptually independent of forms of second-personal address involved in making claims and holding people responsible, the second is not. A *second-personal reason* is thus one whose validity depends upon presupposed authority and accountability relations between persons and, therefore, on the possibility of the reason's being addressed person-to-person within these relations. Reasons of this kind simply would not exist but for their role in second-personal address and in mediating our relatings to one another. And their second-personal character explains their agent-relativity. As second-personal reasons always derive most fundamentally from agents' *relations to* one another, they are invariably agent-relative at the most fundamental level.[5]

It is important also to see, however, that a norm or reason can be agent-relative without being second-personal; in other words, there might be a reason of yet a *third* kind that is agent-relative, like the second, but not yet a second-personal reason. We can imagine someone who accepts and scrupulously observes a universal norm

---

[5] The formulation of the reason may not always be agent-relative, however. Suppose, for example, that the best way of grounding the Categorical Imperative is, as I argue in *The Second-Person Standpoint*, from the second-person standpoint in an equal authority to make claims and demands that persons presuppose when they address one another second-personally (32–5, 115–18, 239–42, 304–9). It is at least conceivable that what the CI itself requires is a principle of conduct that can be specified agent-neutrally. R. M. Hare, for example, believes that the CI can be seen to entail the sort of universal prescriptivism he favors *and* that this entails a form of act-utilitarianism (an agent-neutral theory). See Hare 1993.

I take the relevance of the arguments of *The Second-Person Standpoint* to the problem of justifying of agent-relative (or "deontological") constraints to be the following therefore. Justification from the second-person point of view can provide a compelling rationale for agent-relative constraints, like the demand not to step on another's feet, since, if I am right, any moral obligation or constraint is irreducibly second-personal, and second-personal reasons are agent-relative in their foundations. It is, however, conceptually consistent with this that moral obligations are agent-neutral in their content, and some presumably are, such as the obligation to help those in need. I am indebted to David Sobel and Steven Wall for pressing me to clarify this point.

of foot-avoidance but who also denies, consistently with that, anyone's authority to claim or demand his compliance with this norm, hence denies that he is responsible to anyone for compliance, even to God. Such a person might conceive of the norm as mandatory in the sense of entailing categorical, indeed supremely authoritative reasons, without accepting that he is accountable to anyone for complying with it. However, he could not then consistently accept that anyone has a *right* to his foot-avoidance, and in respecting the norm of avoiding people's feet he would not be respecting *them* as persons, since he would not be recognizing any authority anyone might claim as a person to demand anything, in particular, that he avoid their feet (Feinberg 1980; Darwall 2004). Neither, in my view, could he consistently accept that he is *morally obligated* not to step on others' feet since moral obligation is related to moral responsibility conceptually. It is conceptually impossible for one to be morally obligated to do something but not responsible for doing it, neither to the moral community, nor to God, nor to anyone. So someone who thought he was accountable to no one could not think he was morally obligated not to step on others' feet, whatever priority he might give to a norm requiring him not to do so.

There is thus a significant difference between the idea of an authoritative claim or demand, on the one hand, and that of a valid (and in that sense authoritative) norm or normative reason, or even of a normative requirement, on the other. There can be requirements *on* us that no one has any standing *to require of* us. We are under a requirement of reason not to believe propositions that contradict the logical consequences of known premises, for example. But it is only in certain contexts, say, when you and I are trying to work out what to believe together, that we have any standing to demand that one another reason logically, and even here that authority apparently derives from a moral or quasi-moral aspect, namely, our having undertaken a common goal.[6] Requirements of logical reasoning are, in this way, fundamentally different from moral requirements. I follow Mill and a number of contemporary writers in holding that it is part of the very idea of moral obligation that moral requirements are what those to whom we are morally responsible have the authority to demand that we do.[7]

---

[6] Of course, these further constraints are frequently in the background, as they are, for example, whenever we do philosophy, say, right now. Because of the relationship you and I are currently in, each of us *does* have authority to call one another to account for logical errors, a standing that, without some such context, we lack. But however frequently that or some relevantly similar context obtains, the authority comes, not just from the requirement of reason, but from some other presupposed feature of the context.

[7] "We do not call anything wrong, unless we mean to imply that a person ought to be punished in some way or other for doing it; if not by law, by the opinion of his fellow-creatures; if not by opinion, by the reproaches of his own conscience. This seems the real turning point of the distinction between morality and simple expediency. It is a part of the notion of Duty in every one of its forms, that a person may rightfully be compelled to fulfil it. Duty is a thing which may be exacted from a person, as one exacts a debt" (Mill 1998: Ch. V.¶14). John Skorupski points out that calling an act "morally wrong...amounts to blaming the agent" and maintains that the idea of moral wrong can't be understood independently of that of blameworthiness (Skorupski 1999: 29, 142). Allan Gibbard quite explicitly follows Mill's lead in proposing that "what a person does is *morally wrong* if and only if it is rational for him to feel guilty for having done it, and for others to be

Clearly this is no part whatsoever of the concept of a demand of logic or a requirement of reason.[8]

Now, as I have said, second-personal reasons are related conceptually to, respectively, the authority to make a claim or demand, a valid or authoritative claim or demand, and responsibility or accountability *to*. To appreciate the second-personal aspect of moral responsibility, consider Strawson's famous critique of "pragmatist" or consequentialist approaches to responsibility in "Freedom and Resentment" (Strawson 1968). Strawson argued influentially that social desirability cannot provide a justification of "the right *sort*" for practices of moral responsibility "as we understand them" (1968: 74). When we seek to hold people accountable, what matters is not whether some sanction is desirable, either in a particular case or in general, but whether their actions are *culpable* and whether we have any authority to demand their acceptance of a sanction. Desirability is a reason of the wrong kind to warrant the attitudes and actions in which holding someone responsible consists *in their own terms*.

Strawson's point is an instance of the *wrong kind of reason problem*. To be a reason of the right kind, a consideration must justify the relevant attitude in its own terms. It must be a fact about or feature of some object, appropriate consideration of which could provide someone's reason for a warranted attitude of that kind toward it.[9] The *(morally) responsible* and the *culpable* concern norms for the distinctive attitudes and actions that are involved in holding people responsible and blaming them. The desirability—whether moral, social, personal, or otherwise—of holding someone responsible or blaming her, or reasons why that would be desirable, are simply reasons of the wrong kind to warrant doing so in the sense that is relevant to whether she *is* morally responsible or blameworthy. The former concerns reasons and norms of desire (even if from the moral point of view), and what is thus desirable is simply a different question from whether we are justified in holding someone responsible or blaming her in the relevant sense. The latter concerns reasons and norms that are distinctively relevant to these latter attitudes.[10]

Strawson dubbed the distinctive attitudes involved in holding people responsible "reactive attitudes," with prominent examples being indignation, resentment, guilt, blame, and so on. And Strawson himself pointed out what more recent commentators, notably Gary Watson and Jay Wallace, have since also noticed, namely, that reactive attitudes implicitly address *demands*. They involve "an *expectation of*, and *demand* for"

---

angry at him for having done it" (Gibbard 1990: 42). And we can find versions of this Millian idea in other writers also (Baier 1966; Brandt 1979; Shafer-Landau 2003).

[8] I am indebted to Peter Graham for this point.

[9] Rabinowicz and Ronnøw-Rasmussen put essentially the same point by saying reasons of the right kind also appear in the content of the attitude for which they are reasons: the attitude is toward something "on account of" these reasons (Rabinowicz and Ronnøw-Rasmussen 2004: 414). As W. D. Falk pointed out, a favoring that is relevant to value is "by way of true comprehension of what [the object] is like" (Falk 1986: 117). See also Hieronymi 2005.

[10] That is, to blame as an attitude. We also speak of blaming as an action, but even when we do we normally take it to express the attitude of blame.

certain conduct from one another[11] (Strawson 1968: 85, emphasis added). To feel a reactive attitude is to feel as though one has a warranted expectation *of* someone. Reactive attitudes, and actions that express them, must therefore presuppose the authority *to* expect and hold one another responsible for compliance with moral obligations (which must then be standards to which we can warrantedly hold each other as members of the moral community). Strawson claimed also that holding one another responsible with reactive attitudes presupposes that those we hold responsible have that standing as well. In holding someone accountable in this way, we "view him as a member of the moral community; only as one who has offended against its demands" (Strawson 1968: 93). In these ways, reactive attitudes can mediate *mutual* accountability.

It follows on Strawson's analysis that culpability and moral responsibility are second-personal phenomena in my sense. They implicitly involve the address of authoritative claims and demands and, therefore, of second-personal reasons. Moral responsibility is responsibility *to*—in Strawson's view (and mine), to the moral community or to one another and ourselves as representative persons. It concerns what the moral community can warrantedly expect and demand of each other and themselves. When we hold one another responsible, we express these demands and presuppose the authority to do so. So if Strawson is right, as I think he is, then responsibility *to* is conceptually related to the idea of authoritative demands and, therefore, to practical authority and second-personal reasons, that is, to reasons for acting that are thought to consist in or to derive from authoritative demands.

But the conceptual relations also seem to run in the opposite direction. If one person has practical authority with respect to another, then this would seem to mean, not just that the latter has a reason of whatever priority or weight—whether overriding, silencing, exclusionary, pre-emptive, or whatever—for acting as the former directs, but also that the latter has some responsibility *to* the former for doing so, that the latter is, in some way or other, answerable to the former. This point can be illustrated by altering our earlier thought experiment to imagine someone, call him now B, who accepts a mandatory norm requiring him always to do what someone in a certain position tells him to do. Suppose that A is now in that position. B will then accept that he must do what A tells him to do. We can imagine that B thereby accepts a reason for complying with A's directives of whatever weight or priority. B might think that the reason always overrides, silences, or pre-empts any potentially conflicting reasons. But B could still deny, consistently with all of that, that he is in any way responsible or answerable to A (or, indeed, to anyone). Were he to do so, he would seem also to be questioning A's authority over him. "Just because I always have overriding or

---

[11] Gary Watson stresses this in Watson 1987: 263, 264. Note also, R. Jay Wallace: "there is an essential connection between the reactive attitudes and a distinctive form of evaluation . . . that I refer to as holding a person to an expectation (or demand)" (Wallace 1994: 19). See also Bennett 1980 and Scanlon (1998: 272–90).

pre-emptive reason to do what you say doesn't make me answerable to you or give you authority over me," he might consistently say. A cannot have authority with respect to B, it seems, unless B is in some way answerable to A.

We might put this point by saying that practical authority is not just a relation in the logical sense; it is a standing in a relationship.[12] If A has authority with respect to B, then certain things follow about how A and B may and must relate to one another. If A has the authority to demand that B stay off A's feet, then not only is it the case that B has a reason of whatever weight or priority for doing so on the occasion of such a directive. B is also answerable to A for doing so.

This point is illustrated further by early modern theological voluntarist moral theories, like those of Pufendorf and Locke. The fundamental premise of such theories is that God has superior authority over his creatures. It is absolutely central to the voluntarist picture, moreover, that, because God has authority over us, not only must we do what God says, but we are also accountable to Him for doing so. Unless we were responsible to God for compliance, any sanction God might attach to violating His commands would amount to coercion by threat. Of course, it might be within God's authority so to threaten us, but voluntarists like Pufendorf thought it critical to distinguish between even such justified threats and God's authority *over us*, which essentially includes His authority to hold us accountable with sanctions. For us to be God's *subjects*, so subject to His authority, Pufendorf thought, we must be able to see ourselves as responsible to Him for doing as He directs.[13] (As we shall see, Raz also distinguishes between direction by justified threats and by authoritative directives.)

I take it, then, that there is a strong prima facie case for thinking that the four second-personal notions I mentioned at the outset—practical authority (to claim or demand), valid (authoritative) claim or demand, responsibility *to*, and second-personal reason for acting—are interdefinable in something like the following fashion.

Practical authority: Someone has practical authority with respect to another if, and only if, the latter has a second-personal reason to comply with the former's valid claims and demands and is responsible to the former for so doing.

Responsibility to: Someone is responsible to another if, and only if, the latter has the authority to make some valid claim or demand of the former that the former is thereby given a second-personal reason to comply with.

Valid claim or demand: A valid claim or demand is one that is within the authority of someone having practical authority with respect to another to make of the latter and that the latter thereby has a second-personal reason to comply with and some responsibility to the former for so doing.

Second-personal reason: A second-personal reason is one consisting in or deriving from some valid claim or demand of someone having practical authority with respect to the agent and with which the agent is thereby accountable for complying.

---

[12] I have been helped here by discussion with Jules Coleman.
[13] For discussion see Darwall 2003.

In *SPS*, I argue that many central moral concepts, including those of moral rights, moral obligation (and so, moral right and wrong), culpability, the dignity of persons, respect for persons, and the concept of moral agent or person (subject to moral obligations) are second-personal notions and so within the network of concepts just defined. For example, moral obligations are not just what there are moral reasons to do (of whatever weight); they are what morality demands and, therefore, that to which we can be justifiably *held*.

I claim, again, that the four interdefinable notions of practical authority, valid claim or demand, responsibility *to*, and second-personal reason are all irreducibly second personal. If this is so, then, to the extent that the moral categories I have just mentioned involve these notions, it will follow that they all have an irreducibly second-personal aspect also. In my view, this is a fact of great importance for moral theory. It means that no set of propositions that do not already involve the interdefinable second-personal notions I have identified can possibly entail any proposition of moral right, responsibility, obligation, and so on. To paraphrase a slogan of Bernard Williams's: Second-personal authority out, second-personal authority in (Williams 1985: 181).[14] Of course, it may still be true that, for example, we are morally obligated to maximize overall utility, but this cannot possibly follow simply from the fact that the world would be better if we did. There must be some showing that this is something we reasonably demand of one another and hold ourselves and one another to through warranted reactive attitudes.

The Normal Justification Thesis and Accountability

But what makes it the case that someone has practical authority of any kind (as I contend, for example, that beings with second-personal competence share a basic authority as equal members of the moral community or that one person has authority of some kind over another)? And what makes it the case that any claim or demand from someone to another is valid, one that that person has the authority to make on the other? If it is possible to justify practical authority fully in terms of reasons that are not themselves second-personal, then perhaps the notions I have identified are not *irreducibly* second-personal. Maybe their apparently second-personal character is a superficial aspect that can be explained away or otherwise accounted for at some more fundamental level.

This is the challenge that is posed by Raz's *normal justification thesis* which Raz formulates as follows:

---

[14] Williams's slogan was "Obligation out, obligation in." One way of putting the thesis that moral obligation must be understood in terms of second-personal reasons is to say that the formulation in the text is not just a paraphrase of Williams's slogan, but that the point it formulates is the genus of which that formulated by Williams's slogan is a species.

the normal way to establish that a person has authority over another person involves showing that the alleged subject is likely better to comply with reasons which apply to him (other than the alleged authoritative directives) if he accepts the directives of the alleged authority as authoritatively binding and tries to follow them, rather than by trying to follow the reasons which apply to him directly. (1986: 53)[15]

Now the reasons that already apply to an "alleged subject" independently of the second-personal reasons putatively generated by some *specific* alleged authority may themselves be partly second personal, since they may be conceptually related to claims and demands of some other authority. This will turn out to be important if reasons of moral obligation are themselves second personal in the way I have claimed. On my view, moral obligations conceptually entail an authority all persons share to make demands of themselves and one another.

Of course, if the normal justification thesis is correct, then it may be possible to establish every authority, including whatever authority we have as equal members of the moral community, by reference to independently existing reasons. So it may be true that whatever standing we have to hold one another answerable for moral demands, like any other practical authority, can be accounted for by virtue of its being the case that we would do better, were we to accept this authority, at complying with reasons that apply to us independently of this authority. If, however, we can account for all practical authority by the normal justification thesis, then it would seem to follow that practical authority and the other notions that are conceptually related to it, although second personal on their face, are not irreducibly second personal.

Meeting the standards of the normal justification thesis is not, however, sufficient to establish practical authority. There are cases where one person might very well do better to follow someone else's directives where it seems clear that the latter has no claim whatsoever on the former's will and actions and consequently no practical authority with respect to him. And cases where an "alleged subject" would do better in complying with independent reasons where genuine authority *does* seem to be involved all also seem to involve some assumed background accountability relation that gives the authority's directives standing as second-personal reasons. In these cases, it is the latter that establishes the directives' authority, not the former.

It is worth pointing out that much of what Raz says about practical authority in *The Morality of Freedom* aside from the *normal justification thesis* seems well attuned to practical authority's second-personal character. First, Raz notes that authority of this kind is different, not only from power and coercive threats, but also from *justified* power and coercion. One does not exercise authority over "people afflicted with dangerous diseases," Raz notes, "if [one] knock[s] them out and locks them up to protect the public" even if one "is justified in doing so" (Raz 1986: 25). Such a justified use of

---

[15] We should note that Raz says here that this is the "normal way" to establish authority, not that it is a necessary, or even a sufficient condition. Since the normal justification thesis poses a critical challenge to my irreducibility claims only if it is taken as providing a sufficient condition, that is how I propose to understand it.

coercion would miss, Raz says, an essential element of any exercise of authority purporting to give the person over whom it is exercised a distinctive reason to comply, namely, "an appeal for compliance" and "an invocation of the duty to obey" (25–6). This seems exactly right. Any such appeal would be an instance of what I am calling second-personal address. It would be an appeal *to* the alleged subjects to recognize the alleged authority and comply therefore with directives that are authorized by it. Moreover, someone can credibly make such an appeal only if he can expect his alleged subject to accept that the subject has some duty or obligation to follow his directives. Without such a duty or obligation in place, which an alleged authority cannot of course create by his own directives, no genuine authority exists.

Second, Raz makes an important distinction between the kind of authority that can give one new reasons for *belief*, including beliefs about what there is reason to do, on the one hand, and genuinely "practical authority" (as he also calls it), which can give one reasons for *acting* that one did not previously have, on the other. Raz rightly rejects a "recognitional conception" of practical authority according to which an authority gives agents no new reasons for acting, just new reasons to believe what reasons for acting they already have. Applying the "recognitional conception" to authority *über-haupt* gives rise to what Raz calls the "no difference thesis": "the view that authority does not change people's reasons for acting" (Raz 1986: 30). Raz points out that one way of seeing that the recognitional conception and no difference thesis cannot be correct is to reflect on the role that practical authority can play in solving coordination problems. There are cases where it is important for everyone to coordinate on one of two options that, so far as antecedently applicable reasons go, are equally choice-worthy. It is fine if everyone drives on the right, or on the left, but everyone had better coordinate on one side or the other. "A wise man," Raz notes, "can tell me which options belong" to a set of optimal choices, "but he cannot tell me which option to choose before it is known what others will do" (Raz 1986 30). This is, of course, correct. Raz rightly distinguishes between *practical* authority and the kind of authority that a trusted adviser can have in directing us to independently choiceworthy options. There is, as Hobbes famously noted, a distinction between "counsel" and "law" or "command" (Hobbes 1983: XIV.¶1). Genuine practical authority can give those who are subject to it new reasons for acting by addressing valid claims or demands to those subjects. As I would put it, the relevant reasons are second-personal reasons; their validity depends on the alleged authority's actually having the authority he presupposes when he addresses the demand (or "appeal") for compliance.

Nonetheless, one might still think that what grounds practical authority and so makes it the case that someone can give reasons of this distinctive, second-personal kind are further reasons that are not themselves second personal. This brings us back to the *normal justification thesis*. The basic idea, again, is that someone earns practical authority with respect to another person if the latter would do better in complying with already applicable reasons were she to accept the former's directives "as authori-tatively binding and tr[y] to act on them" than she would if she did not and tried to act on her own assessment of reasons. There is, however, a problem we face right at the outset in interpreting the normal justification thesis. What is it to accept someone's "directives as authoritatively binding"?

If we understand such acceptance to be accepting a directive as a valid demand in the second-personal sense I have been pointing to, then the alleged subject's own normative thought must then be interpreted in second-personal terms. In particular, we must suppose that she not only takes herself to have a reason of whatever weight or priority (exclusionary or pre-emptive, say), but that she also sees herself as *responsible* for compliance, that is, as answerable to the alleged authority. We must suppose that she, at least, takes it that the fact that she is thus responsible is in itself a reason for her to comply of this distinctively second-personal kind. But if this is so, then a version of Strawson's "wrong kind of reason" problem will arise from her perspective. Just as the fact that there might be desirable effects of treating people as responsible and their actions as culpable is a reason "of the wrong sort" for practices of holding people responsible "as we understand them," so also will the fact that an alleged subject would do better in complying with independently applicable reasons seem to her to be a reason of the wrong kind to think that she really is responsible for complying with some (alleged) authority's directives and therefore that his putative practical authority is genuine.

If this is right, then the beneficial effects of the subject's acceptance of an alleged authority may themselves be hostage to the subject's not also accepting the normal justification thesis herself, since the putative authority she accepts may then be susceptible, from her perspective at least, to, as Mill might put it, "the dissolving force of [the] analysis" that the normal justification thesis purports to provide.[16] Were she to think that the only legitimacy the "alleged authority" can claim is that she would do better if she were to accept it, then this may tend to undermine her acceptance of it, and so its beneficial effects.

It seems more accurate to Raz's idea, however, to suppose that by accepting an alleged authority's "directives as authoritatively binding," Raz means nothing essentially second personal, but simply that the alleged subject takes the authority's directives as pre-emptive reasons, that is, reasons that are "not to be added to all other relevant reasons when assessing what to do," but that "exclude and take the place of [at least] some of them" (Raz 1986: 46). Thus A acquires practical authority with respect to B if B would do better in actually complying with independently applicable reasons if B were to treat A's directives as pre-emptive reasons in this sense.

---

[16] The reference is to Mill in a different context: "But moral associations which are wholly of artificial creation, when intellectual culture goes on, yield by degrees to the dissolving force of analysis: and if the feeling of duty, when associated with utility, would appear equally arbitrary; if there were no leading department of our nature, no powerful class of sentiments, with which that association would harmonize, which would make us feel it congenial, and incline us not only to foster it in others (for which we have abundant interested motives), but also to cherish it in ourselves—if there were not, in short, a natural basis of sentiment for utilitarian morality, it might well happen that this association also, even after it had been implanted by education, might be analyzed away" (1998, Ch. III.¶97).

It is the pre-emptive character of the reasons that practical authority purports to create, according to Raz's analysis, that enables Raz to distinguish between genuinely practical authority and the kind of epistemic authority that a trusted adviser might have, that is, to make Hobbes's distinction between command and counsel. The only claim an adviser makes as such is on an advisee's beliefs about independently existing reasons and about what actions these reasons support, not directly on her will. "This is what I think you have good reason to do," an adviser might say, and add, "but I'm not for a moment telling or even asking you to do it," without canceling his advice or anything the advice implied. The improvements to the alleged subject's reason compliance that matter for the normal justification thesis are those that come, not from her being convinced by the alleged authority that there is sufficient independently existing reason to do as he suggests, but from her taking his instructions as *directives* that create *pre-emptive* reasons.

Raz does not consider what might be necessary for us actually to take (whether judge or in some less reflective way regard) someone's directives as giving rise to pre-emptive reasons. In my view, however, there is a problem here that is similar to the problem we set aside before of how it is possible to regard someone as having genuine authority if one holds the normal justification thesis. For as I see it, the normal way of taking someone's directives to provide pre-emptive reasons is to take it that he has practical authority in the second-personal sense I have been pointing to, namely, that one has an obligation to comply with his directives and is responsible to him for doing so. In other words, normally one must have authority to be able to give someone pre-emptive reasons by issuing a directive, and someone must normally regard one as having authority over them to take themselves to be given pre-emptive reason to comply with one's directives. I propose to set this problem aside also.

Now I take it that when Raz says that it is sufficient to establish that A has practical authority with respect to B if it can be shown that B would do better in complying with independently applicable reasons were B to accept A's directives as creating pre-emptive reasons, he means this to entail also that under such conditions A's directives actually do create such pre-emptive reasons. It is important to see, however, that these two theses can be distinguished. In fact, all three of the following theses are different:

I. If B would do better in complying with independently existing reasons were B to treat A's directives as pre-emptive reasons, then B has sufficient reason so to treat A's directives.

II. If B would do better in complying with independently existing reasons were B to treat A's directives as pre-emptive reasons, then A's directives actually are such pre-emptive reasons for B.

III. If B would do better in complying with independently existing reasons were B to treat A's directives as pre-emptive reasons, then A has authority with respect to B (normal justification thesis).

It seems obvious that one could accept I without accepting II and accept both I and II without accepting III. Indeed, one could accept I and II without accepting the normal justification thesis even if one thought that A's having authority with respect to B entails that A's directives are pre-emptive reasons.

For our purposes, however, we can simply put aside any reservations we might have about I and II and simply stipulate that both are true.[17] Our question will still remain, namely, whether the satisfaction of the conditions of the normal justification thesis establishes, not just that the directives of an alleged authority should be taken as pre-emptive reasons or even that they are pre-emptive reasons in fact, but that the alleged authority is genuine.[18]

There seem to be clear cases, however, some that Raz himself considers, where it is hard to see how the normal justification thesis could possibly hold. Raz asks us to imagine that "John is an expert on Chinese Cooking" and that if one wants nothing but "to prepare the best Chinese meal [one] can [one] should just follow John's instructions" (64). Let us stipulate also that one has no reason to do anything other than prepare the best Chinese meal and therefore, following from our acceptance of II above, that John's instructions provide pre-emptive reasons. The question remains, does John thereby acquire any practical authority over one? It is hard to see how he does. Of course, one would be foolish not to follow his instructions, but if one did not it is difficult to see why John would have any standing to complain or otherwise hold one to account. Raz says that those with practical authority "have the right to replace people's own judgment on the merits of the case." But what *right* could John have in such a case? Or recall Raz's remark that, unlike merely justified coercion, genuine practical authority involves "an appeal for compliance" and "an invocation of the duty to obey" (Raz 1986: 25–6). How, in such a case, could John warrantedly expect that one would have any obligation to follow his instructions, however foolish one might be not to do so? It follows from our stipulations that John's instructions are not mere advice; they provide pre-emptive reasons. But it is hard to see how that gives John any right to our compliance with his directives or us any obligation to comply with them.

Raz's position about cases of this kind is somewhat equivocal. He grants that we would not ordinarily think that John would have any authority "over" one even if one's Chinese cooking would "prosper" by following his instructions, but points out that one can accept the normal justification thesis and still resist that John has such authority because one might think one would enjoy self-directed Chinese cooking more or have other goals. No doubt, but we can simply stipulate that one has no reason to do anything other than prepare the best Chinese meal, and it still does not seem to be

[17] For the record, however, I might say that II seems to me, as I argue in Darwall 2010c, almost certainly false. As I see it, the kinds of case where pre-emptive reasons are most plausibly in play are those that depend on the existence of (second-personal) practical authority.

[18] Of course, Raz might hold that A's having authority over B is no more and no less than that A's directives to B give B pre-emptive reasons. I consider this possibility below.

the case that John has genuine practical authority as the normal justification thesis requires (64–5).

However, what if the reasons with which one would better comply themselves concern moral obligations? In such a case, an alleged authority would more plausibly appeal to an obligation to do as he directs. If the only way we can adequately comply with our moral obligations is to treat an alleged authority's directives as pre-emptive reasons, then there seems to be a sense in which it is plausible to suppose that we would be under an obligation so to treat them. Even so, it would not follow from this that the alleged authority himself thereby acquires any actual authority (beyond any he might have had already) to hold others to moral demands. After all, treating some appropriately programmed computer's "directives" as pre-emptive reasons *might* be no less effective, but neither the computer nor the programmer would thereby acquire any special practical authority by virtue of that.

Even if we could extend the scope of authority to an effective moral director by applying the normal justification thesis in such a case, this would still give us no reason to conclude that the second-personal appearances of practical authority can ultimately be explained away entirely by the normal justification thesis. The reason, as I argue in *SPS*, is that moral obligations provide second-personal reasons themselves (Darwall 2006). Moral obligations are what is warrantedly demanded of us, what we can warrantedly be held to. In the kind of case we are imagining, it is, at best, as if the alleged authority functions as a kind of representative who acquires any special authority he comes to have by virtue of the general authority to hold morally responsible. So even if the normal justification thesis tracks genuine practical authority in a case of this kind, it does so thanks to there being an assumed second-personal authority to hold people to moral demands in the background.

But suppose we attempt to explain the authority to hold people to moral demands itself by the normal justification thesis. If we try to do so based on improvements that would come in our compliance with reasons of other kinds then our moral philosophy will "rest on a mistake," in Prichard's famous phrase (Prichard 2002). Reasons of other sorts are reasons of the wrong kind for distinctively moral authority. But what if we say that moral authority derives from improvements that accepting it would make in our compliance with moral obligations themselves? How then are we to specify our moral obligations? If Mill and I are right, there is no way adequately to characterize what it is to be morally obligatory that does not already involve the authority to hold morally responsible.[19] So we cannot explain moral authority itself by the normal justification thesis by claiming that we will do better in complying with moral obligations if we accept that authority, since nothing will count as a moral obligation unless there is already such a thing as the authority to hold morally responsible. I need not assume, of course, that it is impossible to designate moral obligations extensionally in

[19] See note 8.

non-second-personal terms, for example, with some list like: acts of kind A in circumstances of kind C_1, of kind B in circumstances of kind C_2, and so on. The point will nonetheless remain that the mere fact that we will do better in performing acts on the list is impotent by itself to explain the authority to hold morally responsible, since an act's being morally obligatory, and so on the list, is not itself independent of the authority to hold morally responsible and make demands of one another.

Suppose, however, that Raz were to eschew talk of obligation in this sense "all the way down," and simply take the position that all he really means by a duty of obedience is that there are pre-emptive reasons for following an alleged authority's directives. Similarly, he might hold that the latter is all that it is for someone to have practical authority in the sense in which he has in mind. If we interpret the normal justification thesis as applying to practical authority defined in this way, it may seem more plausible. But it should be clear that practical authority so defined is not a thesis that entails anything about any *right* to obedience or about any *obligation* to obey, at least as we ordinarily understand rights and obligations. So understood, the normal justification thesis is simply a thesis about pre-emptive reasons. But if that is so, then it is not even relevant to the question of whether second-personal authority, demands, reasons, and responsibility, in the sense that I have delimited, can ultimately be accounted for in terms of considerations that are not themselves second personal.[20]

My conclusion is that the normal justification thesis poses no serious challenge to my claim that the four notions I have identified constitute a circle of interdefinable, irreducibly second-personal concepts. If we interpret the thesis as concerning practical authority, understood in second-personal terms, then it is either implausible or, in cases where it seems not to be, it borrows plausibility from the implicitly second-personal character of the reasons on which the alleged authority's directives are based (as when she directs us to comply with our moral obligations). And if we interpret the thesis otherwise, it just becomes a thesis about pre-emptive reasons for acting and so has no direct relevance to the possibility of grounding or otherwise explaining second-personal authority in non-second-personal terms.

Of course, even if the concepts of practical authority, valid demand, second-personal reason, and responsibility *to* I am pointing to are irreducibly second-personal in the ways I am claiming, that does not entail that any of these concepts are actually instantiated, that is, that there are any second-personal reasons, is any second-personal authority, and so on. So we might regard a position like Raz's as a kind of skepticism about practical authority of the kind I am pointing to and as offering a "reforming definition" in the style of Stevenson or Brandt in terms of pre-emptive reasons. I cannot, of course, establish here that the unreformed second-personal ideas I have

---

[20] And it may also be the case, as I mentioned in note 17, that pre-emptive reasons themselves normally plausibly exist only when there has been a directive with genuine (second-personal) practical authority.

described are anything other than what Kant calls "figment[s] of the mind."[21,22] However, if what I have said here is correct, it will follow that if these ideas are mere figments, then so are the ideas of moral right, responsibility, and obligation and, indeed, the very concept of moral agent or person itself.[23]

[21] At the end of Chapter II *Groundwork* points out that his arguments that autonomy of the will, the unqualified goodness of the good will, and the Categorical Imperative are mutually entailing has derived from an analysis of our moral concepts, and that nothing yet follows from this about whether any of these are actually realized or valid. That, he says, requires a "critique" of practical reason, to which he turns in *Groundwork* III and, of course, *The Critique of Practical Reason*.

[22] I attempt to vindicate these ideas in Darwall 2006.

[23] I am indebted to audiences at the Bowling Green Practical Reason Conference, Texas Tech University, Vanderbilt University, University of Toronto School of Law, Yale University, The Graduate Center at the City University of New York, University of Chicago, University of California at Irvine, Northwestern University, and Brugge, Belgium, especially, to John Broome, David Copp, James Dreier, Kyla Ebels Duggan, Margaret Gilbert, Aaron James, Shelly Kagan, Richard Kraut, Victoria McGeer, Douglas MacLean, Marina Oshana, Philip Pettit, David Plunkett, Wlodek Rabinowicz, Peter Railton, Arthur Ripstein, T. M. Scanlon, Mark Schroeder, Scott Shapiro, John Skorupski, Wayne Sumner, Candace Vogler, Gary Watson, Susan Wolf, and most especially to David Sobel and Steven Wall.

9

Authority and Reasons: Exclusionary and Second Personal

In *SPS*, I argue that a distinctive kind of reason for acting, a *second-personal reason*, is an ineliminable element of many central moral categories, including rights, moral responsibility, moral obligation, the dignity of (and respect for) persons, and the concept of moral agent or person itself (Darwall 2006). Second-personal reasons are distinguished from reasons of other kinds by their conceptual connection to *authority* and to authoritative claims and demands that must be able to be *addressed to* those to whom they apply. I call these reasons second-personal to highlight this relation to address, which is necessarily always *to* someone (an addressee) and so in that sense second personal, even when the addressee is oneself, the public at large, or anyone at all, real or imagined.

More specifically, I argue that there are four interdefinable, irreducibly second-personal notions that together define a conceptual circle: the authority to make a claim or demand, a valid (authoritative or legitimate) claim or demand, accountability or responsibility *to* someone (with the relevant authority), and a second-personal reason for acting (that is, for complying with an authoritative claim or demand and so discharging the responsibility).[1] Each of these notions entails the other three, and no proposition that does not already involve one of these four concepts can entail any that does. Whenever we take up a second-person standpoint and address or acknowledge a claim or demand, I argue, we necessarily reason within this circle of second-personal concepts. And I argue further that we are thereby committed to a basic second-personal authority we share with our reciprocal others as second-personally competent, that is, as beings able to enter into relations of mutual accountability at all.

In a more recent paper (Darwall 2009), I consider a challenge that might be posed to my claims about the irreducibly second-personal element in these central moral concepts based on Joseph Raz's "service conception of authority," specifically, on what Raz calls the "normal justification thesis" (NJT). The kind of authority that Raz and I are both concerned with is *practical authority*, as distinguished from various forms

---

[1] I take "accountability" and "answerability" to be synonyms that refer to a distinctive kind responsibility *to* someone. There are of course other forms of (ethical) responsibility. Cf. Gary Watson's distinction between "responsibility as accountability" and "responsibility as attributability" in Watson 1996.

of epistemic authority or expertise, including the kind of authority on practical matters that a trusted adviser might have. Raz argues that the claim that one person (A) has authority over another (B), entailing that A has the right to B's obedience and B a correlative duty to obey, can be justified by its being the case that B would be likely to comply better with reasons that apply to him independently already were he to accept as binding and act on the directives of an alleged authority than he would if he were to act on his own assessment of reasons (Raz 1986: 53). In other words, claims to genuine practical authority can be justified if one would better comply with reasons were one to accept these claims and treat them as valid.[2]

The objection to my irreducibly claim would then proceeds as follows. If the reasons with which an agent would better comply were not themselves second-personal reasons, it would then follow that someone could acquire practical authority over her owing entirely to non-second-personal considerations. So there might be good arguments to second-personal claims (e.g., A's authority over B and consequently A's authoritative demands of B) that do not depend on premises in which second-personal concepts and reasons figure in any way.

Against this possibility, I argue (in the paper just mentioned) that our concept of practical authority involves a conceptual connection to accountability and that satisfying the conditions of the Normal Justification Thesis cannot be guaranteed to secure this. The kinds of case in which the NJT has any plausibility, I claim, are those in which the reasons with which following a putative authority's directives secures better compliance already themselves assume background accountability relations that are critical to establishing the directives' legitimacy or authority. The rough idea is that the NJT is only plausible at all in cases where the relevant reasons involve background obligations of some kind or other and that the idea of obligation is itself conceptually related to that of accountability (I argue, ultimately to one another as representative persons or members of the moral community). If the reasons with which I will better comply have no connection to anything I am answerable for doing (independently of the directive), then it is simply not true that someone can come to have authority over me by virtue of the fact that I would better comply with those reasons were I to treat her directives as authoritative and follow them.

For example, I assume that I have prudential reasons to provide for my retirement that are independent of any obligations I might have, say, to provide for others whom I am answerable for supporting or of any obligation to support myself. It seems obvious that I do have such reasons and, moreover, that however important or valuable it might be for me to make my own choices, this latter value might not override (or sufficiently inform) the prudential reasons so that it could indeed make sense for me in prudential

---

[2] For ease of exposition, I will sometimes use "better comply with reasons" as synonymous with "better comply with reasons that apply to the agent already, that is, independently of the putatively authoritative directive."

terms to put myself in the hands of a financial expert and simply follow her directives.[3]
Suppose, then, that I would better comply with the relevant prudential reasons if
I were to do so and that there are no other reasons, or at any rate no sufficient reasons,
for me not to do so. (We should note that the kind of case we need is not just one
where I would do better to follow an expert's *advice*, that is, by treating her as an
epistemic authority on the theoretical question of what there is reason for me to do, but
where I would do better if I were to treat her as having *practical authority over* me, hence
the standing to issue legitimate directives to me, in other words, as being in a position
not just to tell me what I should do, but to tell me *to do* it.)[4]

I argued that however desirable it might be for me to place myself in someone's
hands in this way, even to the point of treating her as though she had practical authority
over me, it simply would not follow that she actually has this authority. In order for her
legitimately to claim authority over me, I would have to be answerable to her, and
actually being answerable to someone cannot follow from the desirability (even,
indeed, the moral desirability (in at least some senses of that phrase)), of regarding
oneself (or of someone's regarding one) as answerable to her. Following Strawson's line
of argument in "Freedom and Resentment," I argued that reasons that establish the
desirability of treating someone as answerable to another person (or of his so treating
himself), specifically, because he would thereby do better in complying with non-
second-personal reasons that apply to him independently, are simply reasons of the
wrong kind to show that he actually *is* answerable to that person (Strawson 1968).
(Reasons of the right kind, I claimed, are irreducibly second personal.) So if, as
I argued, authority entails answerability, then the NJT fails, and no objection can be
mounted on its basis to my claims in *SPS* that central moral concepts, like those of
moral obligation, responsibility, rights, and so on, are irreducibly second personal. No
authority to make claims and demands can be based entirely on non-second-personal
reasons.

Of course, Raz might for his purposes restrict the NJT to cases where the relevant
reasons already entail some kind of answerability (although not, of course, the specific
answerability of B to A that simply follows from A's having practical authority over B).
I did not argue against this possibility, though I believe that, even so restricted, the NJT
is unlikely to be true and that the right way to justify claims of differential practical
authority—e.g., of legal and political authority—is within a contractualist framework
grounded in the premise that all persons share a common basic (second-personal)
authority to make claims and demands of one another at all.[5]

---

[3] This is necessary to satisfy what Raz has recently called the "independence condition" (Raz 2006).

[4] According to the NJT it is accepting "the directives of the alleged authority as authoritatively binding,"
that must produce the improvement in reason compliance. Cf. Hobbes's distinction between law or
command and counsel (Hobbes 1994: XXV).

[5] I discuss the relation between second-personal authority and contractualism in Chapter 12 of Darwall
2006.

And Raz might also simply reject my conceptual thesis that practical authority entails accountability and argue that the NJT applies to a concept of authority that lacks this entailment.[6] I have my doubts that Raz and I really do have different concepts in mind, since he talks also of the authority's "right" to a subject's obedience and the subject's "duty" to obey. But perhaps these notions might be given readings that do not entail accountability also.

Indeed, Raz's *preemption thesis* suggests how this might be done. A core idea of Raz's theory of practical authority is that an authoritative directive provides "a reason for behaving as it directs, as well as an exclusionary reason, that is, a reason for not following (that is, for not acting for) reasons that conflict with the rule" (Raz 2006: 1022). Specifically, an authoritative directive "preempts" or "excludes" any reasons against performing any action it prescribes that the authority can be presumed to have taken into account in deciding to issue the directive.

This suggests that we might attempt to put the idea of accountability to one side and simply ask whether, if the conditions specified by the NJT are satisfied, this guarantees that the relevant reasons are in fact created. According to Raz in *The Morality of Freedom*, an authoritative directive creates a "preemptive reason" to act as it directs (Raz 1986: 42). In the Postscript to the 1990 second edition of *Practical Reason and Norms*, Raz says that "mandatory rules," of which "directives issued by authority are one subspecies," create "protected reasons," which consist in a "systematic combination of a reason to perform the act . . . required by the rule, and an exclusionary reason not to act for [conflicting] . . . reasons" that the authority can be presumed to have taken account of in deciding to issue the directive (Raz 1990: 191). I will follow Raz's earlier usage and refer to *preemptive reasons* as the reasons that a putative authority purports to create, that is, a positive (or first-order) reason for acting as the authority directs together with a (second-order) *exclusionary reason* not to act on conflicting first-order reasons.[7]

Even if, consequently, the NJT were to fail as an account of practical authority as involving a standing to hold accountable, it might nonetheless succeed as an account of authority as the capacity to create preemptive reasons. Similarly, a Razian might understand the idea that authoritative directives create binding obligations in terms of their creating the relevant preemptive reasons.

My object in this paper is to argue that the NJT fails here as well. Although I agree with Raz that the capacity to create preemptive reasons (that is, to create exclusionary reasons not to act on reasons that would otherwise have force along with a new reason that "displaces" or preempts the excluded reasons) is a mark of practical authority, I believe that this capacity itself requires the second-personal relation of accountability. In a slogan: "No preemptive reasons without the standing to hold accountable." If, as

---

[6] As I point out in Darwall 2009.

[7] For discussion on exclusionary reasons and their relation to preemptive reasons, I am indebted to Scott Hershovitz, David Enoch, Steven Wall, and Scott Shapiro.

I maintain, the latter can be established only within a second-personal framework, it will follow that the former requires a second-personal framework also.

Second-Personal Reasons

Before I proceed to attempt to make this case, I should say something more about second-personal reasons and the Strawsonian lesson, as I interpret it, namely, that reasons "of the right kind" for establishing accountability claims can arise only within the second-personal conceptual network.

Suppose someone is stepping on your foot. There might be various different reasons for him to get off. One would simply be the fact that he is causing you pain and that this pain is bad for you or a bad thing period. Whether or not anyone does wrong or violates others' rights by gratuitously causing them pain, there is some reason not to cause them pain simply in the badness of pain or in its being bad for the person who is subjected to it.

Suppose, however, that you take yourself to have a *right* (specifically, a "claim right") not to be caused pain. Were you to think that, you would have also to think that you have as right holder some standing or authority to claim or demand that people not step on your feet without your consent and, specifically, that the person currently stepping on your foot not have done so, that he get off, and so on (Feinberg 1980: 155). Moreover, you must also think that you have some standing, again as the right holder, to hold the person accountable for having stepped on your foot, for example, to object, to ask him his reasons, to demand an apology, to forgive him if he apologizes, and so on. Since the idea of a right is connected in this way to the (right holder's) authority to claim or demand and hold accountable, it is a second-personal reason.

The authority one has as a right holder is not, however, the only relevant standing in this case. Although the victim of wrongdoing has the distinctive standing to resent or forgive an injury, he has no special standing others do not have to *blame* the wrongdoer or to hold him responsible through (what Strawson called "impersonal") reactive attitudes such as indignation.[8] This is an authority that anyone has as a representative of the moral community, indeed, that the wrongdoer has himself and that he exercises when, in blaming himself, he feels guilt.

If it is wrong to cause gratuitous pain, this is a reason not to do so, perhaps, indeed a conclusive reason.[9] And if, as I believe,[10] the idea of moral wrong is conceptually connected to accountability—what is wrong is what we are answerable to one another as representative persons for not doing—then the fact that it would be wrong is a

---

[8] Though it is not distinctively up to the victim whether to have the *attitude* of blame, the victim may have a distinctive standing to blame the wrongdoer overtly. I am indebted to an anonymous referee for prompting me to clarify this point.

[9] I argue for this claim in Darwall 2010a.

[10] And argue in Darwall 2006.

second-personal reason for anyone not to cause gratuitous pain by stepping on your foot.[11] Both reasons—that it would violate your right and that it would be wrong—conceptually entail authorities to address demands (second personally).

Second-personal reasons exist only if the relevant authorities also exist to address and acknowledge claims and demands. The two reasons I just mentioned depend, respectively, on your standing as an individual right holder, on the one hand, and your and any other person's authority as representative persons or members of the moral community, on the other. Both involve an authority to make claims and demands and to hold accountable, although in different ways.

To appreciate the second-personal aspect of moral responsibility, consider Strawson's famous critique of "pragmatist" or consequentialist approaches to responsibility in "Freedom and Resentment." Strawson argued influentially that social desirability cannot provide a justification of "the right *sort*" for practices of moral responsibility "as we understand them" (Strawson 1968: 74). When we seek to hold people accountable, what matters is not whether some sanction is desirable, either in a particular case or in general, but whether their actions are culpable and whether we have any authority to demand their acceptance of a sanction. Desirability is a reason of the wrong kind to warrant the attitudes and actions in which holding someone responsible consists *in their own terms*.

Strawson pointed out what more recent commentators like Gary Watson and Jay Wallace have since also noted, namely, that reactive attitudes implicitly address *demands*. They involve "an expectation of, and demand for" certain conduct from the object of attitude (Strawson 1968: 85).[12] To feel a reactive attitude is to feel as though one has a warranted expectation *of* someone. Reactive attitudes, and actions that express them, must therefore presuppose the authority *to* expect and hold one another responsible for compliance with moral obligations (which must then be standards to which we can warrantedly hold each other as representative persons or members of the moral community).

Reactive attitudes differ from other critical attitudes in that they don't merely have objects; they implicitly address their objects. Compare, for example, blame, indignation, or resentment, on the one hand, with (non-reactive) attitudes like disgust, contempt, or disdain, on the other. The former implicitly address a *charge* to their objects, while the latter do not. This is why the former, but not the latter, involve or presuppose a view of their objects as having some competence to understand or

---

[11] Of course, the fact that it would cause gratuitous pain is a reason why it would be wrong to step on your foot. I believe, however, that the fact that causing pain in this way amounts to doing wrong is a further, second-personal, and conclusive reason for not stepping on your foot that is additional to this wrong-making reason. On this point, see Darwall 2010a.

[12] Watson 1987: 263, 264. R. Jay Wallace: "there is an essential connection between the reactive attitudes and a distinctive form of evaluation... that I refer to as holding a person to an expectation (or demand)" (Wallace 1994: 19).

appreciate the charge.[13] We can think someone an "egregious blockhead," in Hume's phrase, without thinking him capable of understanding our contemptuous criticism. To the contrary, a really egregious blockhead is incapable of seeing what a blockhead he is. However, we can only intelligibly blame and hold accountable individuals we think capable of understanding and internalizing our blame, that is, of seeing themselves as being *to blame*, thereby holding themselves responsible.[14]

It follows on Strawson's analysis that culpability and moral responsibility are second-personal phenomena. Holding someone accountable involves an implicit address of authoritative demands and, therefore, of second-personal reasons. But the conceptual relations also run in the opposite direction. If one person has practical authority with respect to another, then this would seem to mean not just that the latter has a reason of whatever priority or weight for acting as the former directs, but also that the latter is answerable for doing so. Practical authority is not just a relation in the logical sense; it is a standing in a relationship.[15] If A has authority with respect to B, then certain things follow about how A and B may and must relate to one another. If A has the authority to demand that B stay off A's feet, then not only is it the case that B has a reason of whatever weight or priority for doing so. B is also answerable to A for doing so. I take it, then, that there is a strong prima facie case for thinking that the four second-personal notions I mentioned at the outset—practical authority (to claim or demand), valid (authoritative or legitimate) claim or demand, accountability *to*, and second-personal reason for acting form an interdefinable circle of irreducibly second-personal concepts.

The Normal Justification Thesis and Exclusionary Reasons

We can turn now to considering whether the NJT provides an adequate justification for practical authority, specifically, of the sort one person has over another when she has the standing to issue directives to another that the latter thereby has some obligation to obey. Here is Raz's formulation of the NJT in *Morality and Freedom*:

> the normal way to establish that a person has authority over another person involves showing that the alleged subject is likely better to comply with reasons which apply to him (other than the alleged authoritative directives) if he accepts the directives of the alleged authority as authoritatively binding and tries to follow them, rather than by trying to follow the reasons which apply to him directly. (Raz 1986: 53)

As I mentioned above, I argue in the earlier paper that if we take the relevant authority and resulting obligation to analytically entail accountability, that is, that being subject

---

[13] And it explains their distinct connection to the problem of freedom of the will in a way that other critical attitudes are not.

[14] There are of course exceptions, e.g., blaming the dead. I am indebted here to an anonymous referee.

[15] I have been helped here by discussion with Jules Coleman.

to authority essentially involves answerability, then the NJT fails, at least that it does so when the reasons with which the person would comply better are not themselves second-personal reasons. In cases where the reasons do not concern anything one is already answerable for, then the fact that one would comply better with these reasons if one were to treat someone's directives as authoritative and make oneself answerable to that person for complying with the directives cannot establish that one is accountable to her in fact.

This, again, is the lesson of Strawson's "Freedom and Resentment." The fact that I would do better in complying with the prudential reasons concerning provision for my retirement if I were to put myself in the hands of a financial expert to the point of treating her directives as authoritative and myself as accountable to her for complying with them, cannot establish that I actually am answerable to her or that she has any standing to hold me to account for complying with her directives.[16] We can simply stipulate that I have no better reason to do anything other than what is necessary to provide for my retirement, that this is what I have most reason to do all things considered, and it will still not follow that I would actually be accountable in such a case. However weighty the reasons connected with the desirability of providing for my retirement might be, so long as I am not answerable for doing what they recommend, these reasons are simply of the wrong kind to establish that I would actually be accountable. In Hobbes's terms, reasons of this kind are sufficient to establish good "counsel" but not "law" or "command" (Hobbes 1994: xxv.¶1).

But suppose, again, that Raz were to maintain that whether or not the NJT fails for authority as essentially involving accountability, it nonetheless holds for authority as the capacity to create *preemptive reasons*?[17] We can put to one side the question of which concept of practical authority is "ours" and consider whether if we take the capacity to create preemptive reasons as the mark of practical authority, the NJT succeeds for authority so conceived. In other words, is satisfying the conditions of the NJT sufficient (or necessary) to establish that one person has the standing to create preemptive reasons for another?

The Razian idea of a preemptive reason includes that of an *exclusionary reason*. An exclusionary reason is a reason that does not count in favor of or against an action in the way "first-order" reasons do; it is a "second-order" reason against acting on certain first-order reasons. The idea underlying Raz's *preemption thesis* is that in deciding what directives to issue, an authority will take account of first-order reasons, at least within some range, for and against actions that would be prescribed by directives the authority is considering and that an authoritative directive preempts

---

[16] Of course, she might acquire this standing if I put myself in her care, depending on how she and I understand the terms of the relationship into which we voluntarily enter.

[17] Alternatively, Raz might hold that though our concept entails accountability, this is not an entailment we can adequately support or vindicate, and offer an NJT based account in terms of preemptive reasons as a "reforming definition" in the spirit of Richard Brandt or Charles Stevenson.

the reasons for acting that the authority has already taken into account, specifically, it preempts or excludes the reasons for performing any action that would violate the directive. So an authoritative directive both creates an additional reason for doing what the directive prescribes that would not otherwise exist—namely, that so acting is required by an authoritative directive—*and* it creates an exclusionary reason against acting on any reason in favor of actions that would violate the directive, which reasons the authority can be assumed to have taken into account in deciding to issue the directive.

For example, suppose the state decides to impose a certain speed limit, say 65 miles per hour on a certain road. In deciding what speed limit to set, the state will balance complex considerations concerning safety, fuel economy, citizens' convenience, other economic factors, and so on. Once, however, the speed limit has been set, it is no longer permissible for citizens simply to make their own judgments about what speed to drive based on their own assessments of these and other relevant reasons. That is no longer within their discretion. The authoritative directive both gives them a reason to drive no faster than 65 miles per hour that they would otherwise not have had and a reason not to act on reasons for driving faster that they might have otherwise legitimately regarded as counting in favor of so doing, e.g., that they would thereby more conveniently arrive at their destinations sooner, are able to drive safely at a faster speed, and so on.

Suppose then we ask whether the NJT holds for authority as the capacity to create exclusionary reasons along with an additional reason for doing what the authority directs, which together comprise a preemptive reason? I shall argue that it does not. The conditions of the NJT are satisfied when a person would do better in complying with the reasons that apply to him already anyway were he to treat someone as an authority and treat her directives as legitimate. Now again, in my view, when we treat someone as having authority over us, we see ourselves as accountable to that person. But whether I am right about that or not, we are ignoring the element of accountability at this stage. Our question at this point is whether if someone does better in complying with reasons if he treats another person's directives as giving him preemptive reasons, this is sufficient to establish that the preemptive reasons actually exist. Is that sufficient, in other words, to establish the existence of a positive reason to comply and a second-order reason not to act on first-order reasons recommending non-compliance?[18]

It will be useful to have before us now the following three propositions to help us focus the issues:

---

[18] For convenience, from here on when I say "if he treats A's directives as giving him exclusionary means," I will mean, "if he treats A's directives as giving him an additional reason for acting as she directs and as giving him exclusionary reasons not to act on reasons that might otherwise recommend against the action she prescribes."

    I. B will do better in complying with reasons if he treats A's directives as giving him preemptive reasons.

    II. There is reason for B to treat A's directives as giving him preemptive reasons.

    III. A's directives actually do give B preemptive reasons.

Now I am prepared to stipulate that when I is true, II is true also. We can simply agree for purposes of the argument that if someone would comply better with reasons were he to perform some action or adopt some attitude, then there is reason for him to perform that action or adopt that attitude.[19] The question before us is whether if II is true, then III is guaranteed to be true as well. I believe that this is not the case. For III to be true whenever II is true, the reasons that speak in favor of B's believing that A's directives create exclusionary reasons, or B's regarding or treating A's directives as creating them, would also have somehow to make B's belief or way of seeing or treating things true or correct. And that is not generally the case. As D'Arms and Jacobson put the point, not all reasons for having an attitude are reasons of the right kind to show that attitude to be "fitting," that is, that it fits what it purports to represent (D'Arms and Jacobson 2000b). In this case, not all reasons for regarding or treating directives as creating preemptive reasons are relevant to whether the directives actually do create preemptive reasons.

    For example, suppose that I would comply better with reasons for acting if I just had some false belief. Suppose, somewhat like Kavka's toxin puzzle, that someone will give me a prize enabling me to provide better for my children if I just believe, say, that the U.S. invasion of Iraq was an unqualified success in every respect. Assume that what I have most reason to do is to provide for my children, which I will be able adequately to do only if I form this belief and so win the prize. Clearly I would have reason to (try anyway) to form the belief (surrounding myself with relevant political propaganda and avoiding reputable news sources). But the reasons for doing so would not be reasons of the right kind to bear on whether the belief is actually true or credible. Only evidence can do that and pragmatic reasons for forming a belief are not evidence of a belief's truth or credibility.

    Admittedly, this case has a different shape than those where the conditions of the NJT are satisfied. In this case, the false belief is necessary to give me the *means* to accomplish what I have reason to try to accomplish. I might, after all, form the belief, get the prize, and then not actually end up providing for my children. Perhaps I would spend the money foolishly on expensive antiquarian books. But the general point nonetheless still stands, namely, the fact that one has reason to adopt an attitude does not in general make it the case that the attitude is true, correct, or "fitting."[20] We might, therefore, reasonably be suspicious about whether if II is true, III will be guaranteed to be true also. Why should the fact that one has reason to *regard* or *treat*

---

[19] For the record, I doubt that this is true.

[20] This, of course, is just the "wrong kind of reasons" problem.

someone's directives as creating exclusionary reasons make it the case that their directives actually do create such exclusionary reasons?

Let us focus now on that question, and to vary the case, suppose that what B has most reason to do is to get out of bed at a certain time, say, 7 a.m. We can suppose, again, that B has conclusive prudential reasons for doing so and no better reasons to do anything else. One thing B might do, of course, is to use an alarm of some kind. Let us suppose, however, that the usual alarms do not work for B. They wake him up all right, but when they do, he then deliberates about whether to get up and invariably persuades himself (against, let us suppose, his better judgment) that he has more reason to stay in bed a little longer. Suppose further that there is no other technical fix to B's problem. For example, if he puts the alarm far enough out of reach so that he has to get out of bed to turn it off, the ring from that distance is not loud or annoying enough to get him out of bed.

As it happens, however, B has an authoritarian personality. Whereas some people have bumper stickers saying "Question Authority," B's car displays one saying "Respect Authority." And B is the kind of person who, were he a subject in the Milgram experiment, would administer shocks up to the full 450 volts (Milgram 1974). So B gets an "authority alarm clock." The clock has a recording of an authoritative voice that says "You must get out of bed now." And if B stays in bed, the voice says things like "If you don't get out of bed, you will be found in violation and made subject to the full authority of the state," and so on. Suppose that this works and that it is the only way that B can reliably get out of bed at 7 a.m. as he has most reason to do. And suppose that the way it works is by giving B an "authority experience," that is, it is by making it seem to him as if someone with genuine authority is ordering him to get out of bed, that he must comply or be in violation, and so on.

Now if what B has most reason to do is to get out of bed at 7 a.m., then it would seem that B also has reason to treat the voice as actually issuing authoritative directives that create exclusionary reasons, as his "authority experience" indeed inclines him to do.[21] That is, B has reason to treat his authority experience as though it were veridical. But it is also obvious that whatever weight the reasons B might have to get out of bed at 7 a.m. and so to *treat* his experience as veridical, these reasons cannot actually make his experience veridical or even bear on its accuracy. They would be completely impotent to make it the case that the alarm's "directives" actually are legitimate or genuinely create preemptive reasons. When the alarm clock goes off and the voice speaks, B has the very same reasons to get up at 7 a.m. and, by hypothesis, the same less weighty reasons to continue to lie in bed.

---

[21] Of course, it might be argued that there is no actual directive in this case, but only the illusion of one, so that the letter of the NJT is not satisfied. While this seems a fair point, it also seems clear that the psychic mechanism leading to B's "compliance" is the same as might be involved in many cases of genuine compliance with actual directives, for example, in the Milgram experiments themselves, or in the case to be described presently. I am indebted to David Owens for this objection.

Granted, B has pragmatic reasons to respond to the alarm, on the one hand, and, on the other, not even to think about his reasons for staying in bed (since if he does consider them he is likely to act contrary to the weightier reasons and stay in bed). But this does not mean that he may not legitimately think about these reasons, that it is outside his discretion, or that the latter reasons have somehow been displaced, preempted, or defeated, only that he would be foolish to consider them. Clearly, the person who recorded the "authoritative voice" acquires no authority by virtue of the fact that B will comply better with reasons if he treats his voiced directives as creating preemptive reasons.

I should point out, however, that as Raz usually defines the general category of "exclusionary reason," namely, as a second-order reason not to be moved by or to act *for* certain first-order reasons, it simply follows from the fact that it makes no sense for B to consider his reasons for staying in bed that there is indeed an exclusionary reason in this case.[22] But the existence of an exclusionary reason does not guarantee that a preemptive reason of the kind Raz thinks is generated by authoritative directives exists, as Raz himself makes clear. First, a preemptive reason involves an additional new first-order reason that preempts or displaces the excluded reasons, and that is what I am arguing is not created in this case. And second, Raz himself points out that not all exclusionary reasons are "authority-based"; some derive straightforwardly from deliberative incapacities (of the sort, indeed, that seem to be involved here).[23] "Authority-based" exclusionary reasons, Raz says, derive from "a fundamental point about authority, i.e., that it removes the decision from one person to another" (Raz 1990: 193). I take this to be a conceptual claim about practical authority, rather than, say a metaphysical claim about deliberation and action. So understood, it can be interpreted as a point about deliberative *discretion*, about what we may *legitimately* take into account.[24] In this sense, however, it seems clear that no authority-based exclusionary reasons are created for B. B remains perfectly free *in this sense* to consider and be moved by his reasons for staying in bed. However foolish it would be for him to do so, staying in bed while considering the reasons for doing so remains within his discretion. So even if there is an exclusionary reason for B in this case, it is not the kind required to partially constitute a preemptive reason of the sort that genuinely authoritative directives create.

Suppose now that after a while the authority alarm is no longer effective for B. He no longer has a sufficiently vivid "authority experience" when it wakes him. "Oh, you're only a recorded voice," he begins to think. And he begins to talk back to the clock, saying things like "There you go again. I'm going to stay in bed. What are you going to do about it?" Being somewhat unsophisticated, the device is unable to give B a sufficiently vivid experience of being held to account. It simply continues with its

---

[22] I am indebted here to Scott Hershovitz and David Enoch.

[23] See Raz 1990: 48. I am indebted here to Scott Shapiro.

[24] And so, as I would analyze it, about the second-personal character of authority-based exclusionary reasons.

recorded message: "If you don't get out of bed, you will be found in violation and made subject to the full authority of the state."

Finally, B, who really does need to get out of bed reliably at 7 a.m., is at his wits' end. In desperation, he hires an actual person to play the role of a legitimate authority. We can imagine that he hires the very person (call him A) who played the role of the authoritative experimenter in the Milgram experiment. Assume, moreover, that before he issues his directives to B, A deliberatively rehearses the reasons for and against directing B to get out of bed; as it happens A is both wise and concerned for B's welfare. This finally gives B a permanent fix to his problem; it provides B precisely the "authority experience" he needs to get him reliably out of bed at 7 a.m. When B is tempted to continue lying in bed, A speaks to B in an authoritative voice, "reminds" him of his (A's) (putative) authority and that B may not even think about remaining in bed in a sufficiently persuasive way that B "obeys."

Here again, it seems obvious that although B has reason to treat A as an authority and A's directives as giving him preemptive reasons, since this is the only way he will be able to get out of bed at 7 a.m., as he has most reason to do, A does not actually have any genuine authority over B, and A's directives do not actually create preemptive reasons. B continues to have the same weighty reasons for getting out of bed at 7 a.m., and so for responding to the directives, and the same less weighty reasons for continuing to lie in bed. Granted, he has pragmatic reasons for following A's directives (maybe even weightier reasons than he did for responding to the alarm, since, if this does not work, maybe nothing will). And so perhaps he has even weightier pragmatic reasons not even to think about the reasons in favor of continuing to lie in bed. But *however* weighty these pragmatic reasons might be, they do not constitute or create preemptive reasons or authority-based exclusionary reasons. Even if he would be an idiot to think for a moment of the reasons for staying in bed, it is in no way illegitimate or beyond his discretion to do so, and we have no inclination to say, as we do in the case of genuine preemptive reasons, that the reasons for remaining in bed are not just overridden, but are rather preempted or displaced.

I built into the case that A wisely considers the reasons for directing B to get out of bed in order to mirror Raz's thought that genuine practical authorities exclude reasons when they take account of them in deciding to issue directives that conflict with actions the excluded actions recommend.[25] But how exactly is the fact that an

---

[25] It might be objected that Raz intends the Normal Justification Thesis only to concern the justification of claims to authority made by those who already have *de facto* authority; in other words, as what can turn *de facto* authority into *de jure* authority. We can easily modify the case, however, to deal with this. Suppose that A is someone with *de facto* authority, a policeman, say, and that the police claim the authority to enter citizens' homes and wake them up by issuing orders. Suppose that B does not, as a matter of conviction, accept the validity of these claims. Nonetheless, B needs a reliable way of getting up, and he knows that he will treat A's claims as legitimate and comply with them in his sleepy state, so B asks A to come to his house and issue orders daily at the appointed hour. It is hard to see why any of this should give B any reason to believe that A has *de jure* authority as a matter of actual fact. I am indebted to Candice Delmas for this objection and for discussion of it.

authority takes account of the reasons for and against the actions they prescribe supposed to be relevant to establishing practical authority (including the capacity to create preemptive reasons) according the NJT? The fact that genuine authorities have the standing to consider reasons in this way and issue directives that preclude those who are subject to their authority from legitimately taking account of the reasons in favor of actions that violate their directives is a *consequence* of their authority and nothing therefore that can be relevant to establishing it. Of course, one way in which the fact that a putative authority takes good account of reasons in deciding what to prescribe can be relevant to his actually having authority of *one* kind is in establishing his *epistemic authority*. But epistemic authority is not *practical authority*; it involves no standing to create exclusionary reasons. The most it licenses is counsel, not command.

Consider a case that Raz discusses in a recent paper. Raz notes that we "can best avoid endangering [ourselves] and others by conforming to the law regarding the dispensation and use of pharmaceutical products." In doing so we "rely on the experts whose advice [the law] reflects to know what is dangerous in these matters better than [we] can judge for [ourselves]" (Raz 2006: 114–15). The only kind of authority the experts have, however, is epistemic authority. Assume that they know better than we what we must do in order to comply with reasons in the area of their expertise. So far, the only authority they have is to issue advice—to tell us what we should or have reason to do, not to tell us *to do* it. Expertise alone gives them no standing to issue authoritative *directives* that create preemptive reasons. When we have heard their advice, we may, of course, have pragmatic reasons not just to follow it, but also not to deliberate further or even to consider reasons for acting contrary to it. But however inadvisable it might be for us to consider these latter reasons, that would not make it illegitimate or outside of our area of discretion. And it wouldn't preempt or displace the reasons.

So far as the NJT is concerned, the only work that can be done by the fact that a putative authority knows the relevant reasons for acting better than we do is to make it likelier that our treating putative directives based on that expertise as genuinely (practically) authoritative will lead us to comply better with these reasons. Raz's position is not that epistemic authority is transformed into practical authority when we would do better in complying with reasons that would apply to us if we were to accept experts' epistemic authority and follow their *advice*. What the NJT says is that someone acquires practical authority over us when we would do better in complying with reasons if we were to accept her "directives as authoritatively binding." It is the consequences of treating someone as having genuine practical authority that are relevant, not the consequences of seeing her as knowing better than we do what reasons for acting we have. Whether the directives are based on expertise or not has no apparent intrinsic relevance, although of course it can be extrinsically relevant in the way I described.[26]

---

[26] Raz might, of course, modify the NJT to require that the putative authority's directive be based on expertise, and/or that it be believed by those putatively subject to it to be based on expertise as a separate

It seems, therefore, that the most we can say when the conditions of the NJT are satisfied, is that an "alleged subject" has reason to *treat* the alleged authority as having genuine practical authority, and hence to *regard* her directives as creating preemptive reasons. As we have seen, it simply does not follow from the fact that we have reason to treat someone's directives as creating preemptive reasons that they actually do create such reasons. Even if II follows from I (in the cases considered above concerning A and B), III does not follow from II.

There being reason to treat someone as having the authority to create preemptive reasons in the fact that one will comply better with reasons in general is not therefore sufficient to make it the case that he actually has that authority. Now, as I have said, I believe that authority is conceptually tied to accountability. In my view, indeed, the capacity to create preemptive reasons is itself inextricably bound up with accountability. Once an authority sets a speed limit, it is no longer within my discretion to decide for myself whether considerations that would otherwise speak in favor of driving faster are good enough reasons for me to do so, overriding whatever reasons the law might create. I may no longer legitimately take these into account. It seems to me, however, that the reason I may not is because obeying legitimate authority is something I am answerable for doing. In this matter, I no longer simply answer to myself. I answer to the authority and, as I see it, to other representative persons or members of the moral community to whom I am accountable for complying with moral obligations.

So far, I have deliberately constructed examples where the reasons in play concern nothing we are normally answerable for doing, for example, complying with prudential reasons. And I have argued that the fact that treating someone as an authority would enable one to comply better with these reasons cannot establish that he actually has the authority one would thereby take him to have. It cannot establish that his directives create preemptive reasons. If one is not answerable for providing for one's retirement or for getting out of bed at 7 a.m., then, even if one would do better at accomplishing these (and so complying with the relevant reasons) were one to treat oneself as answerable to some authority and so treat his directives as creating preemptive reasons, one does not thereby actually become answerable to him, and his directives do not thereby create preemptive reasons.

But what if the reasons themselves concern moral obligations, which, if I am right, are things we are answerable (to one another as representative persons or members of the moral community) for doing? If we restrict the NJT to reasons that already entail answerability in some form, will it serve to justify differential practical authority claims of the sort Raz is concerned with, e.g., of someone *A over* someone else, *B*, along with A's capacity to create preemptive reasons for B? I do not think so.

Suppose that the reason why B needs to get out of bed at 7 a.m. is that if he does not he will be unable to comply with an important obligation, say, a promise he has made

condition. But this would raise the question of the relation of this new condition to the (unmodified) NJT, since it would seem to have a substantially different rationale from the NJT as Raz has proposed it.

to C. And suppose that the only way B can reliably get out of bed at 7 a.m. is to treat A as a legitimate authority in the way we earlier imagined. Does this create some special accountability of B to A? Does it make it the case that A has the capacity to create preemptive reasons for B? Now, as I analyze things, in having promised to C, and thereby given C a right and created an obligation *to* C, B has become answerable to C in a special way as a right holder.[27] Only C is in a position to release B from his promise, to receive an apology or compensation should B not keep his promise, and so on. However, in being morally obligated *period*, B is not *distinctively* answerable to C; he is accountable to the moral community and, in principle, therefore, to anyone as a representative of the moral community, including A, C, and B himself.

Notice now that none of this involves any *special* accountability of B to A or A's having any special capacity to create preemptive reasons for B. B is no less answerable to A than to any other member of the moral community, but neither is he any more. We might agree that if the only way B can keep his promise to C is to treat A as having authority over him and regarding himself as answerable to A, then he is, as we might then put it, *answerable for answering to A*. He would not, however, be especially answerable *to A* for answering to A. Any special or individual answerability would seem to be to C. Under these conditions, he would be answerable to C, especially, for answering to A, as the only means for complying with his obligation *to* C. B would also be answerable to the moral community, and hence, *inter alia* to A, for answering to A. But this is not the same kind of accountability to A that would be involved in A's having authority *over* B.

Neither, it seems, would A thereby acquire any capacity to create preemptive reasons. We should agree with Raz that mandatory moral norms create preemptive reasons, and therefore, that if it would be wrong for B not to get out of bed at 7 a.m., that B has an exclusionary reason not to consider or act on any reasons he might otherwise have to stay in bed (Raz 1990: 61). If it is wrong for him to stay in bed, then it is no longer legitimate for B to consider staying in bed for the reasons that would otherwise recommend his doing so; this is no longer within his discretion. Similarly, if C were to object to B's remaining in bed, then C's legitimate demand owing to the right given him by B's promise would create a preemptive or authority-based exclusionary reason for B. But none of this gives *A* any distinctive authority to create preemptive reasons for B that other members of the moral community do not have.

As I see it, what explains the capacity of mandatory moral norms to create (authority-based) exclusionary reasons is that they are tied to accountability in the way I have proposed. It is because we are answerable to one another for not violating moral obligations that it is not within our discretion to deliberate on the basis of reasons that would otherwise recommend actions that, as things actually stand, amount to moral wrong. Here we answer not just to ourselves but also to one another and, indeed,

---

[27] I discuss promising as a second-personal relation in Darwall 2011b.

ourselves, as representatives of the moral community. But if that is right, then the capacity to create exclusionary reasons cannot characterize a concept of authority that is an *alternative* to authority as involving accountability. Rather the capacity to create exclusionary reasons would itself *derive* from an accountability relation that is itself essential to practical authority.

But if the NJT fails therefore both for authority as accountability and, consequently, for authority as the capacity to create preemptive reasons, what then can justify differential authority relations, as in legal and political authority? The lesson to draw from the failure of the NJT, I believe, is that the only justification that can succeed is one that proceeds from within the second-person standpoint, beginning with the assumption that we all share a common basic authority to make claims and demands of one another at all, and proceeding from there to consider what differential claims to authority anyone could sensibly accept, or no one could reasonably reject on that basis. The basic premise underlying any successful justification of differential authority, in other words, is that we share a common basic authority to make claims of each other just by virtue of being persons. Or, as Rawls put the point, to be a person is to be a "self-originating source of valid claims" (Rawls 1980: 546).[28]

---

[28] I am indebted to audiences at the Analytical Legal Philosophy conference at Yale University in April, 2008 and a conference on the philosophy of Joseph Raz, held at the University of Manchester in May, 2008, for comments and discussion and to two anonymous referees for *Ethics*.

10

Law and the Second-Person Standpoint

In *SPS*, I argue that there is a distinctive kind of a reason for acting, a *second-personal reason*, that is conceptually implicated in many central moral notions: moral responsibility, moral obligation, rights, respect for and the dignity of persons, and the concept of moral agent or person itself. What is distinctive about second-personal reasons is that they are analytically related to claims and demands that an addresser has the authority to make of, and address to, the agent second-personally. Because this is so, I argue, reasons of this kind always involve an accountability relation between addresser and addressee, that is, that the addressee is answerable to the addresser in some way, if not for compliance, then at least to give consideration or something similar.

Although the claims I argue for in my book concern *morality*—moral obligation, responsibility, rights, and so on—they would seem also to bear on the *law*.[1] One way of viewing my project, in fact, is as trying to bring out the distinctive character of that part of morality that is modeled on the idea of law.[2] Moral *obligations*, I argue, are not just what there are good (or even compelling) moral reasons for us to do; they are what morality demands of us and what we are accountable for doing, where the latter is understood as what representative persons or members of the moral community have the authority to demand that we do. This is why, like Kant, we naturally speak of the "moral law" in such cases.

Similarly, moral *rights* must also be understood in legal or juridical terms. What a person has a moral *claim right* to is what she has the standing as an individual to demand that others provide her, along with the authority to hold them accountable for doing so. What she has a moral *liberty right* to do is what others have no authority to demand that she not do. And so on. Moral rights thus also involve the moral law. If I have a moral liberty to do A, then I do no wrong in doing A, that is, I do nothing that members of the moral community have, as such, the authority to demand I not do. I do not violate the moral law, understood as what members can demand of one another. And if I have a moral claim, as an individual, to your doing A, then the moral law gives me special standing as an individual to demand that you do A and to hold you

---

[1] For a more systematic development of this idea, see Kar 2011.
[2] See "Morality's Distinctiveness" in this volume.

accountable if you do not, say, to demand that you compensate my injury or to release you from compensation or, even, to forgive you for injuring me. This is a standing I have not as a representative of the moral community authorized to hold one another responsible for moral wrongs in general, but as an individual involved in the transaction. It involves, not my *representative authority*, which is in play with moral obligations *period*, but an *individual authority* I have as the person *to whom* a (bipolar) obligation is owed, that is, as the *obligee* (Darwall 2012).

The authority that is involved in moral obligations and rights are forms of *moral authority*, as I see it, the authority of members of the moral community to make claims and demands of one another as such. But the notions of authority, obligations, rights, and responsibility are also all obviously central to law properly so-called (that is, to laws legislated, administered, and enforced by those with *legal authority*). Laws create legal obligations and rights, and the authority to hold responsible is essential both to the criminal and the civil law. Laws are not simply standards that assess conduct in some specific way; laws are *promulgated*, that is addressed, to those who are subject to them, and they make putatively authoritative demands with which addressed subjects are responsible for complying.

Legal sanctions are not just coercive threats, even justified ones. They involve an exercise of putatively legitimate authority that purports to give reasons for compliance that cannot be reduced to the desire to avoid some evil in which the sanction consists, or even to avoid a justified evil. As Hart famously put it, laws purport to *obligate* rather than only to *oblige* (Hart 1961: 6–8). However unwelcome or restrictive sanctions may be, there is a fundamental conceptual difference between putting someone on notice of a legitimate sanction as a way of holding him responsible for complying with law and coercion, even, as Raz has pointed out, justified coercion. Unlike justified coercion, the exercise of authority invariably involves "an appeal for compliance" and "an invocation of the duty to obey" (Raz 1986: 25–6). We respect law not in the same way a fighter might respect his opponent's left jab; we recognize its *authority*.

As I see it, the reasons that the law purports to provide are second-personal reasons. I cannot defend this proposal in detail here, but in what follows I nonetheless want to suggest some reasons in its favor and for thinking that the notions of second-personal address and of what I call *second-personal authority* and *second-personal competence* can be useful in understanding the nature of law and legal obligation. First, however, let me say something about the notions of second-personal reason, authority, and responsibility or accountability that I will be employing in my analysis and that I explore at greater length in *The Second-Person Standpoint*.

Second-Personal Reasons

The intuitive idea of *second-personal reasons* can be gotten across with an example. Suppose someone has stepped on your foot. Compare, to begin with, two different ways in which you might try to give him reason to get off.

One would simply be to get him to see that you are in pain, that this is a bad thing, or, at any rate, bad for you, and that either fact is a reason for him to remove his foot. Nothing in the existence of this reason, or even, indeed, in your being able to get him to see and accept it, need have anything to do with second-personal address, that is, with your having any authority or standing to make any particular claims on him.

A different way of giving someone a reason to move his foot from yours would be to lay a claim or address a purportedly valid demand. "Hey, that's my foot," you might say, implying a right to determine where your foot steps and who may and who may not step on it. Your implicit demand would presuppose a discretionary individual authority that right holders have to exercise their wills, to make demands, to consent to what would otherwise violate their rights, to seek compensation for violations of their rights, and so on. I say "discretionary" because you could consent to his foot placement.

Or suppose you are a third-party bystander to a foot tromping, and say something like, "Hey, you can't just step anywhere you like. You're stepping on someone's foot, and that's wrong." Here again, you would be pressing a claim or demand against the person, and assuming some authority to do so, but not, this time, as the right holder. Rather (I argue), you would be presupposing an authority we all have as representative persons or members of the moral community (Darwall 2006).

Both of these latter two reasons, that someone is violating one's right, or that an action is morally wrong (period), are *second-personal reasons* in the sense that both depend conceptually on second-personal address. The idea is not that the reasons must actually be addressed in order to exist. You have a right that others not step on your feet without your consent, whether you say anything to them about this or not. And the moral wrongness of stepping unbidden on other people's feet depends in no way on anyone's actually demanding that people not do this. The idea is that the concept of a right and the concept of moral obligation implicate second-personal address. It is entailed by the very idea of a claim right that right holders have a distinctive (*individual*) authority to demand certain treatment and hold those who violate their rights personally accountable at their discretion (Feinberg 1980).

I argue that the idea of moral obligation similarly entails accountability, in this case, to any representative person or member of the moral community. What we are morally obligated to do, what it is wrong not to do, is not just what there are good, or even conclusive, moral reasons for us to do. It is what we are morally accountable for doing in the sense that failing so to act, without excuse, is morally *blameworthy*. Blame is what Strawson called a "reactive attitude" (Strawson 1968). It is an attitude with a distinctive "inter-personal" or *second-personal* structure, since it implicitly makes a demand of (and so implicitly addresses a demand *to*) its object.[3] Unlike other critical attitudes—such as disesteem, disdain, and disgust—blame involves a second-personal

---

[3] I bring out these aspects of Strawson's analysis in Darwall 2006.

orientation toward its object that contrasts with a third-personal or, what Strawson calls, an "objective attitude." Unlike other critical attitudes, reactive attitudes bid for reciprocal recognition of the authority they presuppose. They come with an RSVP.

I therefore argue that the concepts of moral rights and of moral obligation, and so moral right and wrong, are second-personal concepts. Therefore reasons that are expressed with these (and related concepts) are *second-personal reasons*. Unlike the first reason for acting, which depends in no way on second-personal address, reasons of the second kind would simply not exist without the possibility their being addressed second personally.

The notion of a second-personal reason is one of a set of irreducibly second-person concepts that can be defined in terms of one another. *Practical authority* legitimates claims and demands that the person having it can make of someone who is subject to her authority and hold him accountable for. Someone is *accountable to* someone else just in case the latter has the authority to make claims and demands of the former. A *valid claim or demand* on someone is one that another person has the practical authority to make. And a *second-personal reason* is any reason deriving from a valid claim or demand.

Again, I argue that the concepts of moral responsibility, moral obligations, rights, respect for and the dignity of persons, and the concept of person or moral agent all involve these irreducibly second-personal notions. As I see it, this is a fact of the first importance for moral theory. It means that no premises not involving these second-personal notions can entail any conclusion that does. It follows that substantive theses about moral obligation or right cannot be convincingly supported simply from premises about how it would be desirable for the world to be. This doesn't rule out utilitarian or consequentialist moral theories, to be sure, but it does mean that for them to be adequately supported, they will have to be advanced within a second-personal framework, that is, from within a set of assumptions about our authority to make claims and demands of one another at all.[4]

Law and Legal Authority

I turn now to ways in which the framework of second-personal ideas I have been sketching might help illuminate the character of law. To begin with, note that nothing I have said about the four interconnected, irreducibly second-personal notions just discussed ties them exclusively to morality. As I see it, the root idea here is of second-personal normative reasons, which reasons always presuppose authoritative claims and demands, hence authority, along with accountability. As I analyze them, second-personal reasons are grounded in genuine, that is *de jure*, authority of any kind. Moral obligations derive from the equal authority of representative persons or

---

[4] As I see it, some such argument lies behind the attraction of preference-satisfaction forms of utilitarianism. The idea that people's preferences are relevant to social choice is more naturally grounded in the idea that everyone has fundamentally the same claim than it is in ideas of general happiness of welfare.

members of the moral community to hold one another morally responsible; obligations within, say, a military chain of command, derive from the authority to issue orders of various kind; and so on. So also, I propose, do legal obligations and responsibilities derive from legal authority.

Now I do not want to take any stand on fundamental issues of jurisprudence that divide legal positivists and their critics, at least those in the mainstream. Whether the existence of law depends on anything ethical or genuinely normative, and how law relates to morality, can remain in dispute even if all parties agree that there is a conceptual difference between law and straightforward coercion or the "gunman writ large." At the very least, all sides can accept that the law *presents itself* as having *de jure* authority, whether it actually has it or not. Or as we might alternatively put the point, in order for law to exist there must be some authority *de facto*, and in order for *de facto* authority to exist, at least some people, maybe just a critical mass of public officials, must be seen to treat some practices or institutions as having authority *de jure* (and maybe, as Hart held, must actually so treat them by taking an "internal point of view") (Hart 1961: 55–7).

Something analogous is true of morality, actually. Even skeptics like Hume's "sensible knave" or Hobbes's "fool" can question whether morality creates genuine normative reasons while agreeing that it purports to do so (Hobbes 1994: XV.4; Hume 1985: 283). So they can accept my analysis of moral obligation and distinguish between the putative existence of second-personal reasons and whether such normative reasons exist in fact. They can, if they like, use "moral obligation" and "moral reason" to refer to the former, that is, to the putative normative reasons that they deny are normative reasons in fact. If they do, they can agree that morality creates "moral obligations" and "moral reasons" for action, but deny that these are genuinely obligating or genuine normative reasons. In so doing, they would deny that the putative authority that morality claims is authority *de jure*. (They may even deny that this is such a thing as *de jure* authority.) My suggestion is that the same is true of legal authority and the law. The law presents its demands as issuing from genuine, that is, *de jure* authority, but this may not be so in fact.

I take it, then, that the concept of law requires that of legal authority, that is, not just authority that is created as a social fact, as when a law is passed that gives some body the authority to issue a permit to ride bicycles within the city limits, but also the authority to make or find law itself, that is, to make it the case that citizens have legal obligations, responsibilities, and reasons at all that they otherwise would not have had. If this is so, the concept of law would seem to be a second-personal concept, that is, one that can only be defined within the set of interdefinable irreducibly second-personal concepts that I outlined in the last section.

There is, then, a truistic or tautological sense in which the concept of law is second personal. By definition, if you like, laws derive from legal authority and create legal obligations, responsibilities, and reasons to comply, that is, "legal obligations" and "legal reasons" for acting in a sense analogous to that in which even a moral skeptic can accept that there are "moral obligations" and "moral reasons." Second-personal legal reasons exist in this sense, whether or not such reasons are genuinely normative and whether or not the authority that law and legal authority purport to have is *de jure*. This much is tautologous or nearly so. Whether or not the relevant reasons, obligations, responsibilities, and authority are genuinely normative or *de jure* or not, it should be clear that they have a facially second-personal structure. The concept of legal obligation seems analytically to entail those of legal responsibility, authority, and reasons. What one is legally obligated to do is what it is one's legal responsibility to do, what one has a legal reason to do, and what legal authority requires or demands that one do. And similarly with the other interdefinable legal concepts. Legal reasons of the appropriate kind just are those that are associated with legal obligations and responsibilities, that is, with what is demanded of us by legal authority. And so on.

Thus legal concepts are at least superficially second personal. Whether or not the law creates genuinely normative second-personal reasons, obligations, and responsibilities, the putative reasons and obligations are nonetheless second personal in their structure. They are situated within a framework of putative authority and accountability relations. They purport not simply to favor action, or even to provide compelling or conclusive reasons for it, but to give distinctive reasons that derive from authoritative demands, hence bear conceptually on what we can legitimately be held responsible for doing. And this points to a second way in which law may be second personal, namely, that the putative second-personal reasons and obligations may actually exist. The reasons that law purports to create are genuine second-personal reasons, that is normative reasons for acting that derive from some genuine, that is, *de jure* authority to make demands and hold responsible.

Now if the argument of *SPS* is correct, the only way any such authority can be established is within the second-person perspective. But how can any such authority claim be justified? I argue that one thing that distinguishes second-personal reasons from reasons for acting of other kinds is that the validity of second-personal reasons depends upon its being the case that the person to whom they apply can be expected to accept the reasons and the authority from which they derive by exercising the capacities in virtue of which the reasons apply to him. The root ideas are, first, that second-personal reasons always presuppose an accountability relation, second, that certain capacities (*second-personal competence*, as I call it) are necessary to be able intelligibly to be held responsible at all, *and*, third, that when we hold someone responsible for doing something, we are committed to thinking that the person we hold responsible is capable of *holding himself* responsible by recognizing and acting on the relevant reason (along with the requisite authority) through exercising the relevant capacities.

Compare the difference in what you must presuppose about someone to believe that there are, say, reasons of prudence for her to do something, or even to give prudential advice to her, on the one hand, and what you must assume to hold someone responsible for complying with some putatively authoritative demand, on the other. You may sensibly think that it would be for my good for me to take my medications, say, and therefore that there is a prudential reason for me to do so, without supposing anything about my having any ability to accept and act on this reason. Even in giving me advice to act for this reason, you do not have to think that this is something I must be able to be brought to see the wisdom of for myself. You might just say, "Trust me, this really is a good reason to do this and you should do it." After all, whether the reason exists just depends on whether it would be for my good so to act, not on whether I can be brought to see this. If, however, you address a putatively authoritative demand to someone to get off your foot and hold him answerable for doing so, you do assume, do you not, that this is something he should be able to see for himself, or at least to appreciate when it is pointed out to him? After all, how can you hold him responsible for doing something for reasons he cannot himself appreciate even when they are pointed out to him? To intelligibly hold someone else responsible at all, it seems, you have to suppose that he is capable of holding himself responsible, that is, that he can comply with the demand by recognizing the authority to make it and that he is therefore responsible for compliance.

If this is right, then second-personal reasons must satisfy a "reasonable acceptance" condition.[5] Unlike reasons for acting of other kinds, their very existence is staked on its being the case that those to whom they apply can reasonably be expected to accept their validity by accepting the authority from which they derive. But what authority can we reasonably expect people to accept? In *SPS*, I argue that when someone takes up a second-person standpoint toward someone and make claims and demands of her of any kind, he is committed to the presupposition that both he and his addressee share a common second-personal authority to make claims and demands of one another at all by virtue of their capacity to enter into relations of mutual accountability (that is, their second-personal competence).

It follows from what we have said already that the addressee of a second-personal reason must be assumed to have the authority to hold himself responsible through making the relevant demand of himself. This is not a trivial thing. Holding someone responsible for doing something is trusting and respecting her, by giving her authority to answer for her conduct, including to herself as well. Of course, this may involve the application of a sanction. But a sanction through which we hold someone responsible is not just a penalty or cost, and the second-personal authority and reasons that it takes to justify sanctions in the right way, that is, as a way of holding responsible, differ from reasons of other kinds that might be sufficient to warrant imposing costs. To be a reason of the right kind, a consideration must be something the sanctioned agent could reasonably be expected to accept as making the sanction *legitimate*, that is as consistent with the respective authorities of addresser and addressee, and hence as fully respecting the addressee's authority also.

---

[5] For related discussion, see Yaffe 2008.

The point can be made with an example drawn from *SPS*. If a sergeant orders a private to do ten pushups, she addresses a reason to him that presupposes her authority to give the order and the private's obligation to obey it. So far, she may assume only a superior authority, that as a sergeant she has the standing to give orders to the private, whereas the private has no standing to give orders to the sergeant. But an order does not simply point to a reason holding in normative space; it purports to address it second-personally, *press* the claim or demand, and hold the addressee responsible for compliance. As second-personal address, an order presupposes that its addressee can freely determine himself through accepting the reasons it addresses and the authority on which they are grounded and hold himself responsible for complying with it. Any second-personal address whatsoever calls for reciprocal recognition of the authority it presupposes (in this case the sergeant's authority). It attempts to direct an addressee's will through the addressee's own free acceptance of that authority.

In assuming that the private is responsible for complying with the order, the sergeant is committed to thinking that the private would rightly be blamed if he failed to comply without adequate excuse. But attitudes like blame address demands from a perspective they presuppose their addressee can share (Strawson 1968). Their content is not just "I blame you," but "You are *to blame* (as you should be able to see and acknowledge yourself)." So although the sergeant assumes she has a distinctive authority to hold the private accountable, which goes with her special authority to issue the order in the first place, any such specially authorized standing must ultimately be grounded in an authority she must assume that the private shares with her (to hold himself accountable). Otherwise, threatening a sanction, even one he could not complain about, would give him a reason of the wrong kind to comply. The reason would not be a second-personal reason to do the pushups whether or not he could escape the sanction, one the acceptance of which is part of holding himself responsible.

In making a claim on the private in this way, consequently, the sergeant must presuppose a distinction between making a legitimate claim on the private's will in a way that respects his authority as free and rational, on the one hand, and, on the other, attempting illegitimately to direct his will by simply imposing her will on him coercively. However hierarchical, therefore, any address of a second-personal reason also implicitly presupposes a common second-personal authority as free and rational.

The upshot, I believe, is that any *de jure* authority must be able to be justified to those over whom it is claimed in a way that is consistent with the equal second-personal authority of all persons, that is, all second-personally competent rational agents. I argue that this basic proposition can provide a grounding of the right kind for contractualist moral theories of the sort advanced by Scanlon (1998) and suggested by Rawls ("rightness as fairness") in *A Theory of Justice* (1971). I conjecture that the proposition can also ground similar approaches to justifying political and legal authority. *De jure* authority of these kinds is also irreducibly second personal and must, consequently, be capable of being justified to those subject to it in ways that are consistent with their (equal) second-personal authority. I turn now to ways in which the criminal and civil law more specifically illustrate this claim.

Criminal Law and Second-Personal Reasons

Broadly speaking, the criminal law is that part of the law where legal punishment is appropriate. But how should we conceive of punishment? It is a familiar idea that punishment essentially involves holding someone responsible for something she has done based on a finding of culpability and guilt. Of course, a legal system may articulate these latter ideas in formal ways with specific standards. But that does not change the fact that the underlying ideas have the same basic (second-personal) shape as those connected to moral obligation, namely, moral responsibility, culpability, and guilt. The moral emotion of guilt is the feeling that one has failed to respect some moral demand, that one is rightly blamed and held responsible; indeed, feeling guilt is itself part of holding oneself responsible. And guilt's natural expressions are second personal also—acknowledgment of fault, apology, making amends, and so on—through which one makes oneself answerable, acknowledging the authority to hold one responsible and, therefore, to make claims and demands of one in the first place.

Although apology is most appropriately to the victim, acknowledging his distinctive authority to determine whether or not to forgive the wrong, and so on, guilt is not the feeling that he alone has a justifiable complaint. One does not blame oneself as if from the victim's standpoint. One sees oneself as being *to blame*, that is, that blame is appropriate from a common perspective that violator and victim share as representative persons or members of the moral community. In other words, one feels that punishment and not just compensation is warranted. (Compare, in this regard, Locke's distinction between the right of compensation that victims of injustice have in the state of nature, and the right of punishment, which is held by everyone (Locke 1988).) And in so feeling, one acknowledges, and thereby respects, the moral community's authority to hold one responsible.

As I see it, viewing legal punishment in terms of accountability can also provide a more adequate conception than typical retributivist or consequentialist approaches. The problem with purely consequentialist accounts of punishment put simply in terms of the desirability of deterrence or defense is the same one Strawson identified with consequentialist approaches to moral responsibility: they do not provide a reason of "the right *sort*" for practices of moral responsibility "as we understand them" (1968: 72, 74). That we have reason to desire to be able to hold people responsible for something is one thing, whereas our having reasons of the right kind that warrant our *legitimately* doing so, that is, that give us the authority to do so, is another. The only reasons that can justify relating toward someone in some way *as an instance of holding him responsible* are second-personal reasons; facts concerning the desirability of likely outcomes of the action are, taken by themselves, simply reasons of the wrong kind. This does not mean, of course, that consequences cannot figure within second-personal reasons.

But consequentialist approaches are not the only ones that fail to honor Strawson's point. That some response to a wrong might make for a more fitting whole does not itself establish any authority so to respond. If punishment is, in its nature, holding someone responsible for violations of law, then the right kind of justification for it must be one that can establish its legitimacy; the reasons must be ones the punished can reasonably be expected to accept concerning what can be expected (by anyone, himself included) of himself. Violations of law are, at bottom, failures of respect, most obviously of legal authority, but also of the *de jure* authority (as I see it, residing in the community of second-personally competent persons) that all legal authority purports to have.

Punishment can be justified in the right way, therefore, only by being called for by the underlying mutual respect that mutual accountability itself involves. This is a crucial difference between the form that respect takes in an honor culture and in one built around the idea of mutual accountability (Darwall forthcoming b). Punishment is not a form of retaliation or vengeance that annuls a dishonoring insult or injury and restores the victim's status while lowering that of his victimizer (Darwall 2010b). It does not return disrespect for disrespect. If and when it is justified by considerations that are rooted in equal second-personal authority, punishment respectfully expresses a demand for respect. Adam Smith writes that when we resent injuries, what our resentment is "chiefly intent upon, is not so much to make our enemy feel pain in his turn, as ... to make him sensible that the person whom he injured did not deserve to be treated in that manner" (Smith 1982: 95–6). Properly justified, therefore, a specific form of punishment is called for as a warranted way of holding someone responsible. By accepting punishment, someone thereby recognizes the authority to be held responsible and to have made the relevant demand in the first place; one thereby takes responsibility for oneself.

To view punishment in this way is to see it as justifiable in fundamentally second-personal terms. It follows that if appropriateness of punishment is distinctive of the criminal law, then criminal law is best viewed in fundamentally second-personal terms also.

Civil Law and Second-Personal Reasons

Aspects of the civil law seem to have a fundamentally second-personal character also (in addition to the general second-personal grounding that, if I am right, any genuine *de jure* authority has, and therefore, any putative authority must purport to have). Take, for example, the law of torts. Torts are violations of (bipolar) duties *to* individuals or, equivalently, rights obligees hold against the obligor (Darwall 2012). They involve injuries of various kinds that we have duties to others not to visit on them, whether intentionally or through negligence. Of course, these same actions may be proscribed by the criminal law also, but whereas what is at issue in criminal punishment is, as we have just seen, a form of holding responsible that is carried out by duly constituted legal authorities (in the name of the moral community from whom they inherit their authority), what is involved in torts is compensation, that is, something the victim has a distinctive right to claim or not at his discretion. No one else has the authority to bring an action in tort, and if the victim would prefer not to, then that is usually the end of it. It is, of course, central to the idea of a society under the rule of law that victims do not have standing to "take the law into their own hands" and hold others accountable in ways they might be legally entitled to as a result of due process. They must proceed through appropriate legal channels, through the courts. Nonetheless, the law gives expression to their distinctive authority to claim such compensation as the right holder. The very idea of torts involves the standing individuals have to themselves decide whether to pursue or waive claims to compensation.

In my view, an influential theory of torts, "civil recourse theory," advanced by John Goldberg and Benjamin Zipursky, is best interpreted in second-personal terms, namely that tort law gives expression to our individual authority to hold those who violate our rights accountable to us (Goldberg 2006, 2009; Zipursky 2003, 2008; Goldberg and Zipursky 2010). What civil recourse theory gets right, in opposition to its competitors, is its focus on the victim's individual authority. However, defenders of the theory sometimes present their view as legitimating retaliation, "vengeance," or "action against" victimizers by victims (Zipursky 2003: 749–50). But as I see it, a second-personal approach can show that tort actions should be seen as expressing a kind of mutual respect that is actually incompatible with retaliation and vengeance.[6] The latter notions, I have argued, invoke a notion of respect that is more at home in honor cultures—where dishonoring, status-lowering disrespect can be annulled by reciprocating disrespect (e.g., revenge) (Darwall forthcoming b and 2010b). In "accountability cultures," disrespect calls for attitudes and treatment that respectfully demand respect.

Conclusion

These remarks about the criminal and civil law and about the putative authority of law in general have been necessarily sketchy. I hope, however, that they have at least indicated some ways in which the framework of ideas that I present in *SPS* might prove helpful in accounting for a number of phenomena concerning the law, including legal authority, obligation, responsibility, and, perhaps, the nature of law itself.

---

[6] For an argument, see Darwall and Darwall 2012.

11

Civil Recourse as Mutual Accountability

(co-authored with Julian Darwall)

In *SPS* and a number of papers since, I have attempted to work out a theory of moral obligations as involving mutual accountability between equals, where the latter, I argue, is irreducibly second personal, since it entails an equal authority we have to address claims and demands *to* one another and ourselves (Darwall 2006, 2010a, 2010b, 2012).[1] As many writers have pointed out, moral obligations concern the part of morality that is modeled conceptually on legal, or as Sidgwick called them, "quasi-jural," concepts of responsibility and authoritative demands and claims (e.g., Sidgwick 1967: 196; Anscombe 1998). What we are morally obligated to do is not just what morality recommends or what there is good, weighty, or perhaps even conclusive reason to do from the moral point of view. It is what morality requires. It is what is legitimately demanded of us as moral agents or persons, just as legal obligations concern what the law demands of citizens subject to it. Illegal and wrongful actions are violations of what the law and the moral law, respectively, mandate or require.

Similarly, both moral and legal obligations conceptually entail distinctive forms of responsibility, or accountability. What we are morally obligated to do is what we are responsible or accountable for doing, just as legal obligations entail legal responsibilities. I argue that moral responsibility is irreducibly second personal since it entails accountability or answerability, and that these are always, as a conceptual matter, *to* someone with the authority to hold us thus answerable (even if that person is we ourselves). When it comes to morality, theological voluntarists, like the early modern natural law theorists Pufendorf and Locke, hold that the moral law implicates our accountability to God. My theory is that moral obligations concern our accountability to one another and ourselves as equal moral persons or members of the moral community.

---

[1] This article is a collaborative attempt by the authors to say something about how the second-personal framework developed in Darwall 2006 and more recent papers, e.g., Darwall 2012, might apply to tort law and, more specifically, to civil recourse theory. In what follows, the authorial "I," "my," etc., will refer to Stephen Darwall, and the authorial "we," etc., will refer to both co-authors of this article, Julian Darwall and Stephen Darwall. "You," will refer to you, dear reader, and "we," used non-authorially, will have its usual presumptive sense, referring to you, the authors, and indeterminate others. We regret any confusion; perhaps, however, presuming on your pronominal sensitivity is appropriate in a paper about "second-personal" matters.

The idea of answerability is no less implicated in our idea of law, pure and simple. Criminal proceedings seem, by their very nature, to involve answering charges, defense, determinations of culpability, mitigation, excuses, and holding the guilty accountable through criminal punishment. Similarly, proceedings in civil or private law, including torts, involve a form of answerability, although one that is importantly different from that involved in criminal cases. Complaints are brought not by the state on behalf of the community as a whole but by individual plaintiffs, who claim to have been injured by the violation of a legal obligation or duty *to them*. In civil proceedings, defendants are required to respond to such complaints, and courts attempt to establish the justice of the complaint, and, if justified, whether compensation of some sort is owed by the defendant to the victim.

In some recent papers, I suggest that the form of authority and accountability that underpins civil or private law is different from that at the root of criminal law, and that this legal distinction tracks a moral distinction between, respectively, obligations that are owed *to* others, so called "relational," "directed," or "bipolar" obligations, and moral obligations, pure and simple, or as I sometimes call them, moral obligations *period* (Darwall 2007b, 2012a; see also Thompson 2004). As a moral philosopher, I have mainly been interested to point to differences between civil and criminal law that I take to be uncontroversial among legal philosophers—that civil cases are appropriately brought by plaintiffs and that criminal cases are brought by "the people" and their representatives— in order to illustrate by analogy differences that I have been arguing exist in morality between relational or bipolar moral obligations and moral obligations period.

Here, however, we want to say something about how the second-personal framework I have been developing might apply to tort law, particularly, to an important and influential theory of torts: the *civil recourse theory* that has been worked out in the writings of John Goldberg and Benjamin Zipursky. In our view, civil recourse theory captures an important truth about the structure of relational or bipolar legal obligations, which we take to be the kind that are normally involved in torts, namely, that injured victims of violated bipolar obligations owed *to them* have a distinctive standing to hold their injurers responsible that neither third parties, nor the community at large, have. I have called the analogous moral standing, *individual authority*. This is an authority that, distinctively, *obligees* (that is, individuals to whom bipolar moral obligations are owed, or correlatively, claim right holders) have to hold obligors accountable *to them individually*. This authority is individual, moreover, in the further sense that it is discretionary; it is distinctively up to the individual who has the authority whether or not to exercise it. For example, a victimized obligee has a distinctive individual authority to decide whether to complain or to seek an apology or to forgive a deadbeat obligor, or, indeed, to pursue any combination of these; she can exercise this authority at her discretion. We believe that the distinctive moral standing that is involved in being owed a bipolar moral obligation and having a correlative claim right against an obligor are *de jure* analogues of (*de facto*) bipolar legal obligations and claim rights that are in play in tort law and that the former plausibly underpin the latter.

By contrast, the authority that is implicated in moral obligation period (and, by analogy, in the criminal law) is no individual's authority, but something we have as *representative persons* or members of the moral (or legal) community. I argue in Darwall 2006 that we presuppose such an authority when we hold one another and ourselves accountable for unexcused moral wrongs, for example, through what P. F. Strawson called "reactive attitudes," such as indignation, moral blame, and self-blaming attitudes like guilt (Strawson 1968). We do not presuppose any such authority as the particular individuals we are, or as having any particular relation to the wrongdoer. We presuppose it rather as representative persons or members of the moral community. Nor is this authority discretionary. When we feel blame toward and thereby imaginatively address a putatively valid demand to someone, we, as it were, "second" or "give voice" to a legitimate demand that we take to be authorized from the third-party (not to say, "third-person"—more on this later) perspective of a representative person.

We shall therefore argue that what civil recourse theory gets right is the distinctive *individual authority* that victims have to hold their victimizing obligors accountable to them. However, defenders of the civil recourse theory sometimes present their view as legitimating retaliation, "vengeance," or "action against" victimizers by victims. Here we shall suggest that an understanding of true mutual accountability between obligees and obligors—correlatively, between claim right holders and those they hold rights against—shows this to be mistaken. To realize genuine mutual accountability between equals, tort actions should be seen as expressing a kind of mutual respect that is actually incompatible with retaliation and vengeance. The latter notions, I have argued, invoke a notion of respect that is more at home in honor cultures—where dishonoring, status-lowering disrespect can be annulled by reciprocating disrespect (e.g., revenge) (Darwall forthcoming b and 2010c). In "accountability cultures," as I have called them, disrespect calls for attitudes and treatment that respectfully demand respect.

As we see it, the idea of justified retaliation is not really central to civil recourse theory, and, to be fair, Goldberg and Zipursky's allusions to it seem off-hand and non-committal. The present article might therefore best be seen as an argument for developing civil recourse in one way rather than another, that is, within a framework of mutual accountability rather than legitimate reprisal. In addition, we suggest a tentative account of tort remedy and process within that framework

Bipolar Obligations and Moral Obligation Period

We shall begin by saying something about how the ideas of moral obligation period and bipolar or relational moral obligations or duties differ conceptually. Here we assume that the kind of relational duties we are concerned with are not merely conventional or even legal, but moral in the sense that violation of a bipolar obligation to someone *wrongs* that person, other things being equal at least.

On a second-personal analysis, both moral obligations period and bipolar obligations involve legitimate demands and so presuppose an authority to make the demand and hold the person who is subject to the obligation accountable. What distinguishes the two is the different authorities they respectively presuppose.

To see moral obligation period's conceptual tie to legitimate demand consider the idea of morally supererogatory action. The concept of a supererogatory act is that of an act that morality recommends but does not require, an act that, as it is said, "is above and beyond the call of duty." Such an act might be thought to be one that it would be morally good for the agent to do but nonetheless one that the agent is not morally obligated or required to do, say, because it involves a level of sacrifice that cannot be legitimately demanded of him or her. Now notice that whether there are any supererogatory actions, whether this concept is actually instantiated, is a substantive normative issue and therefore a conceptually open question. Some normative ethical theories—for example, act consequentialism—hold that there can be no such thing. On an act consequentialist theory of right, moral agents are always under a moral obligation to do whatever morality would most recommend they do—by consequentialism's lights, to perform that action, of those available to them, that would produce the best consequences overall. But act consequentialism is a substantive normative theory, not a conceptual analysis. No normative theory, neither act consequentialism nor any other, could hold that supererogation is conceptually impossible.

If a critic claims act consequentialism to be "too demanding" and a consequentialist denies this, they must employ the same concept of moral obligation to disagree. The consequentialist must agree that the possibility of supererogation is conceptually open, even if she denies as a normative thesis that there is any such thing. She must agree that her critic is not being self-contradictory or conceptually confused when she denies consequentialism because it denies the (normative) possibility of supererogatory action.

The space between the concepts of moral recommendation, however weighty, and moral obligation is explained by the latter's (but not the former's) conceptual tie to legitimate demand and accountability. Any discussion of whether consequentialism is "too demanding" a moral theory assumes, as we all normally do, that what is morally obligatory is what morality *demands*, that is, what we are legitimately held accountable for as moral agents.

SPS follows a number of philosophers, including John Stuart Mill, Richard Brandt, and Allan Gibbard, in arguing that the concepts of moral obligation, duty, right, and wrong are tied to those of legitimate demand, accountability, and therefore conceptually to moral *blame* (Mill 1998: Ch. V; Brandt 1979: 163–76; Gibbard 1990: 41). What is morally obligatory is not just what there are good moral reasons to do, however weighty these reasons might be. It is what it would be morally *wrong* not to do. And a moral wrong is not just any kind of failing, but what it would be *blameworthy* to do, were one to do it without excuse.[2] As Mill put it, "There are other things . . . which we

---

[2] Note that the concepts of moral wrong and of violation of moral obligation are nonetheless distinct from that of blameworthiness. Something is morally wrong, violates a moral obligation, if, and only if, it would be blameworthy *if done without excuse*. Excuses defeat claims of blameworthiness, but not that of having done

wish that people should do, which we like or admire them for doing, perhaps dislike or despise them for not doing, but yet admit that they are not bound to do" (Mill 1998: Ch. V. ¶14). In these cases, Mill adds that "it is not a case of moral obligation; we do not blame them."[3] It is a conceptual truth that an act is morally wrong, if, and only if, it is blameworthy if done without excuse.

Blame, as it functions in this line of thought, is not a speech act, but a Strawsonian *reactive attitude*. When we blame someone in speech, indeed, we normally intend to express, and to be taken by our interlocutor to express, the distinctive attitude of blame. *SPS* follows Strawson in arguing that reactive attitudes have a special role in mediating human practices of responsibility—more precisely, accountability or answerability—because they are essentially "inter-personal," as Strawson put it, or "second personal," in the terms of Darwall 2006.[4] They implicitly address demands *to* their objects in a way that other critical attitudes like disdain or contempt need not. And they presuppose an authority to address the demand and bid for the other's recognition of that authority. They have an implicit RSVP.

Strawson did not give a formal definition of reactive attitudes, but their central features are clear from the role they play in his argument about moral responsibility and freedom of the will. Strawson's core idea is that reactive attitudes involve a characteristic "inter-personal" way of regarding the individuals who are their objects that commits the holder of the attitude to certain assumptions about the object individual and her capacities to regulate her will. Unlike "objective attitudes," such as disdain, disgust, and annoyance, reactive attitudes are essentially characterized by "involvement or participation with others in inter-personal human relationships" (Strawson 1968). There is always a second-personal element to reactive attitudes. Through the attitude we *hold* its object to something and thereby implicitly make a demand *of* (and so implicitly address the demand *to*) him or her. As Strawson put it, "the making of the demand is the proneness to such attitudes" (Strawson 1968: 92–3). The reason that reactive attitudes distinctively implicate freedom of the will, then, is that we can intelligibly address a demand to someone to regulate her will appropriately only if we suppose that she can so regulate it as a result of recognizing our demand's legitimacy. That supposition is, as Gary Watson says, a "constrain[t] on moral address" (Watson 1987: 263, 264). In this way, reactive attitudes like moral blame are unlike other critical attitudes, such as disesteem, contempt, and disgust, which lack an intrinsically addressing, second-personal element, whether these latter take a distinctively moral form, as in moral disesteem or disgust, or not.

---

moral wrong. To the contrary, an excuse itself presupposes that the conduct it excuses was nonetheless wrong.

[3] Also: "We do not call anything wrong, unless we mean to imply that a person ought to be punished in some way or other for doing it; if not by law, by the opinion of his fellow creatures; if not by opinion, by the reproaches of his own conscience" (Mill 1998: Ch. V.¶14).

[4] See also Watson 1987 and 1996.

Strawson makes a distinction, which is important to our argument, between *personal* and *impersonal reactive attitudes*. A personal reactive attitude, like resentment, is felt as if from the perspective of an involved party (like the victim in a tort), while an impersonal reactive attitude is felt as if from an uninvolved, third party's standpoint. It is, however, crucial to Strawson's argument, as it is to that of Darwall 2006 and to our argument here, that both personal *and* impersonal reactive attitudes are essentially "inter-personal" in Strawson's sense (or "second personal" in ours), since both implicitly address demands. Thus "first-party" reactive attitudes, like guilt, second-party attitudes, like resentment, and third-party attitudes, like indignation or moral blame are all *equally* "inter-personal" or second personal.[5] "Second person" does not mean "second party." Reactive attitudes, whether personal or impersonal, are all equally second personal in having implicit *addressees*. As Strawson puts it, they are all equally "participant" as opposed to "object-ive" attitudes, such as annoyance, disesteem, or disgust.

If moral obligations period are what it would be blameworthy to fail to do without excuse, and if blame is an impersonal reactive attitude that implicitly makes a demand, then both obligation and blame presuppose the idea of a standing or *authority* that any third party, or as we might put it, any representative person or member of the moral community, has to hold wrongdoers responsible and implicitly address the demand to them. I formulate this point by saying that each and every one of us has a *representative authority* to address the moral demands we implicitly make of ourselves and one another, as we presuppose when we feel blame (Darwall 2010a, 2010b, 2012b).[6]

I argue that bipolar moral obligations, that is, directed duties whose violation entails that the violating obligor has injured *and*, at least other things equal, *wronged* his obligee, also conceptually entail an authority to address claims and demands. However, the kind of authority distinctive of bipolar obligations is not representative authority but an *individual authority* that the individual obligee has to make claims and demands of an obligor who is obligated *to him* and to hold the obligor personally accountable. To be sure, violations of bipolar obligations not only wrong the obligee; they are also wrong *period*, at least, other things being equal.[7] And this entails, on a second-personal analysis, that third parties have a *representative authority* to hold the wrongdoer accountable as well. But third parties do not have the distinctive *individual authority* that the victim has, and which, moreover, he may exercise at his discretion.

As Hohfeld famously pointed out, bipolar obligations entail correlative claim rights and vice versa (Hohfeld 1923: 65–75). If X is obligated to Y to do A, then Y has a right against X that X do A. I follow Joel Feinberg in maintaining that claim rights

---

[5]   The first two are personal reactive attitudes; the third is an impersonal reactive attitude.

[6]   Note that no authority to express this attitude publicly follows straightway. What standing anyone has to do that I take to be a substantive normative, rather than a conceptual, matter.

[7]   That is, unless the obligor has a *justification* for the violation. In this case, the action is no longer wrong, even if there remains a compensable injury. We take it to be a semantic choice whether or not to say that the obligee is "wronged" in this case. We can follow Jules Coleman and say that in such cases the entailed claim right (and bipolar obligation) are "infringed" rather than "violated" (Coleman 1992: 301).

conceptually implicate a distinctive standing (*individual authority*) to claim that to which they are entitled (Feinberg 1980). It follows that bipolar obligations essentially involve this distinctive second-personal authority also.[8]

We can easily imagine a society (Feinberg's "Nowheresville") in which it is thought morally wrong (period) to step on others' feet, unless, say, they desire or do not mind one's doing so, but where the latter is not seen as a giving of consent, which can only be understood within a framework of bipolar obligations and claim rights. Consent, by definition, is required for actions that would otherwise wrong the person who gives it. In Nowheresville, others' will and preference appear simply as features of the moral landscape that bear on moral obligations period. Others are not regarded as having any prerogative, normative power, or authority to consent, where consent is conceived as something that can be given only through a second-personal address that reciprocally presupposes the individual authority to release one from what would otherwise be a bipolar obligation *to* the other.

Consent in this sense can only be given second personally, and it implicates bipolar obligations and claim rights by definition (Ripstein 2009: 111–32; Darwall 2012b). It is an exercise of a normative power, in this case, to release someone from a bipolar obligation he would otherwise have had, say, not to step on your feet (Raz 1972 and 2002: 98–104). Normative powers, in general, are authorities or standings to enter into reciprocally recognizing second-personal engagements with others that alter bipolar obligations and claim rights between the parties, but that also presuppose that the parties are already obligated to one another in various ways. Other essentially bipolar normative powers include the authority to make promises, to enter into agreements and contracts, and even to exercise such prosaic normative capacities as simply asking someone to do something or acceding to a request (Watson 2009; Darwall 2012b; Enoch 2011).

The power of consent is but one of an ensemble of individual normative powers or authorities that enter into the having of a claim right against someone, and therefore into another's having a bipolar obligation to one. Moreover, these powers or authorities are all essentially second personal. Feinberg emphasizes that the right holder's authority to demand or *claim* her rights enters into the very idea that she has a claim right. "[I]t is claiming," Feinberg writes, "that gives rights their special moral significance" (Feinberg 1980: 151). The authority to claim our rights "enables us to 'stand up like men,' to look others in the eye, and to feel in some fundamental way the equal of anyone" (Feinberg 1980: 151). When we regard persons as having a claim right that others not step unbidden on their feet, part of what we think is that each person has a distinctive set of individual authorities over others' conduct with respect to *his* feet that he does not have with respect to the treatment of other people's feet. And these powers include the individual authority to hold the person against whom the right is held

---

[8] The next several paragraphs draw heavily from "Bipolar Obligation."

personally accountable. If the right is violated, the right holder has an authority or standing that others do not have to decide whether or not to complain, seek apology or compensation, or to forgive.

Right holders have a distinctive authority to hold others answerable for violations of *their* rights that third parties do not have. The point is not that third parties have no authority. To the contrary, I argue that the individual authorities that right-holding obligees have can exist only if obligees share a *representative authority* with third parties, as well as with any obligor who might violate their rights. The point is that there is a special *individual* authority an obligee has to hold the obligor personally answerable that can, like the power of consent, be exercised only by the right-holding obligee herself at her discretion.

One way to see this is to reflect on forgiveness (see, e.g., Griswold 2007). Just as it is uniquely up to the right holder to decide whether or not to consent or to waive her right (assuming the right is waivable), so is it distinctively up to a victim whose right has been violated whether to forgive someone who has violated it. No one else has the same authority or standing.[9] Moreover, just as the power to consent can exist only against the background of bipolar obligations and rights that are in force without consent, so also can the authority to forgive exist only against the background of a distinctive authority that obligees and right holders have to hold their obligors personally responsible. Forgiveness involves the victim's somehow moving past personal reactive attitudes, like resentment, that mediate personal responsibility (Butler 1900: Sermon IX, "Upon Resentment and the Forgiveness of Injuries").

The situation is similar with apology. An apology is, by definition, addressed to someone who receives it and who has the authority to accept it or not. If a victim comes upon an unaddressed admission of guilt and expression of sincere regret in her victimizer's diary, she has not discovered an apology.[10] Apologies are a way of holding oneself personally answerable *to an obligee* whose authority to hold one thus answerable is thereby reciprocally recognized. It is a second-personal acknowledgment of having violated a bipolar obligation to the obligee and of the obligee's special authority to hold one answerable for it.

On a Strawsonian analysis, impersonal or "third-party" reactive attitudes through which we hold ourselves and others accountable, and presuppose the representative authority to do so, are implicated in the concept of moral obligation period. A moral obligation (period) is what it would be blameworthy not to do, were one to fail to perform without excuse. Similarly, *personal* reactive attitudes are implicated in the concept of a directed duty or bipolar obligation. A bipolar obligation exists where failure to perform would warrant the obligee in *resenting* the obligor.

---

[9] Though others who are specially related to the victim may have some standing, it is nonetheless not the same.

[10] Though she might if she came across something with the same content addressed to her.

To summarize, moral obligations period and bipolar moral obligations involve different authorities to address their demands and hold obligated subjects answerable for compliance. Bipolar obligations of the sort underpinning the legal obligations in play in tort law involve, as part of their conceptual structure, an individual authority that obligees have to hold obligors personally accountable to them.

Civil Recourse, Corrective Justice, and Individual Authority

We turn now to tort law and to civil recourse theory as a theory of torts. To this point, we have been considering conceptual claims about moral obligation period and bipolar moral obligations, including arguments that these concepts respectively involve distinctive forms of authority, representative and individual authority, respectively, and distinctive forms of accountability. Torts involve violations of bipolar legal obligations, not moral ones. But though the legal obligations that torts violate are not themselves moral or even necessarily *de jure* in some broader non-moral sense, they arguably nonetheless purport to have *de jure* force, as even legal positivists can allow. If this is so, and if, as we submit, the arguments of *SPS* apply to *de jure* obligation and authority more generally and not just to morality more narrowly conceived, it will follow that torts must purport to involve a distinctive form of accountability that is analogous to that involved in bipolar moral obligations and claim rights, namely, a distinctive accountability of tortfeasors *to their victims*. We believe that civil recourse theory can give theoretical expression to this fact, though we shall suggest that it can do so adequately only if it is developed in a way that stresses the mutual accountability of tortfeasor and victim.

Civil recourse theory seeks to reframe the theory of torts in a fundamental way. As Goldberg and Zipursky see it, torts came in the last century to be viewed primarily in terms of the fair or efficient allocation of costs, an idea whose root they find in Holmes, and in later writers like Prosser and law and economics theorists like Calabresi. Civil recourse theory reframes tort as a law of private *wrongs* and recourse. Tort law defines duties to refrain from injuring others, duties that are directed or bipolar in the sense that they are owed *to* others. When these duties are breached by an action, that action constitutes a wrong *to* the obligee; it wrongs him. An action that breaches a right protected by tort law therefore provides a legal basis for private recourse by the obligee against the obligor in court—a private right of action, through which a plaintiff may attempt to exact damages or relief from an injurer.

Now it might seem that *corrective justice theories* had already offered a substantially similar reaction to views concerned primarily with loss allocation. These theories, developed by Jules Coleman, Stephen Perry, Arthur Ripstein, Ernest Weinrib, and others, take as their wellspring a principle of corrective justice that holds that tortfeasors acquire a duty to repair the wrongful losses that their conduct causes. Coleman's version, in particular, has understood tort law as embodying both first- and second-order duties: first-order duties not to injure and second-order duties of repair (Coleman 1992: 317). When conduct breaches a relevant first-order duty and causes injury, the principle of corrective justice triggers a second-order duty of repair.

For a loss to be wrongful in the sense of requiring repair from the point of view of corrective justice, the wrongdoer need not be blameworthy. Indeed, the tortfeasor need not even be a genuine *wrongdoer* in the sense of having done something wrong, all things considered. A person can be wronged in the sense of being made subject to a wrongful loss even by actions that are morally permissible or perhaps even praiseworthy. Coleman writes:

> Culpability is not a condition of a wronging.... Indeed, in the case of some wronging, the injurer's conduct is actually morally praiseworthy or, at least, permissible.... Wronging can sometimes create wrongful losses even in cases of justifiable conduct. In cases of wronging, neither the absence of blame nor the presence of praiseworthiness is sufficient to defeat a claim that a loss is wrongful. The wrongfulness of the loss derives from the fact that the conduct is... invasive of a right. (Coleman 1992: 335)[11]

The tortfeasor's act need only have fallen below a legal standard of conduct established by the duty not to injure. The tort of negligence, for example, imposes liability on those who injure by conduct that falls below a standard of due care: the conduct of a "reasonable person of ordinary prudence." Coleman emphasizes that people are often not blameworthy for falling below this standard but are nonetheless liable in tort. The sense of "wrong" and "wronging" that is relevant to Coleman's corrective justice theory is simply that of an infringement of the victim's right not to be injured, which is correlative to the wrongdoer's first-order duty not to injure. Breaches of this first-order duty trigger a duty to repair the injury caused by the breach, regardless of whether the tortfeasor's conduct was culpable or perhaps even morally justifiable.

The significance of corrective justice theory, according to Goldberg and Zipursky, is that even if it takes a wronging of a victim to trigger the duty of repair, what matters for the theory is the tortfeasor's duty to repair the victim's *loss* (Goldberg and Zipursky 2010: 925–7). They distinguish corrective justice theories, all animated by the duty to repair a loss, from their own civil recourse view, according to which tort remedy is driven by the defendant's responsibility for having committed *a wrong against* the plaintiff "in a manner that renders her a victim entitled to respond to the wrongdoer" (Goldberg and Zipursky 2010: 944).

Goldberg and Zipursky stress Coleman's insistence that tort law is fundamentally about losses, not about wrongdoing. "Tort law is about messes. A mess has been made, and the only question before the court is who is to clean it up?" (Coleman 1998: 257, 302). If tort

---

[11] Without the ellipsis: "The wrongfulness of the loss derives from the fact that the conduct is a wrong, and the conduct is a wrong because it is invasive of a right." Our elliptical construction is designed to set up the contrast Goldberg and Zipursky wish to draw. Note also, as mentioned in note 6 above that Coleman calls justified breaches of bipolar obligations "infringements" or "invasions" of the entailed claim right.

were a state response to wrongs, Coleman and Perry argue, the state would offer legal remedy or penalty based on the gravity of the wrong, rather than awarding plaintiff damages typically keyed to the losses caused by a wrong (Coleman 1992; Perry 2000).

Goldberg and Zipursky thus align corrective justice theory with "loss allocating" views that are concerned fundamentally with a just distribution of resources to remedy losses. What makes the civil recourse view distinctive, in their view, is that it offers a relational account of tort as a law of *redress for wrongs*, which they claim better fits fundamental features of tort doctrine. According to Zipursky, "The key to tort liability . . . is that plaintiffs have rights to act against defendants, not that defendants have prior legal duties of repair to plaintiffs" (Zipursky 2008: 110). For civil recourse theory, the point is not that tort defendants have a duty, but that they have a tort *liability*. As Zipursky puts it, "Liability is not best explained as a form of duty to those whom one has wronged, but rather as a form of vulnerability to the one who has been wronged" (Zipursky 2008: 110). Tort law concerns the sorts of conduct our legal system defines as wrongfully injurious in the sense that, when committed, "the victim is entitled to exact something from the wrongdoer" (Goldberg and Zipursky 2010: 919).[12]

What do Goldberg and Zipursky mean by a right to "exact something?" Their accounts have evolved and continue to do so. We hope that the present article will contribute to this progression. Goldberg and Zipursky have portrayed the power to exact remedy within the context of what they call a Lockean or "social-contract" view. On this picture, citizens relinquish the liberty to respond aggressively to a wrong and receive in return from the state a certain level of security against responsive aggression by others and additional assurance that a civil avenue of redress against wrongdoers will be supplied (Zipursky 2003: 735; Goldberg and Zipursky 2010: 974). The state is therefore obliged to provide plaintiffs with an avenue of recourse through which they are empowered to act against their victimizers. The private right of action is the state's civil empowerment of individuals who have been wronged against the wrongdoer.

The state recognizes itself as obliged to empower the plaintiff to act in some manner against the defendant and acts on that obligation by permitting the plaintiff to exact damages or have the defendant enjoined against performing certain acts. (Goldberg and Zipursky 2010: 974)

Zipursky notes also that the existence of punitive damages suggests that tort law "permit[s] the plaintiff to 'be punitive,' or to 'be vindictive'—to inflict hardship upon the defendant out of resentment, spite, or the desire for revenge, not necessarily as an aspect

---

[12] Goldberg and Zipursky's contrast with corrective justice may seem somewhat exaggerated. They acknowledge that Coleman calls tortious "infringements" of victim's rights "wrongs." After all, they note, Coleman's influential book is titled *Risks and Wrongs* (Goldberg and Zipursky 2010: 925). Still, they claim that tort law, for Coleman, as for Perry, does not respond to wrongs *as wrongs* even in Coleman's defined sense. It responds to the wrongfully created injury or loss, which the tortfeasor has a duty to repair. For civil recourse theory, by contrast, the tortfeasor does not so much acquire a duty as incur a liability, consisting in victim's right of recourse, her entitlement "to exact something from the wrongdoer" (Goldberg and Zipursky 2010: 919).

of self-restoration" (Zipursky 2003: 751).[13] In a similar vein, Goldberg says that the civil recourse theory's "animating ideas . . . are relational and retaliatory, involving notions of empowerment, response, and satisfaction" (Goldberg 2006: 435–6).

Presently we shall argue that justified retaliation or vindication is not the most promising way of developing civil recourse theory's fundamental insights. We think civil recourse theory is right to stress tort liability as a distinctive "vulnerability" that tortfeasors have to their victims (Zipursky 2008: 110). However, we think it is a mistake to conceive this vulnerability in terms of susceptibility to vindication, vengeance, or retaliation, ideas that are more appropriate to an honor culture or ancient Greek tragedy and myth than to the law of torts (or, indeed, to the criminal law). As we see it, the vulnerability that characterizes torts is a form of accountability or answerability of the same genus as the one involved in bipolar moral obligations. Private law, and the law of torts more specifically, involve the fundamental idea that individuals have obligations to and rights against one another and that each person has an individual authority to hold others answerable for complying with obligations to him and his rights against them, just as others have the same authority to hold him answerable for complying with his obligations to them and their rights against him. Goldberg and Zipursky might well agree with this point. "Even when a particular tort is not also a moral wrong," they write, "saying that it is a legal wrong is similar to saying that it is a moral wrong in at least the following respects: it asserts that the act in question . . . merits some form of account-ability when done" (Goldberg and Zipursky 2010: 950). And even more to the current point: "Individuals who are able to prove that someone has treated them in a manner that the legal system counts as a relational, injurious wrong shall have the authority to hold the wrongdoer accountable to him" (Goldberg and Zipursky 2010: 974).[14]

Goldberg and Zipursky offer a number of reasons to think that the doctrine of tort better fits their view than corrective justice. We focus here on the fact that tort doctrine gives a distinctive right to the injured individual to seek tort remedy, which we suggest is the legal expression of a conceptual point about the normative structure of bipolar obligations and claim rights more generally, namely, that obligees have an *individual authority* and consequently a distinctive standing as victims to hold their obligors responsible for violating obligations held *to them*.

In "Civil Recourse and Separation of Wrongs and Remedies," Arthur Ripstein argues that a Kantian corrective justice of the kind he holds can also explain why it is that only victims have standing to bring a case in torts (Ripstein 2012).[15] However,

---

[13] "It may simply reflect the principle that a plaintiff who has been willfully wronged is entitled to be punitive in this manner, if he or she so chooses" (Zipursky 2003: 751).

[14] "A morally significant aspect of what an actor has done is whether his acts—described in a result-inclusive way—are ones that another person could fairly demand that he be held accountable for" (Goldberg and Zipursky 2010: 944).

[15] It seems to us that Coleman's version might also do the same, along the following lines. It is important that the first-order duty not to injure is bipolar, since it entails the correlative claim right (of obligees) not to be injured. And so also is the duty to repair an injury to a wronged victim bipolar, since it entails the victim's right to have her injury repaired. If, however, Darwall 2012 is right that bipolar obligations and claim rights

while Ripstein's argument establishes that a Kantian account like his can explain victims' distinctive standing to bring tort actions, we believe that it nonetheless falls short of providing a view on which a defendant can be seen to be accountable to a plaintiff; nor, indeed, can it explain a genuinely bipolar obligation of the wrongdoer *to* the wronged individual.

Ripstein also rejects Goldberg and Zipursky's claim that corrective justice cannot view tort as a law of wrongs. Ripstein builds his argument on a Kantian theory of right, according to which each person has an "innate right of humanity" to pursue whatever ends he or she chooses independently of the choices of others and consistently with others' equal right (Ripstein 2009: 30–56). Since pursuing ends is impossible without some means or other, every person must be presumed to have some means by right— most clearly, his own body, but also external things he can rightfully acquire as property (Ripstein 2009: 57–109). Individuals are wronged when others take their means or otherwise infringe on their rights to them. According to Ripstein, tort law remedies wrongs, conceived as violations of such rights, by restoring the means to which individuals have a right (Ripstein 2012: 7).

The Kantian doctrine of right flows, again, from the idea that individuals have the right to use their means to pursue whatever ends they adopt, independently of the choices of others and consistently with others' equal right. From the point of view of tort law, an individual's means are her bodily powers and mental capacities, her reputation, and her property. These individual entitlements taken together create a system of rights through which each is his own master and independent of others.

It is important to Ripstein that the victim's original right to her means continues to exist even if someone takes her means from her in violation of her right (and so wrongs her). She remains entitled to the use of her means even after another person has taken them. The duty of repair that is the cornerstone of corrective justice theories of tort is, according to Ripstein's Kantian theory, just the tortfeasor's duty to restore to someone any means to which she has a right. A remedy simply restores to the wronged individual that to which she is already entitled; it replaces the deprived means to which an individual continues to have a right after the wrong. Ripstein's version of corrective justice conceives of right and remedy as continuous, in that an individual's primary right to her means is the same right for which she claims restoration in demanding remedy. The right to remedy is no different from the primary right to her means.

Having set out his Kantian version, Ripstein's response to Goldberg and Zipursky's charge that corrective justice theory cannot explain why the law of tort gives only an injured person a private right of action is then simple. A right constrains the conduct of

---

conceptually implicate the individual authority of obligees (claim right holders) to hold obligors (those against whom obligees' claim rights are held) answerable for compliance, then victims' distinctive standing to hold their victimizers accountable follows directly from that. And this can explain within a Colemanian corrective justice theory why only victims have standing to bring cases in torts.

others, but only the bearer of the right can determine whether to exercise it. Only the injured victim has a right to *her* means against interference from others. And so only the injured victim has a right to claim the restoration of her means when she is deprived of them. It follows from this analysis that a tort suit must be initiated by a plaintiff simply because a plaintiff is the only one with standing to exercise any right that she has. The law of tort may not afford a plaintiff distinctive standing in the civil recourse sense, but it uniquely affords a plaintiff a private right of action since a plaintiff alone is entitled to determine the purposes for which her means are used. Where she does not claim restoration of means after a deprivation, she effectively allows another the use of her means.

We cannot pursue the matter fully here, but we believe that although Ripstein's Kantian theory of right can explain victims' distinctive standing to bring tort actions, it cannot explain any distinctive *accountability* tortfeasors have to victims, nor indeed, any genuinely bipolar obligations owed to their victims in the first place. The point concerns not Kantian theories in a broad sense, but theories, like Ripstein's, that are based on Kant's theory *of right*. And it derives from the fact of what, according to Kant, a right most fundamentally is. For Kant, a claim right to something is an "authorization" to use coercion in defending or securing that thing (Kant 1996c: 390 (Ak. 6: 230)). As Ripstein puts it, Kant identifies a right as a "title to coerce" (Ripstein 2009: 30). Violations of a right are, Kant says, "hindrances," and since a right is an entitlement to the use of coercion to protect that to which one has a right, Kant holds that it follows from the very idea of right that the hindering of hindrances is itself rightful (Kant 1996c: 526 (Ak. 6: 396)).[16]

If a right is a justification to coerce, then tort law is the mechanism through which victims can rightfully coerce tortfeasors to provide them with the means to which they had a right in the first place, or with its nearest replacement. Our point, however, is that this entails no accountability of the tortfeasor to the victim. In fact, it does not entail any accountability to anyone. It just means that tortfeasors cannot complain if their victim recovers her means, whether by a tort suit or in some other way, just as they could not have complained if she had used force to prevent the tort in the first place.

Would not, however, some kind of accountability flow from the obligations that follow from the original rights that justify victims' tort action? Not necessarily. The sense in which rights "constrain" conduct, on a Kantian view of right, is not that they entail *moral* constraints in the sense of genuinely bipolar obligations to victims that the tortfeasor's tortious conduct violates. The only moral constraint that follows from rights, conceived as justifications for coercion, is that right holders are justified *in constraining* violations of their rights.

---

[16] Kant begins the section of *The Doctrine of Right* titled "The Supreme Principle of the Doctrine of Right Was Analytic": "It is clear in accordance with the principle of contradiction that, if external constraint checks the hindering of outer freedom in accordance with universal laws (and is thus a hindering of hindrances to freedom), it can coexist with ends as such" (Kant 1996c: 526 (Ak. 6:396)).

This is a fundamentally different picture from the view that claim rights entail that the person against whom the right is held is *obligated, and therefore accountable, to* the right holder not to violate her right. No distinctive accountability to the victim is entailed; indeed, no accountability to anyone whatsoever is entailed. We could even say that, on the Kantian theory of right, the fact that one has a right against someone is not *itself* a moral reason of any kind for that person to accord one what one can claim from him by right. Of course, there may, and most usually will, be reasons that a Kantian moral theory will credit that will explain why someone should not violate the right. The point is that the fact that a person has a right is not itself such a reason—that is simply the fact that the right holder will be justified in constraining the person against whom the right is held not to violate the right.

We believe that civil recourse theory has a potentially better account of victims' distinctive standing to bring a suit in torts. To theorize adequately *both* the original rights and bipolar obligations with which tort law is concerned *and* the distinctive standing that tort law gives to victims, it is essential, in our view, to appreciate the way the concept of accountability enters into both. Claim rights and bipolar obligations are, as a conceptual matter, what obligors are accountable to obligees (right holders) for doing, and the law of torts provides an appropriate legal expression of this fundamental idea.

In this respect, civil private law in general, and torts, in particular, are to bipolar obligations as the criminal law is to moral obligation period. Just as representative third parties or the moral community have the authority to hold wrongdoers responsible through accountability-seeking reactive attitudes, so is it appropriately up to the people's representatives to decide whether to bring a criminal action. Even whether to *prosecute* a rights violation is not uniquely up to the victim. But if the issue is civil rather than criminal responsibility, then since this concerns the obligee's individual authority rather than community members' representative authority, obligees really should have special legal standing.

In recognizing the distinctive individual authority of victims, a civil recourse theory of torts is supported by a conception of mutual accountability that is grounded in the second-person standpoint. At the same time, however, Goldberg and Zipursky sometimes present civil recourse theory in terms of "vindication" and "revenge," as we noted above. So we would like to say more about why we think this is a mistake and to suggest that the idea of the mutual accountability of equals can provide a more promising alternative.

At one point Goldberg places a more agonistic interpretation of civil recourse theory within an ideal of equal respect. "Part of the state's treating individuals with respect and respecting their equality with others," he says, "consists of its being committed to empowering them to act against others who have wronged them" (Goldberg 2009: 974). It is important, however, to distinguish two fundamentally different conceptions of (recognition) respect for persons that relate to fundamentally different conceptions of the person and that mediate different conceptions of social order.[17] One is the idea of respect for one another as mutually accountable equals—*second-personal respect*. And the other is the form of recognition respect that mediates a status hierarchy of honor—*honor respect*. Vindication, retaliation, and revenge are responses to disrespect within an order of honor. Dishonoring disrespect (contempt) seeks to lower its victim's status, and when it is unopposed, it effectively does so. The victim's status can only be restored by retaliation against the dishonorer, which avenges the insult. The response to disrespect is a reciprocating disrespect.

The sense of "person" in play in an honor culture is that of *persona*, an individual's social presentation or "face." Someone has a certain status, or occupies a social role, when others respect his person (*persona*) in the sense of allowing him the social role he wishes by playing along with him as supporting actors in a social drama. When, however, they treat his self-presentation with contempt, his persona is no longer supported, and he loses face. The emotional response to contempt is shame, whose natural expression is to cover one's face and hide, to remove oneself (even if only) imaginatively from view.

Even if the ideas of retaliation and vengeance are most at home within a hierarchical status culture, that is not, of course, what Goldberg and Zipursky are proposing. They see the state, through tort law, as "respecting [victims'] equality with others." Nonetheless, the way the state would be doing so would still be within the conceptual framework of an honor culture, by providing victims the opportunity to restore their status by avenging their dishonoring wrong.

Consider in this connection a similar proposal that Jean Hampton made about how to conceive of punishment of rights violations. Those who violate others' rights presume a kind of authority over others. They act toward their victims as though their victims have lesser value. They arrogate a kind of "lordship" over their victims and seek to establish this by making their victims submit to the indignity involved in their crime (Hampton 1998b: 124). According to Hampton, the "retributive idea" is that the appropriate response to such attempted diminishment and "defeat" of the victim is to turn tables and force the wrongdoer's "submission," thereby defeating him and reconfirming or "vindicating" the victim's value. According to Hampton, punishment involves a public humiliation of the arrogant violator that simultaneously brings him down a peg and restores his victim's status or honor.

We might think of Hampton's proposal as the analogue in criminal law of a vengeance interpretation of civil recourse theory in tort law. The point of the tort proceeding is not for the state to humiliate the rights violator, and thereby restore the equal status of criminal and victim, but to provide a public forum in which the victim can do so. In our view, however, this imports the idea of equality into a conceptual structure that is still fundamentally that of an honor culture.[18] Respect for one another

---

[17] We draw here on Darwall forthcoming b.
[18] Other writers who make a similar move are Waldron 2009 and Appiah 2010.

as mutually accountable equals is a different idea, not just in the sense that honor cultures are generally hierarchical, but because respect in this latter sense is essentially second personal and reciprocal in a way that honor respect even between equally honored equals need not be (Darwall 2006: 119–47).

To respect someone as a mutually accountable equal is to hold oneself answerable to him at the same time one holds him answerable to oneself. It is to be in second-personal relation to someone. Respect for persons in this sense is what Strawson calls a "participant's" attitude, an attitude of "involvement or participation with others in inter-personal human relationships" (Strawson 1968). Honor respect and contempt, by contrast, even honor respect for equals or peers, are third personal; they are "observer's" or "objective" attitudes in Strawson's sense. Contempt towards someone, for example, is not necessarily implicitly expressed *to* that person; it is more characteristically expressed to peers who are invited to join in the contemptuous attitude.

When someone in a community of mutually accountable equals violates an obligation, whether an obligation period or a bipolar obligation, she does not thereby become a legitimate object of contempt. To the contrary, she is held accountable for her violation. And this reciprocating response is no form of disrespect that seeks to lower her status or retaliate. It is rather a reactive attitude like moral blame that implicitly seeks to engage the other second personally and demand respect. Because the attitude is essentially interpersonal or second personal, it views another in a way that recognizes him as a mutually accountable equal. As Strawson puts the point, reactive attitudes continue to "view [someone] as a member of the moral community; only as one who has offended against its demands" (Strawson 1968: 93). They demand respect in a way that is itself respectful, at least implicitly.

It is a reflection of this that the "first-party" attitude that responds to (indeed, reciprocates) second- or third-party reactive attitudes is not shame, but guilt. Guilt is the feeling as if being appropriately charged (second personally) with some violation, and its natural expression is also second personal—the desire to acknowledge guilt and take responsibility. That is partly what it is to hold oneself answerable.

When we hold one another answerable, whether for wrongdoing period, as representative members of the moral community, or for wronging us individually, as the individual victim to whom the injurer is bound by a bipolar obligation, we enter into a relation of reciprocal recognition and mutual respect for one another as mutually accountable equals. Holding someone answerable thus precisely does *not* return disrespect for disrespect; it embodies a respectful demand for respect.

If we project these ideas into the law of torts, it would seem that for the legal system to "trea[t] individuals with respect and respec[t] their equality with others," would not be for it, in Goldberg's words, to "empowe[r] them to act against others who have wronged them." Rather, the legal system would enable individuals to hold their victimizers answerable by respectfully demanding respect. Only in this way, we believe, can tort law genuinely express an ideal of mutual accountability.[19]

Tort Remedy, Perspective, and the Community

Having emphasized the role of mutual accountability in civil recourse, our account of tort process and remedy calls for clarification. A tort suit not only is an attempt to exact remedy from a defendant, but also serves to hold a defendant accountable in a characteristic way—according to legal standards that have general application to a community of mutually accountable equals. Thus, although a plaintiff bringing a claim based on her individual authority advocates her own position, her prayer for tort relief is at bottom a call to initiate a legal process that seeks mutual recognition of the rights of each party.

In the course of this judicial process, courts apply norms and directives established for the whole society to individual cases, settling disputes through the application of those norms (Waldron 2010b: 10). Courts accomplish this with hearings structured to enable impartial determination of the rights and responsibilities of particular persons on the basis of evidence and argument from each party. When presented, evidence is made available to be examined and confronted by an opposing party in open court, and each party has the opportunity to answer publicly the arguments of the opposing party on the record. In making and interpreting arguments in court, lawyers and judges conceive of the law as a whole, attempting to discern and articulate coherence by integrating particular propositions into a systematic legal structure. Parties and their representatives frame legal arguments within this integrated system, inviting judges and juries to consider how their position fits into a coherent conception that has general application to the community (Waldron 2010b: 17). The parties' arguments are tailored, of course, to their individual situations and commitments. As Waldron points out, part of the law's respecting individuals is that it treats them as though they "had a view or perspective of their own to present on the application of the norm to their conduct and situation" (Waldron 2010b: 14).

Even so, a tort claim is not simply a demand from the plaintiff's perspective in what Waldron has called a "lobbying sense"; it does not merely say what the law should be from only the plaintiff's point of view. Rather, civil suits allow the parties to influence the court's deliberation about what that law is, such that all members of the community should be held accountable to its requirements. To be sure, a plaintiff asks the court to adopt her arguments, but in order to prevail, these must be offered in a way that is susceptible of general public application to a community of mutually accountable

---

[19] In Solomon 2009, Jason Solomon argues that at an ideal of equal accountability grounded in the second-person standpoint can support a civil recourse theory of victims being given legal standing to demand respect of their victimizers by "acting against" them. As we see it, however, equal accountability is always implicitly mutual, recognizing the equal standing of all to demand respect.

equals. Thus, in a suit arising from a plaintiff's individual authority, a judgment is imposed from a more general perspective.[20]

Focusing on this feature of tort as mutual accountability further illuminates the way in which the institution supports, as others have argued, social equality and the dignity of persons. Waldron and Seana Shiffrin have both recently argued that reasonableness standards, which undergird a significant amount of tort law, respect the dignity of each party in part because they embody this particular conception of persons as capable of holding themselves accountable to each other (Waldron 2010a, 2010b; Shiffrin 2010). Applying reasonableness standards to individual conduct "embodies a crucial dignitarian idea—[that] those to whom the norms are applied [are] *beings capable of explaining themselves*" (Waldron 2010b: 14). The application of legal standards to individual conduct conceives of citizens as capable of apprehending the rationales by which the law governs them and of relating standards to their view of the relation between their actions and purposes and those of the community.[21] Shiffrin further reminds us that rather than requiring application of a rule by rote, reasonableness standards induce deliberation among citizens, requiring that they ask themselves, for example, whether they are taking due care, behaving reasonably, or treating one another fairly (Shiffrin 2010: 1217). This is itself an exercise in mutual accountability. Reasonableness standards make possible "richer forms of moral and democratic relations," and require individuals to actively apprehend and appreciate others' rights (Shiffrin 2010: 1222–5).[22]

Tom Tyler's experimental studies show that tort victims seek, not compensation pure and simple, but to hold tortfeasors accountable through fair procedures that enact mutual accountability. The "primary focus," Tyler observes, is on bringing to account "responsible people" (Tyler and Thorisdottir 2003: 361) Tort claimants "are primarily interested in receiving an apology and restoring social order and respect." "[T]he key issue on people's minds [is] moral accountability." Where an individual has been negligently injured, compensation is generally "a poor substitute for . . . accountability" (Tyler and Thorisdottir 2003: 361). It is important, moreover, that accountability come

---

[20] This account of tort remedy fits an account of a tort suit as a second-personal claim, of the sort Gideon Yaffe has spelled out. "It is a fact, and a non-obvious fact, that the question before the court in any negligence case is whether or not to make successful the plaintiff's act of second-personal address of a second-personal reason" (Yaffe 2008: 959). In deciding for the plaintiff, the court in any civil case is acting on behalf of the plaintiff, enacting her request for damages. In this sense, when the court decides for the plaintiff, the plaintiff successfully conveys to the defendant, "you had a reason to take a precaution that would have prevented my injuries"—one whose validity depends on presupposed authority and accountability relationships between persons.

[21] Waldron finds this idea in Lon Fuller's notion the law has an "inner morality" demanding that it be general, public, prospective, intelligible, consistent, practicable, stable, and congruent (Fuller 1964). Every departure from these principles is "an affront to man's dignity as a responsible agent," because subjecting human conduct to rules involves a commitment to the view that persons are "responsible agent[s], capable of understanding and following rules" (Fuller 1964: 162). Waldron argues that particular aspects of legal procedure, not just form, for example, courts, hearings and arguments, are indispensable to the law's respect for the freedom and dignity of each person (Waldron 2010b: 20–2).

[22] This fits also with Elizabeth Anderson's views in Anderson 1999 and elsewhere.

through fair procedures. Studies of decision acceptance suggest that while both out-come and procedural fairness matter, procedural justice usually matters more (Tyler 2003). People are more likely to accept unfavorable outcomes when they result from procedures they regard as fair (Tyler 2006).

What makes a procedure fair according to litigants?[23] First, having a voice or participating in the process (Tyler and Thorisdottir 2003: 380–1). Second, the per-ceived neutrality and lack of bias of authorized deciders (Tyler 2003: 298; Tyler and Thorisdottir 2003: 381). Judicial openness and explanation of the basis for decisions also bolster perceived fairness, as does the quality of interpersonal treatment by authorities. Acknowledgment of litigants' rights increases their sense that they have been treated with respect and dignity (Tyler and Thorisdottir 2003: 381).

In our view, both remedy and process in the law of torts enact the parties' mutual accountability to one another. We conclude, therefore, that civil recourse theory is best elaborated in these terms. What is at issue is not simply an individual authority that victims have to act against their victimizers, but an authority to hold tortfeasors accountable that victim and tortfeasor share reciprocally or mutually.[24]

---

[23] See Tyler (1988).

[24] We are indebted to the participants in the conference on civil recourse theory at Florida State University College of Law in February, 2011 for comments and helpful discussion.

Works Cited

Allison, Henry (1986). "Morality and Freedom: Kant's Reciprocity Thesis," *The Philosophical Review* 95: 393–425.

Anderson, Elizabeth (1990). *Value in Ethics and Economics*. Cambridge, MA: Harvard University Press.

——(1999). "What Is the Point of Equality?" *Ethics* 109: 287–337.

Anscombe, G. E. M. (1957). *Intention*. Oxford: Basil Blackwell.

——(1998). "Modern Moral Philosophy," in *Virtue Ethics*, ed. Roger Crisp and Michael Slote. Oxford: Oxford University Press, 26–44.

Appiah, Kwame Anthony (2010). *The Honor Code: How Moral Revolutions Happen*. Princeton, NJ: Princeton University Press.

Baier, Annette C. (1993). "Moralism and Cruelty: Reflections on Hume and Kant," *Ethics* 103: 436–57.

Baier, Kurt (1958). *The Moral Point of View*. Ithaca, NY: Cornell University Press.

——(1966). "Moral Obligation," *American Philosophical Quarterly* 3: 210–26.

Bennett, Jonathan (1980). "Accountability," in *Philosophical Subjects*, ed. Zak Van Stratten. Oxford: Clarendon Press, 14–47.

Black, Henry Campbell (1999). *Black's Law Dictionary*. Minneapolis, MN: West Group.

Bond, E. J. (1983). *Reason and Value*. Cambridge: Cambridge University Press.

Brandt, Richard (1979). *A Theory of the Good and the Right*. Oxford: Oxford University Press.

Broome, John (1999). "Normative Requirements," *Ratio* 12: 398–419.

Burton, John Hill (1846). *Life and Correspondence of David Hume*. Edinburgh: W. Tait.

Butler, Joseph (1900). *The Works of Bishop Butler*, 2 vols., ed. J. H. Bernard. London: Macmillan.

Carbonell, Vanessa (forthcoming). "*De Dicto* Desires and Morality as Fetish," *Philosophical Studies*.

Clark, Maudemarie (1994). "Nietzsche's Immoralism and the Concept of Morality," in *Genealogy, Morality: Essays on Nietzsche's On the Genealogy of Morals*, ed. Richard Schacht. Berkeley, CA: University of California Press, 15–34.

Coleman, Jules (1992). *Risks and Wrongs*. Cambridge: Cambridge University Press.

——(1998). "Second Thoughts and Other First Impressions," in *Analyzing Law: New Essays in Legal Theory*, ed. Brian Bix. Oxford: Oxford University Press, 257–322.

Cudworth, Ralph (1996). *A Treatise Concerning Eternal and Immutable Morality*, ed. Sarah Hutton. Cambridge: Cambridge University Press.

Dancy, Jonathan (1983). "Ethical Particularism and Morally Relevant Properties," *Mind* 92: 530–47.

——(1993). *Moral Reasons*. Oxford: Basil Blackwell.

——(2000). "Should We Pass the Buck?" in *Philosophy, the Good, the True, and the Beautiful*, ed. Anthony O'Hear. *Philosophy*, supp. vol. 47: 159–73.

——(2004). *Ethics Without Principles*. Oxford: Oxford University Press.

——(2009). "Moral Particularism," *Stanford Encyclopedia of Philosophy*, <http://plato.stanford.edu/entries/moral-particularism/>. First published in 2001, revised in 2009.

D'Arms, Justin and Daniel Jacobson (2000a). "The Moralistic Fallacy: On the 'Appropriateness' of Emotions," *Philosophy and Phenomenological Research* 61: 65–90.

D'Arms, Justin and Daniel Jacobson (2000b). "Sentiment and Value," *Ethics* 110: 722–48.

Darwall, Stephen (1977). "Two Kinds of Respect," *Ethics* 88: 36–49.

——(1983). *Impartial Reason*. Ithaca, NY: Cornell University Press.

——(1986). "Agent-Centered Restrictions From the Inside Out," *Philosophical Studies* 50: 291–319.

——(1994). "Hume and the Invention of Utilitarianism," in *Hume and Hume's Connexions*, ed. M. A. Stewart and J. Wright. Edinburgh: Edinburgh University Press, 58–82.

——(1995). *The British Moralists and the Internal "Ought": 1640–1740*. Cambridge: Cambridge University Press.

——(1999). "The Inventions of Autonomy," review essay on J. B. Schneewind, *The Invention of Autonomy*, *European Journal of Philosophy* 7: 339–50.

——(2001). "Because I Want It," *Social Philosophy & Policy* 18: 129–53.

——(2002). *Welfare and Rational Care*. Princeton, NJ: Princeton University Press.

——(2003). "Autonomy in Modern Natural Law," in *New Essays on the History of Autonomy*, ed. Larry Krasnoff and Natalie Brender. Cambridge: Cambridge University Press, 110–30.

——(2004). "Respect and the Second-Person Standpoint," *Proceedings and Addresses of the American Philosophical Association* 78: 43–59.

——(2005). "Fichte and the Second-Person Standpoint," *International Yearbook for German Idealism* 3: 91–113.

——(2006). *The Second-Person Standpoint: Morality, Respect, and Accountability*. Cambridge, MA: Harvard University Press.

——(2007a). "Law and the Second-Person Standpoint," in special issue devoted to *The Second-Person Standpoint*, *Loyola of Los Angeles Law Review* 40: 891–909.

——(2007b). "Moral Obligation and Accountability," in *Oxford Studies in Metaethics*, vol. II, ed. Russ Shafer-Landau. Oxford: Oxford University Press, 111–32.

——(2009). "Authority and Second-Personal Reasons for Acting," in *Reasons for Action*, ed. David Sobel and Steven Wall. Cambridge: Cambridge University Press, 134–54.

——(2010a). "But It Would Be Wrong," in *Moral Obligation*, ed. Ellen Frankel Paul. Cambridge: Cambridge University Press, 135–57.

——(2010b). "Justice and Retaliation," *Philosophical Papers* 39: 315–41.

——(2010c). "Authority and Reasons for Acting: Exclusionary and Second Personal," *Ethics* 120: 257–78.

——(2011a). Review of T. H. Irwin, *The Development of Ethics: A Historical and Critical Study*, 2 vols. *British Journal of the History of Philosophy* 19: 131–47.

——(2011b). "Demystifying Promises," in *Promises and Agreements: Philosophical Essays*, ed. Hanoch Sheinman. Oxford: Oxford University Press, 255–76.

——(2012a). "Bipolar Obligation," in *Oxford Studies in Metaethics*, vol. VII, ed. Russ Shafer-Landau. Oxford: Oxford University Press, 333–67.

——(2012b). "Grotius at the Creation of Modern Moral Philosophy," *Archiv für Geschichte der Philosophie* 94: 296–325.

——(forthcoming a). "*Ressentiment* and Second-Personal Resentment," in *Nietzsche's Values*, ed. Kenneth Gemes and Christopher Janaway. Oxford: Oxford University Press.

——(forthcoming b). "Respect as Honor and as Accountability," in *Kantian Reflections on Morality, Law and Society: Critical Essays on the Philosophy of Thomas E. Hill Jr.*, ed. Robert Johnson and Mark Timmons. Oxford: Oxford University Press.

——and Julian Darwall (2012). "Civil Recourse as Mutual Accountability," *Florida State Law Review* 39: 17–41.

Dewey, John (1998). "Three Independent Factors in Morals," in *The Essential Dewey*, vol. II: *Ethics Logic, Psychology*, ed. Larry A. Hickman and Thomas M. Alexander. Bloomington, IN: Indiana University Press, 1998, 315–20.

Dworkin, Ronald (1978). *Taking Rights Seriously*. Cambridge, MA: Harvard University Press.

Enoch, David (2011). "Giving Practical Reasons," *Philosophers' Imprint* 11:4: 1–22.

Ewing, A. C. (1939). "A Suggested Non-Naturalistic Analysis of Good," *Mind* 48: 1–22.

Falk, W. D. (1965). "Morality, Self, and Others," in *Morality and the Language of Conduct*, ed. Hector-Neri Castañeda and George Nakhnikian, Detroit: Wayne State University Press, 25–68.

——(1986). "Fact, Value, and Nonnatural Predication," in *Ought, Reasons, and Morality*. Ithaca, NY: Cornell University Press, 99–122.

Feinberg, Joel (1980). "The Nature and Value of Rights," in *Rights, Justice, and the Bounds of Liberty*. Princeton, NJ: Princeton University Press, 159–84.

Fichte, Johann Gottlieb (2000). *Foundations of Natural Right*, ed. Frederick Neuhouser, trans. Michael Bauer. Cambridge: Cambridge University Press.

Fleischacker, Samuel (2004). *A Short History of Distributive Justice*. Cambridge, MA: Harvard University Press.

Foot, Philippa (1958). "Moral Arguments," *Mind* 67: 502–13.

——(1972). "Morality as a System of Hypothetical Imperatives," *The Philosophical Review* 81: 305–16.

Frankena, William (1973). *Ethics*, 2nd edn. Englewood Cliffs, NJ: Prentice-Hall.

——(1992). "Sidgwick and the History of Ethical Dualism," in *Essays on Henry Sidgwick*, ed. Bart Schultz. Cambridge: Cambridge University Press, 175–98.

Fuller, Lon (1964). *The Morality of Law*. New Haven, CT: Yale University Press.

Gibbard, Allan (1990). *Wise Choices, Apt Feelings*. Cambridge, MA: Harvard University Press.

——(2003). "Knowing What to Do, Seeing What to Do," in *Ethical Intuitionism: Re-evaluations*, ed. Philip Stratton-Lake. Oxford: Oxford University Press, 212–28.

Gilbert, Margaret (2004). "Scanlon on Promissory Obligation: The Problem of Promisees' Rights," *The Journal of Philosophy* 101: 83–109.

——(2006). *A Theory of Political Obligation*. Oxford: Oxford University Press.

Glassen, Peter (1959). "The Classes of Moral Terms," *Methodos* 11: 223–44.

Goldberg, John C. P. (2006). "Two Conceptions of Tort Damages: Fair v. Full Compensation," *DePaul Law Review* 55: 435–68.

——(2009). "Tort Law as a Law of Civil Recourse." Available at: <http://works.bepress.com/john_goldberg/1>.

——and Benjamin C. Zipursky (2010). "Torts as Wrongs," *University of Texas Law Review* 88: 917–86.

Greenspan, Patricia (1975). "Conditional Oughts and Hypothetical Imperatives," *Journal of Philosophy* 72: 259–76.

Griswold, Charles (2007). *Forgiveness: A Philosophical Exploration*. Cambridge: Cambridge University Press.

Grotius, Hugo (2005). *The Rights of War and Peace*, 3 vols., ed. Richard Tuck. From the 1738 English translation by John Morrice of Jean Barbeyrac's French translation, with Barbeyrac's notes. Indianapolis, IN: Liberty Fund. Originally published in 1625.

Hampton, Jean (1998a). *The Authority of Reason*. Cambridge: Cambridge University Press.

——(1998b). "The Retributive Idea," in Jeffrie G. Murphy and Jean Hampton, *Forgiveness and Mercy*. Cambridge: Cambridge University Press, 111–61.

Hare, R. M. (1971). "Wanting: Some Pitfalls," in *Agent, Action, and Reason*, ed. Robert Binkley et al. Toronto: University of Toronto Press, 89–97.

——(1993). "Could Kant Have Been a Utilitarian?" in *Kant and Critique: New Essays in Honor of W. H. Werkmeister*, ed. R. M. Dancy. Dordrecht: Kluwer Academic Publishers, 91–114.

Harman, Gilbert (1977). *The Nature of Morality*. New York: Oxford University Press.

Hart, H. L. A. (1958). "Legal and Moral Obligation," in *Essays on Moral Philosophy*, ed. A. I. Melden. Seattle, WA: University of Washington Press, 85–98.

——(1961). *The Concept of Law*. Oxford: Clarendon Press.

Hartley, Christie (2009). "Justice for the Disabled: A Contractualist Approach," *Journal of Social Philosophy* 40: 17–36.

Hegel, G. W. F. (1977). *Phenomenology of Spirit*, trans. A. V. Miller. Oxford: Oxford University Press.

Herman, Barbara (1993). *The Practice of Moral Judgment*. Cambridge, MA: Harvard University Press.

Hieronymi, Pamela (2005). "The Wrong Kind of Reason," *The Journal of Philosophy* 102: 437–57.

Hill, Thomas E. (1973). "Servility and Self-Respect," *The Monist* 57: 87–104.

Hinchman, Edward S. (2005). "Telling as Inviting to Trust," *Philosophy and Phenomenological Research* 70: 562–87.

Hobbes, Thomas (1983). *De Cive, the English Version, Entitled in the First Edition, Philosophicall Rudiments Concerning Government and Society*, ed. and trans. Howard Warrender. Oxford: Clarendon Press.

——(1994). *Leviathan*, ed. Edwin M. Curley. Indianapolis, IN: Hackett Publishing.

Hohfeld, Wesley Newcomb (1923). *Fundamental Legal Conceptions*, ed. Walter Wheeler Cook. New Haven, CT: Yale University Press.

Hooker, Brad (2000). "Moral Particularism: Wrong and Bad," in *Moral Particularism*, ed. Brad Hooker and Margaret Olivia Little. Oxford: Oxford University Press, 1–23.

——(2003). *Ideal Code, Real World: A Rule-Consequentialist Theory of Morality*. Oxford: Oxford University Press.

——and Margaret Olivia Little, eds. (2000). *Moral Particularism*. Oxford: Oxford University Press.

Hutcheson, Frances (2004). *An Inquiry into the Original of Our Ideas of Beauty and Virtue*, Treatise II. Indianapolis, IN: Liberty Classics.

Hume, David (1978). *A Treatise of Human Nature*, 2nd edn., ed. L. A. Selby-Bigge, rev. P. H. Nidditch. Oxford: Oxford University Press. References are to book, part, section, and paragraph numbers.

——(1985). *Enquiries Concerning Human Understanding and Concerning the Principles of Morals*, 3rd edn., ed. L. A. Selby-Bigge, rev. P. H. Nidditch. Oxford: Clarendon Press.

Irwin, Terence (2008). *The Development of Ethics: A Historical and Critical Study, Volume II: From Suarez to Rousseau*. Oxford: Oxford University Press.

Jaworksa, Agnieszka (2007). "Caring and Full Moral Standing," *Ethics* 117: 360–497.

Kant, Immanuel (1996a). *Critique of Practical Reason*, in *Practical Philosophy*, trans. and ed. Mary Gregor. Cambridge: Cambridge University Press. Page references are to page numbers of the Preussische Akademie edition.

——(1996b). *Groundwork of the Metaphysics of Morals*, in *Practical Philosophy*, trans. and ed. Mary Gregor. Cambridge: Cambridge University Press. References are to page numbers of the Preussische Akademie edition.

——(1996c). *The Metaphysics of Morals*, in *Practical Philosophy*, trans. and ed. Mary Gregor. Cambridge: Cambridge University Press. References are to page numbers of the Preussische Akademie edition.

——(1996d). *Practical Philosophy*, trans. and ed. Mary J. Gregor. Cambridge: Cambridge University Press. References are to page numbers of the Preussische Akademie edition.

——(1999). *Religion Within the Boundaries of Mere Reason*, ed. Allen W. Wood and George Di Giovanni, foreword Merrihew Adams. Cambridge: Cambridge University Press.

Kar, Robin Bradley (2011). "The Second-Person Standpoint and the Law," *Illinois Public Law and Legal Theory Research Papers Series* 10–19. <http://papers.ssrn.com/abstract=1589791>.

Kavka, Gregory S. (1983). "The Toxin Puzzle," *Analysis* 43: 33–6.

Korsgaard, Christine (1996a). "The Reasons We Can Share: An Attack on the Distinction Between Agent-Relative and Agent-Neutral Values," in *Creating the Kingdom of Ends*. Cambridge: Cambridge University Press, 275–310.

——(1996b). *The Sources of Normativity*. Cambridge: Cambridge University Press.

——(1997). "The Normativity of Instrumental Reason," in *Ethics and Practical Reason*, ed. Garrett Cullity and Berys Gaut. Oxford: Clarendon Press, 215–54.

Kraut, Richard (2006). "Doing Without Morality: Reflections on the Meaning of *Dein* in Aristotle's *Nicomachean Ethics*," in *Oxford Studies in Ancient Philosophy*, vol. XXX, ed. David Sedley. Oxford: Oxford University Press, 159–200.

Lance, Mark Norris and Margaret Olivia Little (2006). "Defending Moral Particularism," in *Contemporary Debates in Moral Theory*, ed. James Dreier. Boston, MA: Blackwell Publishing, 305–21.

Leiter, Brian (1995). "Morality in the Pejorative Sense: On the Logic of Nietzsche's Critique of Morality," *British Journal for the History of Philosophy*, 3: 113–45.

Locke, John (1975). *An Essay Concerning Human Understanding*, ed. Peter H. Nidditch. Oxford: Oxford University Press.

——(1988). *Second Treatise of Government*, in *Two Treatises of Government*, ed. Peter Laslett. Cambridge: Cambridge University Press.

McDowell, John (1979). "Virtue and Reason," *Monist* 62: 331–50.

McKeever, Sean and Michael Ridge (2005). "What Does Holism Have to Do With Moral Particularism?," *Ratio* 18: 93–103.

——(2006). *Principled Ethics: Generalism as a Regulative Ideal*. Oxford: Oxford University Press.

McLeod, Owen (2001). "Just Plain 'Ought'," *The Journal of Ethics* 5: 269–91.

McNaughton, David and Piers Rawlings (1991). "Agent-Relativity and the Doing–Happening Distinction," *Philosophical Studies* 63: 167–85.

——(1995). "Agent-Relativity and Terminological Inexactitudes," *Utilitas* 7: 319–25.

Milgram, Stanley (1974). *Obedience to Authority*. New York: Harper & Row.

Mill, John Stuart (1869). *The Subjection of Women*. London: Longmans, Green, Reader, and Dyer.

——(1989). *On Liberty and Other Writings*, ed. Stefan Collini. Cambridge: Cambridge University Press.

——(1998). *Utilitarianism*, ed. Roger Crisp. Oxford: Oxford University Press. References are to chapter and paragraph.

Moore, G. E. (1993). *Principia Ethica*, with the Preface to the second edition and other papers, ed. Thomas Baldwin. Cambridge: Cambridge University Press.

Nagel, Thomas (1970). *The Possibility of Altruism*. Oxford: Clarendon Press.

——(1986). *The View From Nowhere*. New York: Oxford University Press.

Nietzsche, Friedrich (1998). *On the Genealogy of Morals*, trans. and ed. Maudemarie Clark and Allen Swensen. Indianapolis, IN: Hackett Publishing.

Olson, Jonas (2004). "Buck-Passing and the Wrong Kind of Reasons," *The Philosophical Quarterly* 54: 295–300.

Parfit, Derek (1984). *Reasons and Persons*. Oxford: Clarendon Press.

——(2011). *On What Matters*, 2 vols., ed. Samuel Scheffler. Oxford: Oxford University Press.

Perry, Stephen R. (2000). "On the Relationship Between Corrective and Distributive Justice," in *Oxford Essays in Jurisprudence*, vol. IV, ed. Jeremy Horder. Oxford: Oxford University Press, 237–62.

Pettit, Philip and Michael Smith (1990). "Backgrounding Desire," *The Philosophical Review* 99: 565–92.

Platts, Mark (1979). *Ways of Meaning*. London: Routledge & Kegan Paul.

Prichard, H. A. (2002). "Does Moral Philosophy Rest on a Mistake?" in *Moral Writings*, ed. Jim McAdam. Oxford: Oxford University Press, 7–20.

Pufendorf, Samuel (1934). *On the Law of Nature and Nations (De Jure Naturae et Gentium)*, trans. C. H. Oldfather and W. A. Oldfather. Oxford: Clarendon Press. Originally published in 1672.

Quinn, Warren (1993). "Putting Rationality in Its Place," in *Morality and Action*. Cambridge: Cambridge University Press, 228–55.

Rabinowicz, Wlodek and Toni Ronnøw-Rasmussen (2004). "The Strike of the Demon: On Fitting Pro-Attitudes and Value," *Ethics* 114: 391–423.

Rawls, John (1971). *A Theory of Justice*. Cambridge, MA: Harvard University Press.

——(1980). "Kantian Constructivism in Moral Theory," *The Journal of Philosophy* 77: 515–72.

——(2000). *Lectures on the History of Philosophy*, ed. Barbara Herman. Cambridge, MA: Harvard University Press.

Raz, Joseph (1972). "Voluntary Obligations and Normative Powers, II," *Proceedings of the Aristotelian Society*, supp. vol. 47: 79–102.

——(1975). *Practical Reason and Norms*. London: Hutchinson.

——(1977). "Promises and Obligations," in *Law, Morality, and Society: Essays in Honor of H. L. A. Hart*, ed. P. M. S. Hacker and Joseph Raz. Oxford: Oxford University Press, 210–28.

——(1979). *The Authority of Law*. Oxford: Oxford University Press.

——(1986). *The Morality of Freedom*. Oxford: Clarendon Press.

——(2002). *Practical Reason and Norms*, 2nd edn. Princeton, NJ: Princeton University Press.

——(2006). "The Problem of Authority: Revisiting the Service Conception," *Minnesota Law Review* 90: 1003–44.

Ridge, Michael (2005). "Reasons for Action: Agent-Neutral vs. Agent-Relative," *Stanford Encyclopedia of Philosophy*. <http://plato.stanford.edu/entries/reasons-agent/>.

Ripstein, Arthur (2009). *Force and Freedom: Kant's Legal and Political Philosophy*. Cambridge, MA: Harvard University Press.

——(2012). "Civil Recourse and Separation of Wrongs and Remedies," *Florida State Law Review* 39: 17–41.

Ross, W. D. (1930). *The Right and the Good*. Oxford: Clarendon Press.

Scanlon, T. M. (1998). *What We Owe to Each Other*. Cambridge, MA: Harvard University Press.

——(2007). "Wrongness and Reasons: A Re-examination," in *Oxford Studies in Methaetics*, vol. II, ed. Russ Shafer-Landau. Oxford: Oxford University Press, 5–20.

Scheffler, Samuel (1982). *The Rejection of Consequentialism*. Oxford: Clarendon Press.

Schneewind, J. B. (1998). *The Invention of Autonomy*. Cambridge: Cambridge University Press.

Sen, Amartya (1983). "Evaluator Relativity and Consequential Evaluation," *Philosophy and Public Affairs* 12: 113–32.

Shafer-Landau (2003). *Moral Realism: A Defense*. New York: Oxford University Press.

Shah, Nishi (2003). "How Truth Governs Belief," *The Philosophical Review* 112: 447–82.

Shiffrin, Seana Valentine (2000). "Paternalism, Unconscionability Doctrine, and Accommodation," *Philosophy & Public Affairs* 29: 205–50.

——(2010). "Inducing Moral Deliberation: On the Occasional Virtues of Fog," *Harvard Law Review* 123: 1214–46.

Sidgwick, Henry (1964). *Outlines of the History of Ethics for English Readers*. With an additional chapter by Alban G. Widgery. Boston, MA: Beacon Press. Originally published in 1886.

——(1967). *The Methods of Ethics*, 7th edn. London: Macmillan. Originally published in 1907.

Skorupski, John (1999). *Ethical Explorations*. Oxford: Oxford University Press.

Smith, Adam (1976). *An Inquiry into the Nature and Causes of the Wealth of Nations*, ed. R. H. Campbell and A. S. Skinner. Oxford: Clarendon Press.

——(1982). *The Theory of Moral Sentiments*, ed. D. D. Raphael and A. L. MacFie. Indianapolis: Liberty Classics.

Smith, Michael (1994). *The Moral Problem*. Oxford: Blackwell Publishing.

Solomon, Jason M. (2009). "Equal Accountability Through Tort Law," *Northwestern University Law Review* 103: 1765–822.

Stratton-Lake, Philip (2003). "Scanlon's Contractualism and the Redundancy Objection," *Analysis* 63: 70–6.

Strawson, P. F. (1968). "Freedom and Resentment," in *Studies in the Philosophy of Thought and Action*. London: Oxford University Press, 71–96.

Thompson, Michael (2004). "What Is It to Wrong Someone? A Puzzle About Justice," in *Reason and Value: Themes from the Moral Philosophy of Joseph Raz*, ed. R. Jay Wallace et al. New York: Oxford University Press, 333–84.

Tyler, Tom R. (1988). "What is Procedural Justice? Criteria Used by Citizens to Assess the Fairness of Legal Procedures," *Law & Society Review* 22: 103–36.

——(2003). "Procedural Justice, Legitimacy, and the Effective Rule of Law," *Crime and Justice* 30: 431–505.

——(2006). *Why People Obey the Law*. Princeton, NJ: Princeton University Press.

——and Hulda Thorisdottir (2003). "A Psychological Perspective on Compensation for Harm," *DePaul Law Review* 53: 355–92.

Urmson, J. O. (1958). "Saints and Heroes," in *Essays on Moral Philosophy*, ed. A. I. Melden. Seattle, WA: Washington University Press, 198–216.

Velleman, J. David (1992). "The Guise of the Good," *Noûs* 16: 3–26.

——(1996). "The Possibility of Practical Reason," *Ethics* 106: 707–26.

Waldron, Jeremy (2009). *Dignity, Rank, and Rights, The 2009 Tanner Lectures at UC Berkeley*. <http://papers.ssrn.com/sol3/papers.cfm?abstract_id=1461220>.

Waldron, Jeremy (2010a). "Vagueness and the Guidance of Action," in *Philosophical Foundations of Language in the Law*, ed. Andrei Marmor and Scott Soames. Oxford: Oxford University Press, 58–82.

——(2010b). "The Rule of Law and the Importance of Procedure," *New York University Public Law and Legal Theory Working Papers*. Paper 234.

Wallace, R. Jay (1994). *Responsibility and the Moral Sentiments*. Cambridge, MA: Harvard University Press.

——(2007). "Reasons, Relations, and Commands," *Ethics* 118: 24–36.

Warnock, G. J. (1971). *The Object of Morality*. London: Methuen.

Watson, Gary (1987). "Responsibility and the Limits of Evil: Variations on a Strawsonian Theme," in *Responsibility, Character, and the Emotions: New Essays in Moral Psychology*, ed. F. D. Schoeman. Cambridge: Cambridge University Press, 256–86.

——(1996). "Two Faces of Responsibility," *Philosophical Topics* 24: 227–48.

——(2009). "Promises, Reasons, and Normative Powers," in *Reasons for Action*, ed. David Sobel and Steven Wall. Cambridge: Cambridge University Press, 155–78.

Weinrib, Ernest (1996). *The Idea of Private Law*. Cambridge, MA: Harvard University Press.

Williams, Bernard (1981a). "Persons, Character, and Morality," in *Moral Luck*. Cambridge: Cambridge University Press, 1–19.

——(1981b). "Internal and External Reasons," in *Moral Luck*. Cambridge: Cambridge University Press, 101–13.

——(1985). *Ethics and the Limits of Philosophy*. Cambridge, MA: Harvard University Press.

——(1995). "Internal Reasons and the Obscurity of Blame," in *Making Sense of Humanity*. Cambridge: Cambridge University Press, 35–45.

——and J. J. C. Smart (1973). *Utilitarianism: For and Against*. Cambridge: Cambridge University Press.

Wolf, Susan (2006). "Deconstructing Welfare: Reflections on Stephen Darwall's *Welfare and Rational Care*," *Utilitas* 18: 415–26.

Yaffe, Gideon (2008). "Reasonableness in the Law and Second-Personal Address," *Loyola of Los Angeles Law Review* 40: 939–76.

Zimmerman, Michael J. (2007). "The Good and the Right," *Utilitas* 19: 326–53.

Zipursky, Benjamin C. (2003). "Civil Recourse, not Corrective Justice," *Georgetown Law Journal* 91: 695–756.

——(2008). "Two Dimensions of Responsibility in Crime, Tort, and Moral Luck," *Theoretical Inquiries in Law* 9: 97–137.

Index